Being and Blackness in Latin America

UNIVERSITY PRESS OF FLORIDA

Florida A&M University, Tallahassee
Florida Atlantic University, Boca Raton
Florida Gulf Coast University, Ft. Myers
Florida International University, Miami
Florida State University, Tallahassee
University of Central Florida, Orlando
University of Florida, Gainesville
University of North Florida, Jacksonville
University of South Florida, Tampa
University of West Florida, Pensacola

Being and Blackness in Latin America

Uprootedness and Improvisation

Patricia D. Fox

University Press of Florida
Gainesville/Tallahassee/Tampa/Boca Raton
Pensacola/Orlando/Miami/Jacksonville/Ft. Myers

Copyright 2006 by Patricia D. Fox
Printed in the United States of America on recycled, acid-free paper
All rights reserved

11 10 09 08 07 06   6 5 4 3 2 1

A record of cataloging-in-publication data is available from the Library of Congress.
ISBN 0-8130-2931-7

The University Press of Florida is the scholarly publishing agency for the State
University System of Florida, comprising Florida A&M University, Florida Atlantic
University, Florida Gulf Coast University, Florida International University, Florida
State University, University of Central Florida, University of Florida, University of
North Florida, University of South Florida, and University of West Florida.

University Press of Florida
15 Northwest 15th Street
Gainesville, FL 32611-2079
http://www.upf.com

For Mom, Dad, Mama, Papa

Contents

Acknowledgments

I am happy to have the opportunity to thank many who have helped me along the road, in ways great and small. First to my family, for love and support and understanding beyond measure. Thanks to my teachers Hans Ulrich Gumbrecht, Mary Louise Pratt, Francisco Lopes Caetano, Cynthia Steele, and especially Sylvia Wynter who stayed the course with comments, questions, and good stories; my colleagues Mary Jo Muratore, Marvin Lewis, Gordon Brotherston, Francis Wyers, Eileen Julien; my collaborators and friends, especially Donna Gates and Angel Acosta Martínez, who provided materials, a table at which to work, idle and fruitful conversation, and the occasional outing; Annette and her staff at Columbia Books; Martin Northway and Martha Ruíz García for editing, coffee, and encouragement; Gordo Neto for help with printing a crucial (but now distant) version of the manuscript and Amy Gorelick for first taking an interest in the project and her help and dedication throughout the process. The Center for Cultural Studies at the University of California at Santa Cruz deserves special mention for a residency during fall 2000 which provided an office, a view of the ocean, and the intellectual climate that aided in the birth of this project.

Introduction

Opening Salvo

For anyone who likes a good story, most tales about Blackness—fact or fiction—represent something of a challenge. Lush scenery is at a premium; the likelihood of a happy ending seems a statistical impossibility; and however redeeming the plot as an example of human triumphant over adversity, the neat sense of equilibrium—moral or otherwise—promised in other well-conceived stories is, at best, elusive. Not surprisingly, in tales sober and silly, Blackness often proves discomfiting and invariably complicates the characterization of the protagonist, whether drawn as entertaining caricature; painted as a being consumed by a belligerence difficult to gauge and impossible to contain; or sculpted as a figure of such superhuman strength and resolve that suffering seems a gift. Hmmm. What is it about Blackness that plays havoc with good stories?

How discourse premises Blackness is very much at the crux of the matter. For instance, Robert Park's 1919 allegation that the Negro in the Americas had "left behind him almost everything but his dark complexion and his tropical temperament" (qtd. in Levine 4) echoes a long-lived argument that has shaped the conception of Blackness in the Americas. Indeed, the perception of a trace or remnant culture contributes to bad storytelling: "To think of [the cultural production of Blacks] as 'survivals' is to prejudge the issue, to make the prior decision that even if they did continue to exist within the contours of a slave world they did so vestigially, as quaint reminders of an exotic culture sufficiently alive to render the slaves picturesquely different but little more" (Levine 5). Culture—in the broader sense suggested by Chinweizu as the less tangible and infinitely more portable "style of life"—signifies more than survival or the "recuperation" of Africanisms, supposedly waylaid on the journey into the Western imaginary. A more compelling storyline argues for unbinding such as historical and theoretical constrictions and assumptions that continue to be imposed on interpretation.

Lawrence W. Levine concurs, explaining that

[t]o insist that only those elements of slave culture were African which remained largely unchanged from the African past is to misinterpret the nature of culture itself. Culture is not a fixed condition but a process: the product of interaction between the past and present. Its toughness and resiliency are determined not by a culture's ability to withstand change, which indeed may be a sign of stagnation not life but by its ability to react creatively and responsively to the realities of a new situation. The question, as VèVè Clark put it, is not one of survivals but of transformations. (5)

The transformation of knowledge, however, cannot go forward without the transformation of the terms and the narratives that ultimately frame discourse.

In Latin America, as just one example, prolonging into the present narrations of empty-handed arrival results in insisting that "class not race" represents the heart of the uneven treatment of peoples of African descent. As a consequence, a troubling image surfaces of the "material negro"—the target of market research for goods tailored to tailor tastes: hair products, clothes, CDs, cars, and other emblems of the dream of upward mobility. Yet, this *homo economicus* negro, like the "folk negro" of yore, is a figurative device, a caricature, whose appearance serves certain narrative ends exemplified in tales of African-descended Cinderellas and Cinderfellas plucked from poverty and the backward tug of racial heritage.[1] The fantasy is as alluring as it is unattainable and serves largely to underscore the distance between reductive fictions and a complex reality.

Clearly, another type of transformation is needed: a critical vernacular that can decipher what is at stake in such representations and that can proffer a methodology that meaningfully links culture and consciousness in the analysis of Africana artistic production. This is not the first time for such a call. In the 1960s (and beyond), North American Harold Cruse bitterly criticized the lack of a Black intelligentsia able to clearly enunciate paradigms constructed on fictions and facts that emerged *from* the Black community.[2] Early in his writing on Afro-Hispanic canon formation, Richard L. Jackson expressed the hope that the dispersed evidence "which is indicative of a black consciousness, could very well form the core of a Black Aesthetic should systematic and radical literary theories based on ethnic affiliation develop" (4).

While the aim of the present project is not to discern a Black Aesthetic per se, it does attempt to posit an explanatory model that can first acknowledge the interconnectedness of representations of Blackness, high and low, scripted and spoken. Secondly, beyond the appreciation of the improvisational creativity of peoples of African descent or their vitality in the face of serial uprootings, the project aims to explicate how and *why* peoples of African descent have been strategically mapped into/onto the narratives of the Americas, often without receiving the benefits of such intimate association. In order to decipher a cultural-studies position that reflects the community it describes and to which it is accountable, Blackness needs to be seen as a cultural agent. In that storied context, Blackness "locates" and "transforms" the experience and expression of peoples of African descent (and vice versa). And, despite claims of "racial harmony" and the "invisibility" of racial practices in Latin America, the dynamics of Blackness provide the necessary clues with which to challenge one version of reality and to suggest another. In that light, the commercialization and folklorization of Black culture; the reiterated projection of Cinderella scenarios of upward mobility (material gain); and the discomfiting caricatures of the nonideal Black can be coherently linked.

More and more, many have taken up these issues in narratives both social scientific and artistic. However, what gets lost under the radar "is not so much a question of the controversial *content* expressed in art forms, as it is a question of what methods of social change are necessary to achieve freedom of expression within a national culture whose aesthetic has been cultivated by a single, dominant, ethnic group" (Cruse 456). Accordingly, the issue of conflicting narratives calls for not yet another rebuttal but rather a fundamental challenge to prevailing methodology and method.

This project concerns the relationship between the experience of peoples of African descent in the Americas as a result of the Middle Passage and the attendant artistic expression produced and shaped in diaspora. Much has been written, filmed, and recorded under what might be termed the rubric of a "culture" of Blackness, including transcribed oral tales; genteel and touristic incursions into music, religion, social practices, and popular culture; apologist historiographies that explain (away) the harshness of slave trade and race relations; flights of local color that pastorally describe difference in order to inscribe the other within an overarching narrative of empire, colony, or nation; and critical "interruptions" that post-theorize the dynamics between native and settler, machines and markets, and that, by turns, subalternate and mechanize (that is, relativize or erase) the participation and contribution of peoples of African descent. As varied as these explorations might seem, they coincide in discursively framing entries and exits, and no less the intervening appearances, of peoples of African descent in the landscapes of the Caribbean and Latin America, insinuating a disconcerting blend of myths and realities, both overarching and peculiar.

Thus, the present effort identifies and deciphers, within the wider context of the Black Diaspora, those rhetorical strategies, tools, tropes, formulae (paraphrase of Wynter "Eye," 9), which retroactively order and "make sense" of New World Blackness even in the face of the most glaringly obvious discrepancies, distortions, and dissonances. This reconsideration entails the comparison of texts and textualities; the juxtaposition of modes of conception, reception, and interpretation; and the contrast of the theoretical contexts and paradigms that blinder both reception and interpretation. This approach affirms that Blackness, like culture, is "not a fixed condition but a process" and as such possesses the "ability to react creatively and responsively to the realities of [each] new situation" (Levine 5). The stagnant "vocabulary" of slavery-based narratives and their derivatives cannot mount a fundamental challenge to the problematic representations of peoples of African descent in Latin America, or elsewhere.[3]

If the beginning of a narrative determines how events are understood and predicts conventional ends, this project then proposes to rethink Blackness as a narrative not about slavery, lack, and open-ended neediness, but rather as a journey propelled by *uprootedness* and expressed with *improvisation*, responsively shaping life strategies as much as world views and behaviors. That shift emphasizes the process of dispersal rather than the survivalist pose in order to better and more dynamically contextualize the complex and layered stylization of Blackness, accented in Spanish, Portuguese, and English. Since both uprootedness and improvisation appear in other contexts, often largely descriptive, the first of two sections carefully clarifies the meaning and usage of these terms in the present model. The second section employs the suggested paradigm to analyze representations of Blackness, both "typical" visions of orality and musicality and "recuperated" tributes re-created in poetry, novel, and theatre.

In Section I, "Coming to Terms," the opening chapter discusses uprootedness as presented in Paul Ilie's examination of Spanish Civil War exile, takes issue with the term as interpreted in Antonio Benítez-Rojo's *Floating Islands*, and embraces transculturalist Sylvia Wynter's suggestive article "We Must Learn," which proposes uprootedness as a paradigm for deciphering the construction of Blackness. The chapter cites examples in film, literary genres, and social scientific texts from the Black Diaspora in the Americas, North and South, to illustrate the pervasiveness of the concept, arguing that the focus on this term fundamentally dislodges the slavery-based imagery that has heretofore defined and constricted the reality of this community. The companion chapter "Territoriality: Becoming Places" historicizes the efforts of the African descended in Latin America—with echoing illustrations from the Caribbean and North America—to refashion space, be it in runaway settlements, enclaves, and associations or as a central motif in creative production. Chapter 3, "Coming to Terms: Improvisation," references Black musicality, as discussed by Amiri Baraka, Paul Gilroy, Antonio Benítez-Rojo, and Eileen Julien among others, in order to discuss the wider concept of cultural improvisation as a reiterated strategy for peoples of African descent in the Spanish- and Portuguese-speaking Americas. The companion chapter, "Temporality: Telling Times," explores the centrality of timing and systems of time (that is, the writing of history) in the formation and deformation of human consciousness and identity.

Section II, "Coming to (Cultural) Consciousness," opens with the chapter "Talking Drums or Trying Times: The Off-Timed Tale," which contrasts and compares the parallel official and extraofficial histories of drums: one version that derides and the other that celebrates the philosophical worldview evident across diasporic borders and genres. The following chapter, "Orality: A Word-World View," studies the deep structures of verbal contest in manifestations of the peculiar experience of uprootedness and improvisation. Questioning the writerly use of orality as a device, a further discussion in chapter 7, "Refashioning Spoken Souls," critiques prose and poetic texts that struggle to remain accountable to both the "vernacular" experience and the philosophical expression of the African descended. The final chapter, "Blackness Unbound: A Tale of One's Own," examines in two subsections,

"Staging Blackness: Race as (High) Drama" and "Novel Performances of Caliban's Blackness," the changing dynamics of the performance of Blackness in theatre practice and in prosaic experimentation, which move from merely "darkening" the protagonist to enunciating a peculiar cosmogony through the clever use of stylistics based in popular traditions, including musicality, orality, and religiosity.

All in all, it's a good story.

I

Coming to Terms

Coming to Terms

Uprootedness

—Yo siempre lo he dicho-interrumpía un zauro viejo-pero no me hace caso. El que no tiene casa es como el que no tiene nombre: ni la gente lo respeta, ni el frío le tiene la menor consideración, ni la lluvia se detiene a meditar si puede mojarlo o no. Uno no puede ni dar su dirección cuando quiere que le escriban. . . . Esos zamuros serán siempre lo mismo; calaveras, vagabundos, seres sin fundamento, condenados a no tener jamás una posición decorosa en sociedad.

—Antonio Arraíz, *Tío Tigre y Tío Conejo*

["I've always said," interrupted an elderly fox, "but no one pays any attention to me. He who does not have a home is the same as he who does not have a name; other people do not respect him, nor does the cold have the least consideration for him, nor does the rain stop to meditate if it will soak him or not. One cannot even give an address to others who want to write to him. . . . These peasants will always be the same, madcaps, vagabonds, beings without foundation, condemned to never have an important position in society."]

Briefly, uprootedness here refers back to the unifying experience of the Middle Passage that molds into the present the lives of peoples of African descent, especially those whose ancestors were kidnapped to be enslaved in the Americas.[1] Yet, as employed by Paul Ilie and Sylvia Wynter ("We Must Learn") and dismissed by Antonio Benítez-Rojo, the term insinuates much more than that event and thus requires careful clarification. Each writer's interpretation reflects a specific and different context: Spanish exile, one version of Caribbean history and the outline for another. Their at once diverging and converging perspectives provide, in juxtaposition, a crucial understanding of how the dynamics of uprootedness—the lure of territoriality, the practice of improvisation and the sense of countertiming—ultimately affect the varying representations of Blackness: experience, identity, culture, expression.

In *Literature and Inner Exile: Authoritarian Spain 1939–1975* (1980), Paul Ilie employed the term to describe a distinct type of displacement, expatriation, which commingles "[b]oth the act of driving out a fellow man and the private unrest that drives man to emigrate" (1). In his reexamination of the semantics of exile and its psychological, philosophical, and aesthetic implications, Ilie bases his reading on Paul Tabori's *The Anatomy of Exile* (1972), which discusses uprootedness as "a story of compassion and charity running parallel with man's inhuman cruelty to man" (12), signaling "the unintended benefits of uprooting: the hospitality no less than the unfriendliness awakened in the host country" (Ilie 1). In the context of Latin American Blackness, a discomfited paradigm of expatriation or "forced" immigration often merely glances the inhumane and inhospitable, aspects reserved for pious comparisons with United States segregation and South African apartheid. Instead, the discussion digresses to random (and rare) acts of compassion and the "unintended benefits" of the African presence in the New World (for example, metonymically predictable orality, rhythm, and sensuality on the one hand, and, on the other, the redemptive utility of *blanqueciamiento, transculturación,* and *sincretismo* [whitening, transculturation, and syncretism]. While those terms seem value-laden positive if considered an additive to master discourses (for example, Vasconcelos, Fernando Ortiz, Nina Rodrigues, Arthur Ramos, Benítez-Rojo, etc.), many who recognize the erosive and deculturizing potential of these concepts, including Jamaican Elsa Goveia and much earlier Incan-Peruvian Felipe Guamán Poma de Ayala, assert that such egalitarian pretensions disguise a hierarchical order wherein Western civilization, white blood, Christian religion, or Greco-Latin–based European culture hold a privileged place in discourse, negatively marking its other as biologically dis-selected, "incapaz de civilização" (Luz 23) or "invincibly ignorant" (Sepúlveda), over space and time.

Notwithstanding the ill-fitting semantic of immigration underlying Ilie's discussion of expatriation, two concepts prove useful to the present "anatomy" of uprootedness: deculturation and permutability. The historical process of deculturation or erosion posits a parallel divergence from an original cultural and civic wellspring (for example, Africa in its Yoruba, Mina, Carabeli, etc., manifestations) and, concomitantly, from dominant discourses such as those into which the kidnapped Africans were inserted.[2] On the one hand, deculturation as practiced on peoples of African descent then aims

> to detach the primary loyalty of its members from all other groups
> (subnational as well as supranational), and to attach it to their new na-

tion and its symbols. This has always required the making of new myths of origin, the invention of national heroes and heroic traditions, and the legitimation of the new national system of authority. Thereafter, preservation of cohesion among the members of the nation becomes a matter of reaffirming allegiance to the symbols of that national identity. (Chinweizu "Literature," 216)

In other words, this process attempts to erode, by turns, tribal, communal (racial), and diasporic allegiances and altruisms in order to reaffirm an exclusive/excluding identity. On the other hand, the effort to make that denatured entity reaffirm dominant imaginings fails to fully understand the complexity and reach of cultural systems. In "Literature and Nation Building" Chinweizu advises that

> it is useful to look at culture as the fabric of mental, emotional and physical activities whose threads hold a people together within and across generations. It does so by shaping their feelings, by ordering the routines of their days, by defining their interests, by determining and interpreting their experiences and by inculcating in them the values and beliefs with which they conduct their lives. . . . culture defines the range of what they wear, eat, talk about, aim for, argue and fight over; it organises the memories they share, the games they play and even the disputes they feel party to. It determines their religious rites, work procedures, leisure habits, culinary styles, economic attitudes, judicial practices, manners, customs and other behavioural regulations. (215)

Logically, these intertwined systems cannot so easily be undone or acquired. Ilie's scheme first allows the acknowledgment of those transplanted cultural bits and pieces—here, in their similarly fragmented African and European aspects—without mystifying their unique confluence in the Americas, further modified by aboriginal contacts. He also makes clear that arguments that posit the totality of either, suggesting the overriding primacy of nature or nurture, represent illusions that misleadingly rely on static points of reference in a disingenuous bid for an imagined authenticity and, consequently, bear little resemblance to an ever-changing cultural historical reality.

Thus, a second important point offered in Ilie's discussion concerns the permutability of uprootedness. That phenomenon insinuates an instability set in motion by an upheaval whose character and implications likewise change as they are nurtured by the travails of expatriation. In the face of this instability, the exile or the emigrant understandably maintains a stead-fastly backward gaze toward a fixed, specific, and known/knowable point of origin. Thus, even as the temporal distance grows, requiring adjustments, the solution to the ever-changing set of "psychological, philosophical and aesthetic" concerns continues to be set in terms of rupture or return in a (vain) effort to recuperate the past and to sabotage the uncertainty attend-ing permutability. The intransigence of the Cuban exile community despite varying political and social climates provides a glimpse of the drawbacks of a framing that constricts its adherents to wait—for the moment of return, for the end of communism, for the death of Fidel Castro.[3] Such a conception of uprootedness remains formulaic rather than fluid.

Absent the surety of a definitive, defining point of origin (as enunciated in immigrant narratives), as is the case in the displacement of peoples of African descent in the Americas, the permutability of uprootedness takes on added significance. *Uprootedness* becomes the point of origin, where this community enters the historical record. An initial instability replicates itself at every step and thus necessitates other conceptualizations and strategies, especially in light of the added significative fluidity that describes the con-comitant permutability of Blackness. In an aptly pragmatic tone in *Notes on Dialectics* (1948), C.L.R. James reasons that "thought is not an instrument you apply to a content. The content moves, develops, changes and creates new categories of thought, and gives them direction. . . . Now one of the chief errors of thought is to continue to think in one set of forms, categories, ideas, etc., when the object, the content, has moved on, has created or laid the premises for an extension, a development of thought" (1980: 15). In other words, uprootedness does not proffer a tangible cause, effect, and solution but germinates a thought that admits variations on the theme, each requiring a situationally appropriate—and layered—response. This plea to consider thought a process rather than a static explanatory tool provides a crucial dis-tinction between Ilie's embrace and Benítez-Rojo's rejection of uprooted-ness—a puzzling catalyst for one, a spent conclusion for the other.

In *The Repeating Island: The Caribbean and the Postmodern Perspective* (1992), Antonio Benítez-Rojo dismisses uprootedness, lumping the concept into a laundry list of other terms employed to explicate Antillean reality.[4] Such a swift and offhand dismissal would hardly deserve mention except for the explanatory frame within which the concept appears—and indeed that which motivates that text—and the implicit exclusion of peoples of African descent. The expatriate Cuban writer considers those concepts as "the main obstacles to any global study of the Caribbean's societies," (1) equating such vocabulary to "judgments and intentions that are like those of Columbus" that apply "dogmas and methods [which] refer only to realities back home" (1–2). In consequence, he suggests, "the reader inevitably reads himself," privileging the Columbian view and necessarily obfuscating the "over here."

In place of those "spent" framings, Benítez-Rojo instead proposes chaos theory that, since it comes from "the scientific disciplines" (that is, physics),[5] is made to seem a more objective approach toward "a new way of reading"(2) the "processes, dynamics, and rhythms that show themselves within the marginal, the regional, the incoherent, the heterogeneous, or, if you like, the unpredictable that coexists with us in our everyday world" (3) and a "Nature [that] is the flux of an unknowable feedback machine that society interrupts constantly with the most varied and noisy rhythms" (16).[6] Earlier, the concept of cultural relativism—based on the theory of relativity and also borrowed from physics—had sought to account for cultural differences by "allowing" for variations on a theme, while all the time privileging the teleological endpoint of developed Western civilization, schemes, and ways of doing. One reason for the attractiveness of that acultural model lay in its seeming distance from the troublesome aspects of locality-specific ideology. Such is also the case with chaos theory when transposed into the literary realm. Employing gear-driven imagery (Benítez-Rojo 5) that recalls the mechanistic images of 1920s Russian constructivism, this postulation seeks to explicate heretofore misunderstood "random" cultural phenomena and multiplicities. Benítez-Rojo asserts:

All machines have their mastercodes, and the codebook to the cultural machine of the Peoples of the Sea [that is, the Caribbean] is made up of a network of subcodes holding together cosmogonies, mythic bestiaries, remote pharmacopoeias, oracles, profound ceremonies, and the mysteries and alchemies of antiquity. . . .

The Caribbean machine . . . is a technological-poetic machine, or, if you like, a metamachine of differences whose poetic mechanism cannot be diagrammed in conventional dimensions and whose user's manual is found dispersed in a state of plasma within the chaos of its own network of codes and subcodes. (17–18)

More than a question of mere semantics, that machine-driven imagery has some perhaps unintended—and contradictory—consequences, particularly the series of displacements that culminate in inextricably marrying the thought of uprootedness and the content of Blackness.

Attempting to reread fifteenth-century incipient modernity and therefore revise twentieth-century modernism, the mechanized approach presents two major difficulties: the objectification of the other and the continued privileging of the traditional subject. First, that mechanized approach, despite poetic flourish, necessarily favors the material world and the study of how specific *objects* function systematically. Thus Benítez-Rojo chooses to focus materialities—inventions that gave birth to factories and products such as mills and printing presses or sugar and (written) texts—in order to metaphorically describe how technologies (of production, transportation, and communication) and economic relations affect objectified human entities (for example, slave, labor power, machine fodder).[7] However, as cultural investigator Edward T. Hall asserts in another context, "The danger is that real life problems are dismissed while philosophical and theoretical systems are treated as real" (*Beyond Culture* 39). Consequently, the present approach asks how *living organisms* function within systems, in the spirit asserted by Hall: "There is an unbroken continuity between the far past and the present, for culture is bio-basic—rooted in biological activities. *Infra-culture* is the term that can be given to behavior that preceded culture but later became elaborated by man into culture as we know it today" (*Silent Language* 37).

Here, continuity does not imply a unitary narrative, but rather suggests that "Without context, the code is incomplete since it encompasses only part of the message" (Hall *Beyond Culture*, 86) or in other words, "It is like talking about bricks without saying anything about houses" (Hall *Silent Language*, 106). Thus, Benítez-Rojo's text that purports to focus an "over here" perspective ironically reinforces that face of colonialism that privileges the colonizer as initiator—code bringer and culture giver—and his creations as pedagogue.

In his essay "Deriding the Derridians," Chinweizu anticipates Benítez-Rojo's methodology of rereading, suggesting "texts are approached as if they are arbitrary codes. Therefore, reading a text . . . consists in deciphering the code and inventing some 'real' meaning that might have been left out, or was even unintended, by the text maker" (236–37). Texts seem to talk among themselves:[8] "it seems clear . . . that critical theorists are making the elementary mistake of endowing lifeless objects called texts with some of the properties of the human minds which create the texts." Chinweizu continues:

> This attempt to give ontological autonomy and active powers to literary objects strikes me as coming, in part, from those anxieties that used to trouble the social sciences, namely, to imitate the assumptions and procedures of the prestigious physical sciences. In other words, they are the anxieties of those who deal with a world in which things, alas, are not the way they are postulated to be in classical physics or chemistry. . . . If you happen to believe that the classical physical sciences are the most prestigious branch of human pursuit of knowledge, and that their epistemological procedures are the best for exploring the nature of things, you might be tempted to imitate them by importing their assumptions and procedures into other fields of knowledge. You might then be tempted to endow the objects of humanistic and social science studies with the kinds of autonomous activism which have proved successful in the physical sciences. But such assumptions and procedures are not applicable in every domain as the social sciences found out. . . . Thus the failure of the attempt to import into the social sciences the basic assumptions and procedures of the physical sciences might have been predicted. However, and unfortunately, since their main motive was to acquire the prestige of the physical sciences failure only heightened the anxieties and complexes of the social sciences leading them to go in for a jargon which echoed the physical science vocabulary. . . . Now, it seems, literary studies have been tempted to the same enterprise. ("Deriding the Derridians" 234–35)

A second unintended consequence of the mechanized approach necessarily favors the *colonizer's* gaze. Discarding thought for theory, Benítez-Rojo's blanket rejection of uprootedness tacitly forgets other theres/the others' there—which is to say, Africa. In rightly tabling the myopic vision that concerns only the displacement of the dominant (Eurocentric) group in its formulaic and intransigent aspect, the new scheme "unintentionally" overlooks or demeans the significance and effect of that same experience for the African descended in the Latin American landscape. Conversely, in "El país de cuatro pisos (Notas para una definición de la cultura puertorriqueña)" [The four-storied country: Notes for a definition of Puerto Rican culture],[9] José Luis González—in what might be termed an extension of Hall's paradigm of biologically based interactions—provides pivotal insight into the discourse of cultures that subsume/reflect/replay the paradigm of fitness into schemes of cultural dis-selection/alienation.

González notes: "La [cultura] que se presenta como 'cultura general,' vale decir como 'cultura nacional,' es, naturalmente, la cultura dominante" (13) [Culture that is presented as 'general culture,' which is to say 'national culture,' is, naturally, the dominant culture]. As this Puerto Rican critic observes, the divergence of cultural experience resides not in a question of conflicting personalities "sino una visión histórica versus otra visión histórica" (14) [but rather in one historical vision versus another historical vision]:

> [L]o que conoce como "cultura nacional" es generalmente la cultura de los opresores, entonces es forzoso reconocer que lo que en Puerto Rico siempre hemos entendido por "cultura nacional" es la cultura producida por la clase de los hacendados y los profesionales a que vengo aludiendo hace rato. Conviene aclarar, sin embargo la aplicación de esta terminología de "opresores" y "oprimidos" al caso puertorriqueño, porque es muy cierto que los opresores criollos han sido al mismo tiempo oprimidos por sus dominadores extranjeros. . . . Pero esa clase oprimida por la metrópoli era a su vez opresora de la otra clase social puertorriqueña, la clase formada por los esclavos (hasta 1873), los peones y los artesanos (obreros, en rigor, hubo muy pocos en el siglo XIX debido a la inexistencia de industrias modernas propiamente dichas en el país). La "cultura de los oprimidos," en Puerto Rico, ha sido y es la cultura producida por esa clase. . . . Y de ahora en adelante, para que podamos entendernos sin equívocos, hablemos de "cultura de élite" y de "cultura popular." (18–19)

[What is known as "national culture" is generally the culture of the oppressors, so it is then necessary to recognize that what we in Puerto Rico have always understood as "national culture" is that culture, referred to earlier, produced by the landowning class and the professionals.[10] It is necessary to clarify however the use of this terminology of "oppressors" and "oppressed" in the Puerto Rican case because it is just as certain that the creole oppressors have been at the same time oppressed by their foreign dominators. . . . But that class group oppressed by the metropolis was in turn the oppressor of the other Puerto Rican

social class, the class formed by slaves (until 1873), the laborers and arti-
sans (there were very few workers, in the classic sense, in the nineteenth
century given the nonexistence of modern industry, strictly speaking,
in the country). The "culture of the oppressed" in Puerto Rico has been
and is the culture produced by this class. . . . Thus, from this point
forward, so that there is no confusion, let us say "elite culture" and
"popular culture."]

That juxtaposition delineates a fundamental difference in the conception of
uprootedness earlier signaled by Ilie and overlooked by Benítez-Rojo: uprootedness as deculturation.

Historically, in the Caribbean and Latin America, elite concerns concomitantly reread, revise, and recode metropolitan practices *and* subsume and
consume all but the rawest forms of popular expression in an effort to create
a distance from both. For their part, popular practices, whose relation to the
metropolis—international and national—is filtered and seemingly fragmen-
tary then tend to parody and erode elite expression while at the same time
employing and innovating on cultural wellsprings "unavailable" to the elite
gaze. Cuban historian Walterio Carbonell explains:

Ya mucho antes del triunfo de la Revolución, la burguesía estaba
profundamente debilitaba por el imperialismo, no sólo en el poder
económico sino también sus valores culturales habían sido socavados
por las tradiciones y manifestaciones de los negros. Es así que los ritmos
musicales africanos, considerados por la burguesía como salvajes hasta
1930, terminan por ser adoptados como propios. Los ritmos musicales
de los barracones coloniales, ritmos por los cuales los propietarios esclavistas daban azotes a sus negros, se convirtieron en ritmos musicales
para divertir a la burguesía. La música de la población blanca de la
época de la colonia desapareció y su vacio fué llenado por la música de
los negros. (*Crítica* 24)

[Already, long before the triumph of the revolution, the bourgeoisie
was profoundly debilitated by imperialism, not only in terms of its
economic power but also its cultural values had been undermined by
Black traditions and manifestations. Thus, African musical rhythms,
considered savage by the bourgeoisie up until 1930, were in the end
adopted by them. The musical rhythms of the colonial slave quarters,

rhythms for which slaveholders punished their Blacks with a hundred lashes of the whip, became the musical rhythms that entertained the bourgeoisie. The music of the colonial white population disappeared and the vacuum was filled with Black music. ("Birth of a National Culture" 197–98)]

One vision of history—for example, one version of the history of Cuban music—then favors revision in an effort to inscribe denatured cultural forms and practices within a unitary (national) narrative, as Chinweizu's earlier commentary indicates. Much in the manner described by Eric Hobsbawm and Terence Ranger in *The Invention of Tradition* (1997), creation transpires in a vacuum that only difficultly (or never) recognizes precedents or influences.[11] Another vision—for example, Black music in Cuba—attempts to root its forms and practices (whether reified religious rhythms or their innovation into kitchen rumba or its public, commercial, and *orquestral* equivalent) within not only *cubanidad* but Blackness as well. While each version contains a part of the other, the emphasis varies: the first hastily compiles a tradition, masking or "forgetting" its derivations, while the second improvises *on* tradition, deliberately weaving that cultural fabric "whose threads hold a people together within and across generations."

In *La música en Cuba* (1946), Alejo Carpentier in his discussion of elite cultural forms and practices makes the case that the well known *guajiro* "La guantanamera" represents a "folklore estático" (304) [static folklore], which repeats the selfsame melody found "en cualquier romancero tradicional de Extremadura" (303) [in any traditional romancero from Extremadura] or "la del *galeron* venezolano" (304) [that of the Venezuelan popular song and dance]:

> El movimiento iniciado por algunos compositores, en favor de la música afrocubana, provocó una violenta reacción por parte de los adversarios de lo negro. A lo afrocubano se opuso entonces lo guajiro, como representativo de una música blanca, más noble, más melódica, más limpia. Sin embargo, los que pretendieron utilizar la música guajira en obras de largo aliento, tuvieron la sorpresa de observar que, después de una primera partitura, nada les quedaba por hacer. Y esto, por una razón que no habían advertido: el guajiro cantó sus décimas con acompanamiento de tiples pero *no inventa música*. (302)

[The movement initiated by some composers, in favor of Afro-Cuban music, provoked a violent reaction on the part of those adverse to Blacks. *Guajiro*, as representative of a nobler, more melodic, purer white music, was placed in opposition to the Afro-Cuban. However, those who pretended to use *guajiro* music in longer compositions were surprised to find that after a first score, nothing else was left for them to do. And this, for an unforeseen reason: the *Guajiro* sang his ten octo-syllable verses to the accompaniment of treble guitars, but he *does not invent music*.]

Any claim to "cubanidad integral" (304) [an integral Cubanness] remains greatly exaggerated. Accordingly, uprootedness, for the expatriate or Euro-centric, tends to redundancy, aping the same mechanistic systems that turn out facsimiles according to code. Conversely, recalling the incoherent, un-predictable—and constant—interruptions of "the most varied and noisy rhythms" (Benítez-Rojo 16), another version of uprootedness fosters the creation of "un algo no escrito . . . inventado, entre las notas impresas" in-sinuating "una serie de acentos desplazados, de graciosas complicaciones, de una 'manera de hacer' que creaban un hábito, originando tradición (Carpen-tier 141–42) [something unwritten . . . invented, between the notes on the score, (insinuating) a series of displaced accents, of pleasing complications, of a "way of doing" that creates a habit, originating tradition]. This drama replays itself wherever peoples of African descent have been dispersed in the Americas—from savory stews, to saucy musical forms, to toothsome tales, spiced with curious syllables and syntax.

Consequently, if not specifically "Columbian," Benítez-Rojo's version of cultural history, even in its reconfigured Caribbean context, nevertheless re-mains unwittingly Western—through a gaze implicitly racialized as white. When inserted into denatured postindustrial, postmodern mastercodes, Benítez-Rojo's "objective" rejection of uprootedness and the other terms insinuates that those framings represent little more than personal problems, which presumably interfere with the disciplined objectivity that dismisses them.[12] As Franco Moretti observes in another context, "That's the point."[13] Indeed, Blackness—similar to the concepts of world literature, Antillean re-ality, or national culture—"is not an object; it's a problem, and a problem that asks for a new critical method: and no one has ever found a method by just reading more texts [or rereading the same texts, as the Benítez-Rojo methodology suggests]. That's not how theories come into being; they need a leap, a wager—a hypothesis, to get started" (Moretti 55).

Not surprisingly, the dynamics of Blackness—interruption, interference, countering—provide the needed leap or wager for thinkers whose collective version of reality does not represent a postindustrial second reading, but rather "an-other" methodology—complex and layered, formed, informed, and deformed by Africana uprootedness, doubly conscious and belligerently counter.[14] For instance, always, already steeped in the realities of the "over here," the critical productions of Cuban Walterio Carbonell, Dominican Aída Cartegena Portalatín, Martinican Aimé Césaire, and Puerto Rico's quarrelsome Isabelo Zenón Cruz recognize that "Los negros son doblemente colonizados, son colonia dentro de la colonia" (Zenón Cruz 199)[15] [Blacks are doubly colonized, they are a colony within the colony], the openly racialized extension of González's assertion of bifurcated national culture: "cultura de élite" and "cultura popular." Thus, while both Ilie's and Benítez-Rojo's approaches are instructive, the relationship between thought, content, and categories suggests that uprootedness cannot remain simply a theme but need be deemed, in the context of the African descended, a paradigmatic way of thinking about a *condition* in constant flux, a challenging and difficult-to-decipher set of peculiarities.

For errant Jamaican Sylvia Wynter, the Caribbean *is* "back home."[16] Admittedly "tainted" by her sojourns in the metropolis, she offers a transculturalist vision of uprootedness that is foundational here. Anticipating Ilie's usage and González's framing, Wynter had earlier employed uprootedness (1968–69) to denote the very specific historical experience and discursive reality of the Caribbean:

> Our condition is one of uprootedness. Our uprootedness is the original model of the total twentieth century disruption of man. It is not often appreciated that West Indian man, qua African slave, and to a lesser extent, white indentured labourer, was the first labour force that emergent capitalism had totally at its disposal. We anticipated by a century the dispossession that would begin in Europe with the Industrial Revolution. We anticipated, by centuries, that exile, which in our century is now common to all. ("We Must Learn" 307)

Ilie and Wynter illuminate the real spatial and temporal displacement-dispersion that separates a people from their land *and* the attendant dispossession-disruption that wrenches a people from their "own corner of reality" ("We Must Learn" 308), from the cosmological context within which they make sense. Miriam DeCosta notes as much in her introduction to *Blacks in Hispanic Literature* (1977): "Primary is the shared experience of the apocalyptic holocaust and the 'deliberate desecration and smashing of idols, the turning inside-out of symbols.' It is the destruction of past beliefs (those of the Other) that *determined* our ethos, our aesthetic, our ontogeny and even our cosmogony" (6).[17] The attendant disassociation of being-in-culture, noun or gerund, establishes a distance between apparent mastery in one context (popular culture) and seeming incapacity in another (elite culture). Thus, just as Wynter states that her "concern is with connections" ("We Must Learn" 307), so too is that of this project: "not the 'actual' interconnection of 'things,' but the conceptual interconnection of *problems*" (Max Weber, qtd. in Moretti 55). And Blackness in tandem with uprootedness as they were uniquely "invented, constructed and formally instituted" (Hobsbawm and Ranger 1) in the Americas represents a problem of competing historical versions and interests.

In that light, uprootedness represents the accumulated and "moving" experiences common to peoples of African descent, a continuity of permutations—to use Italo Calvino's terminology—despite a discontinuous and disorienting history of "vulturistic isms," including "imperialism, racism, and color conscious colonialism" (Jackson 8, 13).[18] Those in turn insinuate a shared history of serial disruptions in various guises beyond the Middle Passage: chattel slavery, abolition, wars of independence, ghettoization, systemic marginalization, tacit proscription, neighborhood gentrification, urban renewal. Thus, Black slave, Black tenant farmer, impoverished or homeless Black corralled in *favelas*, barrack yards, or project ghettos, and even those trespassers who have leased space in bourgeois estates or ivory towers—"a rootless class of displaced persons who are refugees from the social poverty of the black world" (Cruse 454)—carry the indelible stain of uprootedness and therefore remain, in the context of the reigning discourse, racially, socially, economically dead to all autonomy, "totally at [the] disposal" of alienating paradigms. As Eileen Julien explains in *African Novels and the Question of Orality* (1992), those paradigms champion a version of history or culture that employs concrete—albeit accidental—context and material conditions in order to accustom an essentialist (static) description of Blackness. Hence, peoples of African descent are described as ontologically impoverished, primitive, ever challenged by the demands of dominant culture and the canceling atavism of raw nature.

Explicitly or tacitly reaffirming the "ontological" presuppositions signaled by Julien, countless sources "overrepresent" the institution of chattel slavery in the discussion of the condition of New World Blackness, in its financial or atavistic manifestation. In fact, if an investigator looks for material on Blacks in Argentina, whether in a bookstore or a national archive, she or he is ushered to the section on slavery.[19] In card catalogues and computer inventories "negros" are not a category, but "esclavos" are. While seeming to announce a different tack in the highly problematic *Cosas de negros* (1926, revised 1958, 2001), Vincente Rossi (1871–1945) reestablishes that essentialistic image as a prelude to discuss the lurid "black" roots of tango:

> Singularmente constituídos para el dolor, tan oscuros de cerebro como de piel, los hombres negros concluyeron por creer natural y justa su condición de animales domésticos, y sacrificaron al capricho del "amo y señor" hasta el oculto derecho de pensar.
>
> El hombre-fiera de las selvas africanas tranformado por el sufrimiento en hombre-perro . . . (49)

> [Singularly constituted for pain, as dark of brain as of skin, Blacks ended up believing natural and just their condition as domestic animals and they sacrificed even the hidden right to think to the "owner and master's" caprice.
>
> The wild man of the African forests transformed by suffering into a man-dog . . .]

A more sophisticated exposition, *The Black Atlantic: Modernity and Double Consciousness* (1993) by sociologist Paul Gilroy, "looks in detail at the master/mistress/slave relationship that is foundational to both black critiques and affirmations of modernity" (x). He stresses "the unspeakable terrors of the slave experience" and the resulting mistrust "of the complicity of racial terror with reason" (that is, venial rationalizations of man's inhumanity to man) and "the ways in which closeness to the ineffable terrors of slavery was kept alive—carefully cultivated—in ritualised, social forms" (73). Such a narrative beginning reaffirms the catatonic and downtrodden image of peoples of African descent consigned to react to the whims of dominant discourses rather than to negotiate their own contributions and participation. In contrast, uprootedness proffers a tactical advantage: a step back, a shift in focus that dislodges the problematic meanings associated with the "accidental."

Despite the differing propositions, both Rossi and Gilroy seem to concur in presupposing generations of physically, then intellectually, indentured automatons who can do little more than offer reactionary comment or contest on their founding victimization.[20] Rossi's strident polemic is more easily countered by citing the contradictions within the text itself. Gilroy's truncated and anglicized vision of the Black Atlantic that presupposes a wider applicability to the "African diaspora in the New World" requires contextualization. Given diverging—often illusorily so—racial practices and dynamics in the Hispanic World and the Americas (North and South), at least three points structurally constrict the very premises the sociologist attempts to elucidate. First, historically, peoples of African descent were "incorporated into Western civilization, its fact and fiction" (Wynter "Eye," 9)—earlier in the Iberian case as *negros*, the outcome of the *exploration* of Africa, and later in the English context as slaves, predicated on the *exploitation* of Africans. Each agent of civilization offered justifications for the ensuing kidnap and bondage of Africans, (at first) in religious terms in the Iberian instance and in economic terms in the Anglican instance. The focus on uprootedness recognizes both terms, which a focus on slavery cannot.

Second, while Gilroy rightfully decries "the dualistic structure that puts Africa, authenticity, purity, and origin in crude opposition to the Americas, hybridity, creolisation, and rootlessness" (199), one must also be aware of the perils of an approach that does not recognize in modernity those premodern presuppositions that set that duality in motion. The imaginary of the West, as it is wont to do, remains masterfully backgrounded as the unseen authoritative, universal source of delocalized veracity and the effaced point of contact that hold together those "competing" elements and processes. Conversely, uprootedness attempts to place those dynamics within the culturally and locality specific—and interested—historical versions to which they pertain.

Third, the focus on a Black Atlantic *political* culture that carefully cultivates its rituals and genres as the terrified response to the slavery heritage sabotages *popular* culture. As the deculturation model shows, that perspective tends to privilege stylized interpretations over "unofficial" cultural sources. As a result, the narrow parameters of dominant discourse seek to aesthetically and semantically tame the other's demonstrative cultural displays. Critically, the persuasive politics of studied re-creations and interested rereadings then obfuscate the "out of awareness" patterning that regulates human behaviors.

Consequently, uprootedness implies a changing series of peculiar problems. The connective experience of Blackness in the Americas stresses negation based in displacement and dispossession, an outgrowth of a dominant logic of oppositions between chaos and order; nature and machine; and popular display and elite invention, with the unmistakable message of an ontological incapacity to assume the favored term. However, the challenge of the dispersion and deculturation that result from uprootedness motivates a series of innovative negotiations, that is to say, improvisations. Thus, another version argues a mastery of the precarious and oxymoronic equilibrium between negation and affirmation. Thoughts are "linked together" (Mbiti 35)—or "married together" in W.E.B. Du Bois's terminology—propelled by the logic that "nothing can stand alone, there must always be another thing standing beside it" (Achebe *Morning*, 131). Such linkings appear in varied contexts and bear witness to the tangible thread of a layered cultural fabric that has shaped the outlook and that continues to regulate the responses of a proposed amalgamation: consider, for example, Zapata Olivella's use of compressed substantives in his 1983 novel *Changó, el gran putas*—ritmo-agua (69), Hombres-Bosques (71), Hijos-Luceros (82), pájaronoche (136), caraluz (139), nochedías (139), dedosríos (141)—and, in Cuban Santería and Brazilian Candomblé, Tambor de Mina, and Macumba, the Janus-aspect deities such as Changó-Santa Barbara. As the circularity and fancifulness of such linkings suggest, uprootedness implies that one stands outside the "progressive," text-based time-space continuum, tangential to the most fundamental conceptions of being, real or otherwise, and that one remains relegated to nebulous prehistories or parallel narratives of the timeless folkloric. Not surprisingly, the strategies to confront the layered condition of uprootedness invariably raise the question of territoriality.

Territoriality

Becoming Places

Territoriality does not pose as the opposite of uprootedness nor as its solution, but rather as a reminder of the fundamental importance for living organisms of what Stefan Immerfall calls the "space of places" (10). The reconfiguration of maps, localities, and boundaries, and allegiance to the same—once the transitory reality of the explorer, colonizer, exile, or immigrant and now a condition "common to all" (Wynter "We Must Learn," 307)—necessarily signals a dramatic shift in the conception of the human and human order. Yet, territoriality tempers the pervasiveness and persuasiveness of the conceptualization of an "abstract, universal, placeless and disembedded" flow of peoples, ideas, information, and trends seemingly "indifferent to constraints of space, time and location" by situating "the changing means by which space and society are interrelated" (Immerfall 4, 8). One historical version establishes the fundamental import of space as "an organizing principle for social life" that, once lost, has devastating and unsettling consequences; another version, inextricably intertwined, argues that uprootings "simply 'refashion territory' to use Colin Williams's felicitous phrase, rather than make it redundant" (Immerfall 7, 8). Key to understanding uprootedness in the experience and expression of peoples of African descent, territoriality pins down *in real places* the interplay of "aggregate historical changes" (Immerfall 1) and of diverging/converging historical versions—insinuating differing points of reference and offsetting trajectories—and their combined implications in both the local space of community and the global space of diaspora.

In the conceptualization of bio-basic culture offered by Edward T. Hall, a lack of territory proves damning since spatiality determines destiny and distance on the one hand and affects dominance and status on the other:[1]

> *Territoriality* is the technical term used by the ethnologist to describe the taking possession, use, and defense of a territory on the part of living organisms. . . . The history of man's past is largely an account of

his efforts to wrest space from others and to defend space from outsiders. A quick review of the map of Europe over the past half century reflects this fact. A multitude of familiar examples can be found to illustrate the idea of human territoriality. Beggars have beats, as do the policemen who try to get them to leave, and prostitutes work their own side of the street. Salesmen and distributors have their own territories which they will defend like any other living organism. (*Silent Language* 45–46)

While in the context of postmodern globalization "terms that evoke limits resonate as old-fashioned and almost obsolete" (Immerfall 2), "territory" and "territoriality" play a significant role in the dynamics of Blackness and represent a favored topic, from the fanciful to the factual. The Brazilian film *Quilombo* (Diegues 1984) enacts the importance of space in its carnivalesque recreation of the possession, use, and defense of the utopian maroon republic of Palmares (during the period between 1650–1695) from challenges mounted by Dutch and then French forces, the Portuguese crown, Brazilian creole landowners, miscellaneous glory seekers, and internal intrigues.[2] In their 1995 staged dramatizations of the Zumbi legacy, leader of the commune, Bando de Teatro Olodum (Salvador da Bahia, Brazil) and the Black Theatre Collective (London, England) variously explored the respective Brazilian and Anglican modern-day, diasporic realities that continue to suggest that "[t]o have a territory is to have one of the essential components of life; to lack one is one of the most precarious of all conditions" (Hall *Silent Language*, 46).[3]

Another example, the Jamaican movie *Dancehall Queen* (Elgood and Letts 1997), begins with an attempted land grab. The overall-clad protagonist Marcia pushes her cart loaded with foodstuffs through Kingston's congested city streets. As the vendor approaches her usual patch of sidewalk, undistinguished against a backdrop of graffitied corrugated tin, she comes upon a red-haired, hazel-eyed trespasser unloading his wares in a location hers by tradition and prior claim, that is, by primordiality. She leaps to defend her territory, and almost immediately her (male) backup arrives deus ex machina: a likely indication that such incursions are not an unforeseeable or rare occurrence. Her brother and friend run off the intruder but not without setting in motion the central conflict of the film. Thus this initial confrontation over territoriality motivates rippling frictions that affect the destiny of these players—two who die, two who triumph—as well as the dominance among the heretofore-unseen power brokers, licit and extralegal and, ultimately, the status of the high, mighty, and haughty, reordered through their comeuppance or reversal of fortune.

Likewise, colonizer, settler, and immigrant tied their identities and destinies to land in the New World. The conquering Spaniards coveted land because, in the feudal system, acreage signified status for both landed first sons and its lack thereof for landless second siblings, some of whom would seek their turf in the New World. For his part, Argentinean Domingo Sarmiento worried that the atavistic gaucho personality—the reflection of the rough reality of the *pampas*—would derail modernization and the country's bid for European styled metropolitan urban civilization. When the landowning class in Puerto Rico—composed of "españoles, corsos, mallorquines, catalanes, etc" (González 34) [Spaniards, Corsicans, Majorcans, Catalans, etc.]—could no longer covet the land as theirs after the arrival of the North Americans in 1898, they would find a literary outlet to ameliorate their territorial and cosmological displacement, tying nature and emotion (which on "the other side of the pond" also stirred the angst of Spain's Generation of '98):

> El telurismo[,] característica de la literatura producida por la élite puertorriqueña en el siglo XX[,] no responde ... a una desinteresada y lírica sensibilidad conmovida por las bellezas de nuestro paisaje tropical, sino a una añoranza muy concreta y muy histórica de la tierra perdida, y no de la tierra entendida como símbolo ni como metáfora, sino como medio de producción material cuya propiedad pasó a manos extrañas. En otras palabras: quienes ya no pudieron seguir "volteando la finca" a lomos del tradicional caballo, se dedicaron a hacerlo a lomos de una décima, un cuento o una novela. Y estirando un poco (pero no demasiado) la metáfora, sustituyeron, con el mismo espíritu patriarcal de los "buenos tiempos," a sus antiguos peones y agregados con sus nuevos lectores. (González 33)

> [The tellurism, characteristic of literature produced by the Puerto Rican elite in the twentieth century, does not respond to a disinterested and lyrical sensibility moved by the beauties of our tropical landscape,

but rather to a very concrete and very historical yearning for land lost, and not of the land understood as symbol nor as metaphor, but rather as a means of material production whose ownership passed into foreign hands. In other words: those who could no longer continue "surveying the back forty" astride the traditional horse, dedicated themselves to sit astride a décima, a short story or a novel. And extending a bit (but not too much) the metaphor, they substituted, with the same patriarchal spirit of the "good old days," their former peons and anyone else available with their new readers.]

Less prosaically, nineteenth-century slave owners in northeastern Brazil, seeing their net worth slough off to impenetrable *quilombos*, placed their wealth not in *piezas de india* but in hectares of land. Clearly, the reconfiguration of human territory plays a significant role in the construction of identity.

Sheltered by neither status, wealth, nor privilege, peoples of African descent in the Americas found themselves in truly "the most precarious of all conditions":

> O território nacional brasileiro pertence ao conquistador branco, já que os proprietários naturais, os índios (sem cultura, sem governo, sem religião) foram dizimados. Os negros não têm direitos sobre este território, desde quando não são nativos nem conquistadores. (Peixoto 68)

> [Brazilian national territory belongs to the white conqueror since the natural proprietors, the indigenous (without culture, without government, without religion) were decimated. Blacks do not have rights over this territory since they are neither natives nor conquerors.]

Neither founders, nor conquerors, Blacks were always, already poignantly out of place, especially in the immediate postslavery era.

In *Tarmas: historia y tradición* (1993), Daniel Benítez offers one such example. He first affirms that "Según la tradición oral, transmitida de generación en generación, Tarmas es un pueblo antiguo" (13) [according to oral tradition, transmitted from generation to generation, Tarmas is an ancient town], founded by indigenous peoples and later parceled out in *encomiendas* to be assigned to the conquering Spanish.

> Cuando se promulga la abolición total de la esclavitud, los negros al sentirse liberados no sabían qué hacer. Muchos salieron de las haciendas

alegres y contentos, pero sin ningún rumbo fijo. Algunos llegaron a
Tarmas y, después de deambular por las calles, se convirtieron en peones
de las haciendas. Uno de estos casos es el de Felicia, una negra que no
hablaba bien el español, alta, gruesa, con su dentadura completa, pelo
abundante, chicharrón y muy blanco, a veces con moñitos que vagaba
descalza por el pueblo. Después de su libertad, se vio obligada a volver a
las haciendas, a pesar de no tener amo, para poder vivir. En Curiana, en
tiempo de cosecha, Felicia recogía café; en Cangonga ayudaba a sacar
quinchoncho y tomates. Siempre se ubicaba donde se estaba pilando,
sembrando y trabajando la tierra, ayudaba a los que trabajaban y ayudaba a las mujeres fregar y lavar la ropa. Ese fue el destino común de los
negros recientemente libertados. (22)

[When the complete abolition of slavery was proclaimed, Blacks, re-
alizing that they were liberated, did not know what to do. Many left
the plantations happy and content, but without anywhere to go. Some
arrived in Tarmas and, after wandering the streets, they became wage
slaves on the former plantations. One of these cases is that of Felicia, a
tall, stocky Black woman who did not speak Spanish well, with a complete set of teeth, very full, curly white hair sometimes in braids, who
roamed barefoot through the town. After her liberation, she saw herself
obliged to return to the haciendas, despite having no master, in order
to survive. In Curiana, during harvest time, Felicia harvested coffee; in
Cangonga she helped to gather reeds and tomatoes. She always turned
up wherever the earth was being plowed, planted and toiled, she helped
those that labored and she helped the women wash dishes and clothes.
That was the usual fate of recently liberated Blacks.]

Thus for peoples of African descent, landless and adrift in a politically reconfigured world, this juridical "liberation" did little more than reenergize the
dynamics of uprootedness.

This sentiment provides the central motif in Adalberto Ortiz's *Juyungo*
(1943). A picaresque novel with a healthy dose of romanticism, the coming-
of-age saga follows Lastre Ascensión who flees from a dysfunctional family
to roam from one precarious, poverty-stricken situation to another until finally senselessly succumbing in the long-lived border dispute between Peru
and Ecuador. At one point, however, the errant protagonist finds respite
as a member of the settlement (Pepepán) considered the ancestral home

of don Clemente Ayoví and his extended clan, which includes grown sons, their spouses and offspring. The resident clan welcomes the return of errant daughter don Cristo (also known as Cristobalina), and with her, her godson and fellow migrant workers, among them Lastre and his pregnant paramour, María de los Ángeles. The troupe settles in, harvesting tobacco and *tagua*, partially isolated from Esmeraldas, the nearest mercantile and political metropolis, a "spacing" that contributes to the stability of the community. Their level of comfort is such that they host a celebration of San Juan, providing music and catering with homemade delicacies for sale, in a pleasingly pastoral moment. Into what might have been a happy ending, tragedy intrudes in the guise of the double-dealing, unscrupulous businessman who sells the island out from under the clan to a German speculator. Sweat equity and good faith prove no match to "legal" claim, and the conflict culminates in a violent uprooting that causes the death of Lastre's newborn son—victim of arson—and the dementia of María de los Ángeles. Lastre exacts a bloody revenge but cannot stem the dispersion of the community, nor the slow march to his eventual death, naked in a no-man's-land on the contested border between Ecuador and Peru.

Two decades later, the interplay between (threatened) uprootedness and territoriality again provides a central motif in *Chambacú, corral de negros* (1963)[4] [Chambacú, a Black Ghetto] by Colombian author Manuel Zapata Olivella.[5] The novel focuses the implosion of the outside world on the *barrio*: the forced conscription of its denizens to fight in the Korean war and "the attempt to dislocate them in order to construct tourist hotels" (Lewis *Treading*, 102). Máximo, the protagonist (in a phrase remembered by his mother) asserts "Para mí no hay sino Chambacú. Ni siquiera Cartegena" (37) [For me there is nothing more than Chambacú. Not even Cartegena.] Since his identity is singularly tied to the place, that situated identity guides his response to both dilemmas and will lead first to Máximo's imprisonment as a conscientious objector and later to his death as he demonstrates against the Peace Corps presence—which the community "sees as an arm of Yankee imperialism" (107), an extension of patterns of dependency (external and internal colonizations) into the present.

With little modification, this same drama continues *in real places* such as Nicaragua's Atlantic Coast; on the border that Ecuador contentiously shares with Peru; in rural northeastern Brazil in the effort to secure legal rights for former *quilombos*; in "gentrified" or "renewed" urban centers in Salvador da

Bahia, Brazil (dramatized in Bando de Teatro Olodum's *Trilogia*); and in Montevideo, Uruguay (represented in Cardoso's 1992 *El desalojo de la calle de los negros*), among other contested sites. In the last two instances, the uprooting and dispersal of the Black community ironically strengthened and extended Blackness throughout the respective cities, ironically reenacting the diasporic expansion set in motion during the Middle Passage. Discussing Black land rights in Latin America, Edmund Gordon, professor of anthropology and Black studies at the University of Texas at Austin, juxtaposes Nicaraguan land-title struggles dictated by indigenous claims considered primordial tradition—and therefore self-evident—and those European discourses that exclude both natives and peoples of African descent based on the tenets of modernity; these tenets include, one, proprietorship, the ultimate aim of empire/nation and mercantile progress and, two, the pretense/allegation of the capacity to tame, to settle, and to control the land. In modern-day struggles for land rights and titles, these Blacks, similar to their fictional counterparts, are therefore viewed as latecomers, squatters, trespassers who lack legitimate claim, a subtext that impacts national land redistribution strategies as well as funding decisions of international nongovernmental entities, including the World Bank.

Thus, the concept or idea of territory contains political, cultural, and economic considerations. In an attempt to decipher the promise and predicaments of postmodern globalization in that layered context, Stefan Immerfall observes

> Territory means bounded and marked social space. Territoriality refers to human behaviour as it is spatially organized or oriented. It works as a resource control strategy, proscribing specific activities within spatial boundaries. *Space, boundaries, boundary control,* and *boundary transgression* are the key words of the territorial approach. It is important to emphasize that none of these are naturally given. The territorial approach is about power as well as identity. Territory both constrains and impacts movements. Territory enables far-flung contacts as it symbolizes protection and community. (7)

Hence, at least conceptually, the "taking possession, use and defense" of space described by Hall becomes more nuanced in the configuration, control, and transgression of boundaries.

Compelled by the undeniable interconnectedness of political, economic, and social systems, what i term *metropoly* (offspring of the West's earlier monopoly over meaning) embraces relative and hybrid modes of the human—in their Westernized, secularized, liberalized aspect—much like the (elitist) colonizer's earlier embrace of sanitized and homogenized expressions of Black popular culture. Consequently, in the play of identificatory and discursive power, ever-more-distanced peripheries persist precisely because their most meaningful linkages are to origins and coherencies necessarily counterintuitive to metropolizing, deculturizing, deterritorializing paradigms, systems of signs into which those communities are nevertheless inserted—and expunged—as needed. Hence, for example, the unique experience and expression of peoples of African descent in the Americas (and in the Black Diaspora) focus the continuing negation and negotiation of Blackness, its role (constitutive function/fiction), its representation (languages, textualities), and its relation to power. At once coherent and contestatory, their cultural production necessarily stems from the formative import of a "premodern" globalization that begins in Africa in the 1440s: a nature-culture conception of being at odds with those technologic-economic paradigms that, in privileging metropolitan ascendancy, contributed to the physical enslavement, the material impoverishment, and the discursive marginalization of Africa, her diaspora, and her descendants; to racial dynamics that laid bare the relativity of equality; and to the endurance of hierarchies, both tacit and overt. As a result, a peculiar and belligerent liminality, distinct from the labored construction of hybridities and resistance, situates the Africana imaginary—accented in Spanish and Portuguese—as doubly conscious, doubly colonized, doubly marginalized, and doubly tangential, at best, to meanings—and territories—favored by monopoly/metropoly.

Accordingly, the experience of peoples of African descent in the Americas attests to a tenuous and at the same time tenacious relation to territory in which they work a land not their own, fight for the independence of a nation in which they are not free, and occupy a space at the whim of systems disinterested in their well-being. Therefore to "refashion territory" is to refashion both identity and one's relations to power. An early response by peoples of African descent to uprootedness and the dynamics of territoriality can be seen in the central role played by *cabildos*, associations and social clubs in communities of African descent in the New World.

In *The Black Diaspora* (1995), Ronald Segal writes that while church and state encouraged *cabildos* in Cuba "in the hope that these would promote among their members the spread of Christianity," in reality "[m]ost cabildos were apparently more concerned with measures of welfare"(431), that is, "con fines de hermandad, socorro, ayuda mutua, cooperación y religiosidad" (Padilla Pérez 140) [toward the aims of brotherhood, assistance, mutual aid, cooperation and religious ends]. Allowing for a supervised reconfiguration of territorialities, these associations proved useful in teaching new arrivals their "place," functioning according to gentleman-anthropologist Fernando Ortiz "a manera de cónsul de los extranjeros, que servía de lazo político con los importados africanos" (4) [similar to a consulate for foreign nationals that served as political connection for the imported Africans]. With the interested blessing of official entities—church and state—hoping to "promote disunity" between tribal groupings on the one hand and "cohesion" within a particular group, on the other, these societies "were organized along 'national' lines, to associate those extracted or descended from a particular African people" (Segal 431). Similar disunities would be encouraged in later generations: territories between *bozales* and *criollos*; between *negros* and *mulatos* (and other possible configurations of Black and Amerindian); between field and house slaves, slave and free.

Borrowing liberally from undocumented sources,[6] Rossi describes similar associations in the context of *candombe* festivities in the River Plate region:

> En la época *colonial* los *locales* se titulaban "canchas" porque la fiesta se hacía al aire libre, en la parte de la ciudad vieja, donde hoy corren las calles Reconquista y Residencia, lugar que llamaban "Cubo del Sud." . . . Cada "nación" tomaba su parte de terreno, y esas eran las canchas, como también los son hoy y así las llamamos en todos los casos análogos, sea cual sea su objeto. (67)

> [In the *colonial* period the *localities* were called "fields" because the celebration took place in the open air, in the old part of the city where today the streets Reconquista and Residencia run, a place called "Cubo del Sud." . . . Each "nation" had its own territory and these were the fields just as they are today and so we call them in every similar instance, whatever might be their objective.]

These fugitive territories, established and dismantled each Sunday, provided a unique configuration of space and society. Chronicler Isidoro De María in

Montevideo antiguo (qtd. in Rossi) explains that in "esos barrios, de notoriedad y distinción" [those notorious/well-known and distinguished neighborhoods]

> [s]e observaba verdadera democracia, se respectaban las expansiones del humilde aunque fuera negro. Todo ha desaparecido menos el Cubo, escondido tras el templo de los ingleses, prefiriendo el constante castigo del mar a la contemplación del estado social a que hemos llegado, en la Plata como en todas partes, a base de la indisoluble combinación de Progreso y Miseria. (243)

> [one observed a true democracy; the expansions of the humble, even if he were Black, were respected. All of that has disappeared except for Cubo, hidden behind the English church, preferring the constant punishment of the sea to the contemplation of the social condition to which we have come, in River Plate as in other places, as a result of the indivisible combination of Progress and Misery.]

In the era of the republic, various neighborhoods, in the "suburbios" [outskirts], hosted "salones de bailes" [dance salons] and "academias" [(dance) academies] for the enjoyment of *milonga*. Those more permanent spaces and the derived musical form represent the offspring of the rudimentary "candombe canchas" (Rossi 115–47).

Fugitive territories sprang up throughout the Black Diaspora. Writing of the U.S. Black migration/exodus northward in the 1920s, Amiri Baraka offers another example of the permutability of space and society, observing, "The move north, for instance, had broken down the old communities (the house parties were one manifestation of a regrouping of the newer communities: The Harlems and South Chicagos). . . . The dance bands or society orchestras of the North replaced the plot of land for they were the musician's only means of existence" but still retained a "more intense sense of self in its most vital relationship to the world" giving tone to a "wonderfully extended version of . . . communal expression" ("Swing," 44–45).

In Bahia (Brazil), a similar migratory phenomenon took place:

> The [Candomblé] houses gained support and adherents among the lower class by providing a well-organized social structure for a displaced population. Migrants who had left the traditional social structure and patronage networks of rural Bahia for the uncertain life of a burgeon-

ing urban center found an extended family and a renewed sense of social position in Candomblé. Relationships within the *candomblés* were couched in familial terms; mothers- and fathers-of-the-saints (*mães-* and *pais-de-santo*) initiated daughters- and sons-of-the-saints (*filhas-* and *filhos-de-santo*). Patronage relationships also developed as members became part of larger social networks, allaying the sense of urban isolation. (Wimberly 79)

Intriguingly, in many instances the melding of practice (dance) and space share the same name, indicating the interwovenness of experience and expression in the context of territoriality. Over time, the location and dimensions of the "plot" may have changed but the uses to which it was put—cohesion and altruism—did not.

In another case, the migration of meanings reflects a "moving" history of refashioned territory. Blas Matamoro argues that the word *tango* referred first to "los lugares de concentración de africanos previos al embarque," then "al lugar donde se ofrecía en venta esta población esclava, ya en tierra americana," and finally designated "las sociedades de negros libertos y libres" (59) [the places where Africans were housed/stored prior to embarkment, (then) the place where this enslaved population were put up for sale in America, (and finally designated) the societies of freed and freeborn Blacks]. Similar to the Cuban *cabildo*, these mutual aid associations, also called "naciones" (in the sense of ethnicities), were structured according to ethnic groupings and

solían juntar dinero para redimir negros esclavos y conservaban la identidad tribal de orígen por medio de celebraciones periódicas, la elección de los "reyes" de la nación y la conservación del culto a sus santos regionales, a menudo una síncresis o mixtura de viejas deidades africanas con santos católicos. (Matamoro 59)

[used to gather money in order to manumit slaves and they preserved the original tribal identity by means of periodic celebrations, the election of ethnic-group "royalty" and the preservation of the cult of regional saints, often a syncretism or mixture of ancient African deities with Catholic saints.]

Not surprisingly, the "official" decline of *cabildos* and *canchas* coincided with the end of slavery and the beginning of another patriarchal institution—the nation: "De la abolición de la esclavitud arranca la decadencia de los cabildos" (F. Ortiz 11) [The decline of the *cabildos* stems from the abolition of slavery]. Concomitantly, "standard" language began to nationalize formerly racially coded designations, separating the artistic expression from spaces—and peoples—associated with Blackness. In some cases the demise, abetted by legal prohibitions, revealed a general distrust of a potential "Black-lash" in the "emancipated" nation reminiscent of earlier uprisings, such as those depicted in the play and movie *Plácido*—which dramatized events surrounding the 1844 Ladder Rebellion in Cuba—and in the stage spectacle *A Conspiração dos Alfaiates* (Aninha Franco, 1992) [The Tailors' Conspiracy] in Salvador da Bahia.[7] In other cases, the assisted suicide, as described in contemporary writings, stressed Black incapacity and paid homage to the capacity of the nation.

> Estos datos demuestran la imposible adaptación de los cabildos a la legislación moderna; la inconstancia e incapacidad de sus directores para las formalidades escritas y de una administración seria, propia de una civilización jurídica adelantada; la vida artificial de algunos de esos cabildos sin existenica real y positiva, y la única razón de persistencia de unos pocos: el culto fetichista traído de África y todavía vigoroso y extendido en toda Cuba. (F. Ortiz 16)

> [These facts demonstrate the impossibility of the societies adapting themselves to modern legislation; the inconsistency and incapacity of their directorate for written formalities and serious administration, proper of an advanced juridical civilization; the artificial life of some of these societies, neither real nor positive, and, the only reason for the persistence of some few: the fetish cult brought from Africa and still vigorous and extended in all of Cuba.]

Earlier writing on the subject suggests that these associations represented an inroad by European organization that structured, legislated, and adjudicated the lives of peoples of African descent (for example, F. Ortiz). Juridical prohibitions and police records attest to just how shaky that control was in reality. Padilla Pérez cites *Enciclopedia Universal Sopena*, which tellingly defines the *cabildos* in the following terms: "En Cuba, corporación de personas ineptas, reunión tumultuosa o desordenada" (137) [In Cuba, corporation of inept persons, a tumultuous and chaotic meeting]. In Brazil, Black religious fraternities sanctioned by the Catholic Church and Candomblé *terreiros*, who enjoyed no such blessing, offer examples of the inefficacy of state authority. In the introduction to *Afro-Brazilian Culture and Politics* (1998), Hendrik Kraay explains: "Until well into the twentieth century, campaigns against Candomblé and other manifestations of Afro-Bahian culture such as the dance and martial arts of capoeira came and went with some frequency, sometimes brutal violence, and singular lack of success" (14).[8] Analyzed in the context of a response to uprootedness, the tenacity and belligerence of these spaces becomes more readily understood. Thus the strategic motivations—destiny, distance, dominance, and status—imply a context and a continuity for this aspect of Blackness, not only through the Middle Passage or during slavery but also into the present with numerous groupings: expatriated Cabo Verdeans and more recent formal and informal associations and networks of African immigrants from Nigeria, Senegal, and Ivory Coast in Buenos Aires Argentina; sociopolitical entities such as Mundo Afro (Uruguay), Instituto Negro Continuo (Peru), Movimiento Negro Francisco Congo (Peru); Centro Indio-Afro-Americano (Santa Fe, Argentina); Centro Cultural Afroecuatoriano, associated with Instituto Nacional de Pastoral Afroecuatoriano (Quito, Quayquil); Federación de organizaciones Grupos Negros de Pichincha (FOGNEP) (Quito);[9] and race-based *blocos de carnaval* in Rio de Janeiro, São Paulo, São Luis, and Salvador da Bahia (for example, in the last city, Filhos de Ghandi [1949]; Ilê Ayê [1970], Olodum [1979]).

Racial segregation also played a part in nurturing the mimetic desire of peoples of African descent to establish their own social and recreational territories that aped those of the whiter community from which they were barred by color, as well as by class and caste:[10]

> Como no tenían acceso a ningún club social, en el caso de las familias; y ni siquiera los hombres podían hacer tertulias en los cafés de los suburbios . . . era entonces imprescindible un lugar de reunión de la colectividad. . . .
>
> A partir de ese momento, el proceso fundacional del Club Uruguay es un poco la columna vertebral de las actividades de los negros de Melo, a través de su historia encontramos intelectuales, poetas populares, deportistas, vinculación con grupos políticos liderados por negros en todo el país y la participación de la mujer. En 1927 es ya un propósito la construcción de la sede del club, que sigue siendo la única entidad social con estas características en el país. (Ruíz 74)

[Since they had no access to social clubs, in the case of the families; and not even the men were able to hold meetings in the outlying cafes . . . it was therefore necessary to have a meeting place for the community. . . .

From that moment on, the idea of founding Club Uruguay is the backbone of Black activities in Melo, and through its history we find intellectuals, popular poets, athletes, association with political groups headed by Blacks throughout the country and the participation of women. As early as 1927, a goal was the construction of a central seat that continues to be the sole social entity in the country with these characteristics.]

While other types of discrimination disappeared or diminished, the more long-lived segregation of social clubs was seen in a different light. In Uruguay one observer attests: "No lo van a dejar entrar en un club a un negro que va incorrecto, lógico. Por supuesto" (Porzecanski and Santos 20) [They're not going to let into the club a Black who has no business there anyway, logically. Of course]. In Brazil, persons judged "socialmente brancas ou brancas na cor" [socially white or almost white] can gain membership, although as one informant noted, "[quem] admitem é o doutor, não o preto" (T. Azevedo 141) [(whom) they admit is the doctor, not the Black]. Hence, members of African-descended communities throughout Latin America clearly understood the literal and figurative importance of a territory of their own, as one informant testifies:

"Planteábamos los problemas, las necesidades de la colectividad, las necesidades de la sede propia. Imaginesé que había una base muy importante que era el predio. . . . Ese edificio se hizo a pulmón ahí, entre todos." (Ruíz 74)

[We outlined the problems, the needs of the community, the needs of the central seat itself. Think about it, there was a very important base that was the physical structure. . . . That building became the heart, for all of us.]

In another response to the juridical dislocation-dispossession-disruption of territoriality, recent works that could be termed *land biographies* map Blackness by prioritizing place, both geographical site and discursive space. In those works, the experience of uprooting—whether Middle Passage, shipwreck, or expulsion—makes for an exemplary prototypical being: the freedom-seeking escaped slaves of Esmeraldas and Palmares (Zumbi, Ganga Zumbi, and followers) and former Cuban slaves (*mambises*) who planted the seed of freedom in the wars of national liberation. Their images will reappear in fact and in fiction as this passage from Adalaberto Ortiz's *Juyungo* demonstrates:

[S]egún cuentan, hace ya mucho tiempo, allá por el año 1553, frente a las costas de Esmeraldas, naufragó un barco negrero que llevaba veintitrés esclavos negros y negras, aprovecharon el momento para ganar tierra e internarse en estas montañas. Otros aseguran que los esclavos se sublevaron, y acabando con la tripulación, encallaron la nave y saltaron. (238)

[(A)ccording to legend, many years ago in 1553 off the coast of Esmeraldas a slave ship that carried twenty-three male and female Black slaves ran aground; they took advantage of the event to get to land and hid themselves in the mountains. Others swear that the slaves revolted and after having done away with the crew, set the boat adrift and jumped ship.]

Thus *esmeraldeanos* see themselves as a part of a "fuerza humana elemental que casi intuitivamente buscaba un camino de libertad . . . un símbolo de su raza en marcha, creciendo y creciendo" (239) [elemental human force that almost intuitively sought the road to freedom . . . a symbol of their race in movement, growing ever stronger], based in historical personalities such as Alonso de Illescas. Historical chronicles of the area that postdate *Juyungo*'s publication reiterate this tie between belligerency and enclave (for example, *El negro en Esmeraldas* by Julio Estupiñán Tello). In much the same way, the poetry collections *De la tierra brava: Poemas Afroyungas* (1938) by Peru's Enrique Lopéz Albújar (1872–1965) and *Animal fiero y tierno* (1977) by Puerto Rican Ángela María Dávila employ geographical space and sense territories to ground their lyrical search for identity. In "Homeaje a Julia de Burgos," Dávila writes

desde nuestro dolor
hay mucho espacio mudo de fronteras continuas

hay mucha sombra y mucha canción rota
hay mucha historia. (32)

[as a result of our pain
there is the endless mute space of uninterrupted frontiers
there is endless shadow and unending broken song
there is endless history.]

Again and again uprootedness *becomes* the motivating pretense for a version of history overlooked or underrepresented in the dominant version of world events.

By narrating place in both its material and potential dimensions, subjects also purport to narrate themselves, a theme discussed by anthropologist Jacqueline Nassy Brown in her study of Black participation in Liverpool's Age of Sail. Several Latin American works of situated Blackness repeat this territorial thematic of the effects of uprootedness on destiny and distance, dominance and status.[11] For example, in the monograph *Blacks in Colonial Veracruz* (1991), Patrick J. Carroll describes the racially determined distribution of space in urban areas, ripe for the transgression of established boundaries. "Naturally," Spaniards occupied the nucleus: "*Pardos*, mulattoes, and mestizos ranked below Spaniards. This lower rank relegated them to residence on the fringes of the urban core. Hispanicized Indians represent a second subordinate group. They made their homes in the most distant urban *barrios*" (115). This unwittingly strategic placement coupled with the absence or always-threatened security of the family structure "within the slave community induced many Afro-Veracruzanos to seek social bonds in the broader population" (115). Thus

> Not fully accepted into either the creole Hispanic or the native Indian community, Afro-*castas* and blacks lived in both. As a result Afro-Veracruzanos consistently represented the most socially outgoing element with the developing regional populations. . . . This interrelating proved a remarkable tribute to the resilience of their spirit. Afro-Veracruzanos entered a strange and demanding setting restrained . . . [by] slave status, white racism and ethnocentrism, and Iberian law [which] reduced the level and degree of . . . opportunity with the setting. Vera Cruz's Afro-American population not only survived this opposition,

they made positive contributions to the development of the area in the process. (Carroll 147)

In other situations, in Peru for example, the proximity to Spanish colonials in the coastal region and the distance from the majority indigenous population in the *serrano* or *selva* regions, fostered allegiances and fomented mistrust described by Afro-Peruvian *indigenista* writer Enrique Lopéz Albújar in his memoirs, *De mi casona* (1924). Place and proximity would in turn determine loyalties in the colonial wars for national liberation from Spain. On this subject, Peruvian José Carlos Mariátegui had strong opinions. On the one hand, the renowned writer asserted that Black contact with the Spanish colonizer negatively impacted the indigenous and worked "bastardearlo comunicándole su domesticidad zalalmera y su psicología esteriorizante y mórbida" [to bastardize (the aboriginal) by communicating (the Black slaves') fawning domesticity and their barren and moribund psychology]. On the other hand, similar to the scenario offered by Argentine Rossi, Mariátegui soundly criticizes the continuing relationship between the former Black slave and the former (whiter) master:

Para su antiguo amo blanco ha guardado, después de su manumisión, un sentimiento de liberto adicto. La sociedad colonial, que hizo del negro un doméstico—muy pocas veces un artesano, un obrero—absorbió y asimiló a la raza negra, hasta intoxicarse con su sangre tropical y caliente. Tanto como impenetrable y huraño el indio, le fue asequible y doméstico el negro. . . . El mulato, colonial aun en sus gustos, inconscientemente está por el hispanismo, contra el autoctonismo. Se siente espontáneamente más próximo de España que del Inkario. ("El proceso" 220–21)

[For his former white master he has guarded after his manumission an attitude of the recovering addict. Colonial society, which made the Black a domestic—very rarely an artisan or worker—absorbed and assimilated the Black race to the extent of intoxicating itself with their hot tropical blood. The Black was as detestable and tamed as the Indian was inscrutable and distant. . . . The mulatto, colonial even in his tastes, unconsciously favors things Hispanic, not autochthony. He naturally feels closer to Spain than to the Incan world.]

The Marxian thinker will advise that only with socialism could the Peruvian Black be redeemed.

Thus, Blackness—always, already negatively marked—was predictably further corrupted by the slave-master relationship and, what is more, spread contagion when in contact with indigenous peoples. Both attitudes underscore the experiences of *urban* slaves in countries such as Mexico and Peru, with a smaller number of bondspeople, in terms of social mobility, economic opportunities, speed of manumission, and the proximity of free and indentured peoples of Africa descent (Hünefeldt 9–17), liberties more difficult to access in the rural plantation setting of slaveocracies such as those of Cuba, the United States, Brazil. Brazil's relentless attacks on Palmares contrasts with "treaty arrangements with rebellious Blacks" in Mexico that led to the free Black townships of "San Lorenzo de los Negros (founded in 1609), San Lorenzo Cerralvo (1635), and Nuestra Señora de Guadalupe de los Morenos de Amapa (1769) in the mountains of Vera Cruz" (Robinson 15). Carroll writes that the first of these was earlier called Yanga after its original founder, who established the *palenque* [runaway settlement] in 1580 and saw it evolve from a base for marauders into a home for villagers, from "fugitive to legal settlement" (92). In Peru, during the republic, census records show that between 50 and 60 percent of the population were of African descent (Hünefeldt, Mariñez): "Hasta el siglo XVIII había más negros y mulatos que blancos en el Perú" (Clave, qtd. in Mariñez 13) [until the eighteenth century there were more Blacks and mulattos than whites in Peru]. Internal migration and immigration (openly encouraged by national governments all over Latin America), intermarriage, epidemics, wars, and the unreliability of the information itself are variously presented as possible explanations for greatly reduced present-day percentages. However well into the 1950s, Lima hosted a concentrated and vibrant Peruvian Africana community. In that context, Pablo Mariñez writes of renowned Afro-Peruvian cultural historian and performer Nicomedes Santa Cruz Gamarra

> nace el 4 de junio de 1925, en el barrio de La Victoria, por lo que le toca no sólo crecer en la Lima que todavía preservaba sus tradiciones populares negras y mulatas, de origen africano, sino también vivir y conocer la mutación cultural que a mediados de la década de los cincuenta se produciría en la capital peruana. (14)

[he was born on June 4, 1925 in the La Victoria neighborhood which meant not only did he grow up in a Lima which still preserved its Black and Mulatto popular traditions of African origin but that he also lived and witnessed firsthand the cultural change that would take place in the mid 1950s.]

In two interviews with Mariñez, Santa Cruz reminisced,

"En esta Lima que yo nací, que era una Lima mulata, que ignoraba al resto del país, desde el gobierno en su centralismo hasta el mismo pueblo mulato se sentían diferentes de la mayoría andina y la ignoraban, aunque vivían de ella. Esa Lima ya no existe más. . . . Lima era un enclave que estaba ligado más al Caribe que al resto del Perú, porque había desarrollado una cultura mulata en trescientos años y entre murallas." (14)

[The Lima where I was born was a Mulatto Lima that ignored the rest of the country; both the government with its centralism and the same mulatto people felt themselves different from the Andean majority and they ignored it even though they were surrounded by it. That Lima no longer exists. . . . Lima was an enclave that was more tied to the Caribbean than to the rest of Peru because, in three hundred years, they had developed a mulatto culture between walls.]

That "Mulatto" Lima proved a fertile creative base for the Santa Cruz dynasty, including Nicomedes' sister Victoria Santa Cruz Gamarra, founder of *Compañía Cumanana* (1959) and *Teatro y Danzas Negros del Peru* (1966).

The enclave approach submits that geographical isolation can, to some extent, control, or at the least ameliorate, the categorical space of negation that Blackness typically occupies in the larger context of the nation-state and on the global scene as well. While not immune to globalized discursive significations (endoracism, systemic racism, anti-Blackness), geographical isolation or segregation—whether accidental or intentioned—oddly allows "native" values and perspectives to intervene and infringe on dominant enunciations since experience stands at odds with and expression goes against the grain of knowledges elsewhere assumed or accepted. Hence, in *Barloventeñidad: aporte literario* (1997), a study of Black space and expression, Venezuelan

Jesús "Chucho" García asserts that "la especificidad cultural barloventeña se fue configurando a través de su historia y su espacio" (18) [the Barloventan cultural specificity was configured by its history and its space]. By extension, his impulse to that examination also resides in the question/questioning of how writers-intellectuals-professionals "locate" themselves and their local practices in the context of the critical and theoretical paradigms or sacred "truths" propounded by the disciplines—history, sociology, anthropology— and that have shaped their analyses. Not infrequently, "objective" disciplines' universalizing discourses run afoul of "subjective" observation and pertinent case studies, creating a conflicted fealty and an evidentiary gap revealed in praxis and autobiographical self-reflexivity.

Likewise, the uprootedness of peoples of African descent and the result-ing need to refashion territory ironically promoted their paradoxical impor-tance in New World practices and paradigms. According to González, Span-ish presence "fue sumamente inestable" (20) [was highly unstable], with those colonial settlers and later immigrants who could do so going to richer colonies to be replaced by new arrivals who continued to see themselves as Spanish nationals. Conversely, "los descendientes de los primeros esclavos eran ya *puertorriqueños* negros" (20) [the descendants of the first slaves were already Black Puerto Ricans], no longer recorded as *bozales* (born in Old World Africa) but rather *criollos* (born in the New World Americas). It was from these "natives" that the new immigrants would take their cue:

> Por lo que toca al campesinado blanco de esos primeros tiempos, o sea los primeros: "jíbaros," lo cierto es que era un campesinado pobre que se vio obligado a adoptar muchos de los hábitos de vida de los otros pobres que vivían desde antes en el país, vale decir los esclavos. En rel-ación con esto, no está de más señalar que cuando en el Puerto Rico de hoy se habla, por ejemplo, de "comida jíbara," se está hablando, en realidad, de "comida de negros": plátanos, arroz, bacalao, funche, etc. (González 21)

> [In regard to what affects the white peasant in those early times, that is to say the first Puerto Rican nationals, is that he was undoubtedly a poor peasant who saw himself obliged to adopt many of the ways of the other poor who lived up to that time in the country, which is to say, the slaves. In that context, it is not unreasonable to suggest that when

in today's Puerto Rico one speaks, for example, of traditional Puerto Rican cuisine, the topic in reality is Black food: plantains, rice, dried fish, polenta, etc.]

González goes on to posit,

Si la "cocina nacional" de todas las islas y las regiones litorales de la cuenca del Caribe es prácticamente la misma por lo que atañe a sus ingredientes esenciales y sólo conoce ligeras (aunque en muchos casos imaginativas) variantes combinatorias, pese al hecho de que esos países fueron colonizados por naciones europeas de tan diferentes tradiciones culinarias como la española, la francesa, la inglesa y la holandesa, ello sólo puede explicarse, me parece, en virtud de que todos los caribeños—insulares o continentales—comemos y bebemos más como negros que como europeos. (21)

[If the "national cuisine" of all the islands and littoral regions of the Caribbean is practically the same as far as their essential ingredients and only evinces small (although in many cases imaginative) combinatory variations, despite the fact that those countries were colonized by European nations of culinary traditions as varied as the Spanish, the French, the English and the Dutch, this can only be explained, it seems to me, by virtue of the fact that all Caribbean people—island or continental—eat and drink more like Blacks than like Europeans.]

Even in the reportedly *negro*-free zone of Argentina, what are considered national dishes, like *mondongo*, represent by name, preparation, and ingredients concoctions unmistakably *à la Africana*.

It is this dissonance with theory that Hall recognized: "For years, blacks have been regarded as underdeveloped whites, when in fact black culture is very rich and has its own unwritten rules governing behavior. Recognition of black culture has always been important. Now it is critical" (*Beyond Culture* 82). Puerto Rican thinker González echoes that sentiment:

Ya es lugar común decir que esa cultura tiene tres raíces históricas: la taína, la africana y la española. Lo que no es lugar común, sino todo lo contrario, es afirmar que de esas tres raíces, la más importante, por razones económicas y sociales, y en consecuencia culturales, es la africana. (19)

[It is quite common to say that (Puerto Rican) culture has three roots: the Taina (aboriginal), the African and the Spanish. What is not so common, but quite the contrary, is the assertion that, of these three roots, the most important, for economic and social, and consequently cultural, reasons, is the African.]

Likewise in Carpentier's discussion of music and the Spanish immigrant—colonizer and settler—the Cuban writer concludes that, because of the preoccupation with recreating Iberian ways, "nada les quedaba por hacer" (302) [nothing was left for them to do] in terms of the invention of a *sui generis* culture in the Americas. That phenomenon reproduces itself in the "on hold" posture of enclave societies such as Little Havana, Little Italys, and Chinatowns, confirming the Wynterian assertion that the uprootedness of the Black "qua African slave" heralded a condition that would in the twentieth century become common to all. That "all" would include peoples of African descent; one might wonder if postmodern and globalized uprootedness had other dynamics for Black immigrants in the twentieth century who arrived as "guest" workers or political refugees.

Not unexpectedly, Africans or those of African descent who neither passed through the Middle Passage nor survived chattel slavery nor descended as a "minority" from this history, confront uprootedness distinctly. Throughout the 1990s a number of films dealt with uprootedness in the sense of expatriation discussed by Ilie. *Otomo* (Schlaich 1999, Germany) dramatizes the case of an African killed by police in Germany: he carries among his meager possessions an earth-filled baggy, his material and spiritual tie to the abandoned territory. *Cartas de Alou* (Armendáriz 1990, Spain) and *Bwana* (Uribe 1996, Spain) trace illegal male African immigration to Spain. *Flores de otro mundo* (Bollaín 1999, Spain-Dominican Republic) treats female emigration, examining paper marriage and the plights of domestic and sexual workers. *Pieces d'identite* (Ngangura 1998, Belgium/Congo/France) and *Les noms n'habilitent nulle parte* (Loreau 1994, Belgium) explore discomfited cultural encounters of Old World Africa in New World Europe. The Dominican movie *Nueba Yol* (Muñoz 1995, Dominican Republic) follows the peregrinations of a caricatured protagonist, as much Black buffoon as rural naïf, who long has yearned to move to the gold-paved streets of New York and who, once there, is assailed by the intense desire to return to his island roots.

In some cases, displaced immigrants attempt to distance themselves from the denigrating ontological tie to the slave descended. For example, the Maryse Condé historical novel *Tree of Life* (1992) [*La vie scélérate*, 1987] sympathetically traces the peregrinations of various family members, underscoring the hard-fought gains of hard-working and industrious immigrants—in Panama during the building of the transoceanic canal, in France, at home. However, the novel paints an oddly if not inexplicably disparaging picture of North American Blacks, descendants of slaves, represented by their superstitious Pentecostal religious practices, drug-addicted or imprisoned offspring, and impoverished or welfare-dependent lives. In *The Crisis of the Negro Intellectual* (1967), Harold Cruse offers another example of this distancing:

> This is true even in the case of former Virgin Islanders: They identify with the British West Indies proper, even though all Virgin Islanders have been American citizens since 1927. The stereotype of America Negro inferiority is so strong among many West Indians that to them an extra-intelligent American Negro either has distant West Indian antecedents, or else the ability to "think like a West Indian." This has led to another West Indian myth—that the British West Indies were peopled by a different breed of African slaves (when indeed West Indians will admit to slavery) than those landed at American ports. (424)

Similarly, in *Haitian Immigrants in Black America* (1996) Flore Zéphir discusses the constructed aloofness between displaced/exiled Black Haitians and slave-descended Black North Americans based on the Caribbeans' desire to disassociate themselves from the negativity—fictionally scripted in Condé's novel—of Middle Passage uprootedness.

In contrast, Cuban Marta Rojas's historical novel *El columpio de Rey Spencer* (1993) adroitly plays with this opposition, recognizing the coherency wrought by serial uprootedness. The fictionalized chronicle combines personal memory, carefully guarded love letters, diaries, oral histories, and the great wash of unfiltered Internet information to recount the intra-Antillean flight from the harsh conditions of pre–World War II Jamaica. The hopeful immigrants seek their fortunes in eastern Cuba but find themselves working as little more than slaves on the same *ingenios* [sugar plantations] as had their bonded ancestors. Competing for scarce jobs and resources, at the whim of nature (hurricanes) and the price fluctuations of anonymous and distant monocultural agribusiness, the outsiders see their situation exacerbated by racism, economic disparities, and linguistic and cultural bigotry.

Intra-Antilles migration also provides the theme in the Dominican novel *Tiempo muerto* (1997) by Avelino Stanley (whose very name announces a bifurcated identity), which tells the story of the so-called *cocolos* through *testimonio* and letters in the unassuming tone of the opening paragraph:

> La historia de un negro no le interesa a nadie. Y menos si es un viejo que nada notable ha hecho en su vida. Sólo a ti se te ocurre escucharme. Sé que lo haces porque me quieres mucho. Por eso te cuento lo que me pides. Pero de nada servir lo que te diga. Porque de nosotros lo único que ha interesado siempre es nuestro trabajo. Después, más nada. Y, a cambio, nos han devuelto mucho rechazo, mucho desprecio por ser negros. (9)

> [A Black man's story is of no interest to anyone. And less so if he is an old man that has done nothing notable in his life. It would only occur to you to listen to me. I know that you do it because you love me very much. For that reason I'll tell you what you ask. But what I tell you has no point. Because the only thing about us that is of interest is our labor. Beyond that, nothing. And, in return they have given us, for being Black, rejection, disrespect.]

These novels make the connection between the hardships of displacement that clearly have multiplied over time, yet the permutated territory of Blackness continues to evoke an easily recognizable trail of signifiers.

In that light, all of the "immigrant" narratives variously replay the paradigms and paradoxes of uprootedness in the Americas, "the original model of the total twentieth century disruption of man . . . that exile, which in our century is now common to all" (Wynter "We Must Learn," 307). Consequently, the "new-comer" African and African-descended are beset by the same "vulturistic isms" that marked the reception of their fellows in the world that was new in the fifteenth century: racism, elitism (classism), sexism, national chauvinism, etc. Indeed, the same mentality that equated *negro* (lack) and *esclavo* (drone) now reveals itself in color-conscious immigration policies that assume neediness and criminality on the one hand and expects, on the other, that nonnatives content themselves with the most meager of conditions and consideration. As in the cases of the thinly fictionalized prose and filmic immigrants examined above, their human counterparts find themselves becoming yet another labor force totally at the disposal of capitalism—the cause, aim, and bane of their migratory quest. In that sense, African uprootedness anticipated both the dispossession propelled by modernity's Industrial Revolution and the predicament of the migrant Black propelled by postmodernity's Technological Revolution. Thus, in the contemporary context, deterritorialization continues to determine destiny, distance, and dominance—or the lack thereof. The stakes are high, including the harsh realities of death, deportation, marriages of convenience, economic disparities, and a web of legal statuses (refugee, resident, citizen), as elusive as they are difficult to negotiate. Those variables continue to negatively mark the newly uprooted other of African descent as, once again, biologically disselected, "incapaz de civilização" (Luz 23) or "invincibly ignorant." Yet again, that's the point: whether for the historically dispersed African descended or the newly displaced Africans and Afros, the problem of uprootedness begs a response, "something that not only conditions people to cope with disjuncture and change but also provides them with a basic survival technique that is commensurate with and suitable to the rootlessness and the discontinuity so characteristic of human existence in the contemporary world" (Murray 113). Improvisation represents just such a strategic wager, a wager that needs a "hypothesis, to get started" (Moretti 55).

Coming to Terms

Improvisation

Perhaps thinking of the matador's deft movements in the bullring, Ernest Hemingway described "guts" as "grace under pressure."[1] That phrase provides an apt point of departure for this discussion of improvisation as the gutsy intersection of skill and serendipity. Just as the bullfighter relies on a prescribed ritual, costume, and a particular choreography in the confrontation with a knowable yet always unpredictable taurine foe, so too peoples of African descent in the face of permuting and layered uprootings—spatial, cosmological—favor culturally bound and sanctioned "tools, tropes and formulae" that bespeak a praxis. Their pressured and patterned responses, often misread as a series of seemingly random actions, reveal a peculiarly versioned sense of timing, rhythmicity and, at its height, mastery—most recognized in orality and musicality, but part of the "fabric of mental, emotional and physical activities whose threads hold a people together within and across generations" (Chinweizu "Literature," 215). Although the notions of uprootedness and improvisation could apply to other groups, the particular combination of motivating events and possible responses remains peculiar to the marriage of the unifying experience/context and expression/devices of African-ancestored peoples in the Americas.

That music has provided an explanatory model for the dynamics of Blackness is nowhere new: consider Vincente Rossi on tango in Argentina, Hermano Vianna on samba in Brazil, Lauro Ayestarán on candombe comparsas in Uruguay (1953), Alejo Carpentier in Cuba, Amiri Baraka in *Blues People* (1963),[2] and Albert Murray, Stanley Crouch, and countless others on jazz in the United States. Paul Gilroy touched upon the theme in *The Black Atlantic* as did Antonio Benítez-Rojo in *Repeating Island*. All these works configure the participation as well as the contribution of peoples of African descent in the Americas. Likewise, numerous texts address one or another aspect of orality in this same community: *decimistas*, *payadores*, *pregoneros*, spinners of folk tales (Santa Cruz, *Décimas*; Marvin Lewis, *Afro-Argentine*; Cabrera, *Cuentos negros*; Carpentier, *La música*).

As a function of the frame into which each study is inserted, narrative tends to create and confirm a particular worldview or version of history, and everything around it makes it true. Accordingly, this project deliberately juxtaposes national or regional offerings in order to see both coherencies and inner contradictions. This discussion of improvised artistic production gives a good idea of how Black culture-creation came to be viewed—as quaint local color, the atavistic potential undercutting of civilized forms, divisive countergenres, or "inexplicably" sophisticated manifestations by the descendants of a barbarous race. Latin American texts based on those suppositions—and on the centrality of slavery—aim to recuperate the unformed and fragmented and to locate those manifestations in a diffusely homogenized national context. In many cases, enthusiastic intuition tends to fossilize creative/popular cultural practices rather than recognizing that music-content "has created or laid the premises for an extension, a development of thought" (James *Notes*, 15). In contrast, without postponing sensibilities and sensualities, music as a "category of thought," which is to say evidence of wider cultural values, offers a strategic rather than a merely descriptive premise:

> Black music may be defined as a musical tradition of peoples of Sub-Saharan African descent, which consists of a shared core of conceptual approaches to the process of music making. These concepts reflect deeply-rooted values of this culture and, in essence, consist of fundamental ways of approaching musical experience. An analysis of any genre of black music will reveal the presence of these underlying conceptual approaches, and it is precisely the pervasive existence of these qualities which gives the music its distinctive character. (L. Wilson 99)

Unhappily, with few exceptions, many Latin American commentaries often fail to define or stop short of specifically delineating those values and then envisioning them within the system of beliefs that they promulgated and reflected.

The hope here is to suggest the value of improvisation for peoples of African descent in the diaspora.

> Improvisation is the ultimate human (i.e., heroic) endowment. It is, indeed; and even as flexibility or the ability to swing (or to perform

with grace under pressure) is the key to that unique competence which generates the self-reliance and thus the charisma of the hero, and even as infinite alertness-become-dexterity is the functional source of the magic of all master craftsmen, so may skill in the art of improvisation be that which both will enable contemporary man to be at home with his sometimes tolerable but never quite certain condition of not being at home in the world and will also dispose him to regard his obstacles and frustrations as well as his achievements in terms of adventure and romance. (Murray 277)

Attesting to the importance of territory and belligerence in the face of uprootedness, improvisation invites participants to feel "back home" and that depends on strategy, convention, and, ultimately, play.

The linking of uprootedness and improvisation is crucial to understanding Blackness. Uprootedness refers to Blackness as a state or condition and, more importantly, as a process resulting from the earliest European incursions into Africa, the Middle Passage, and other unsettling manifestations. If, as Martha Cobb and Richard L. Jackson suggest, experience affects expression, the reiterated experience of deculturation and permutability propels the continual extension and development of expression, that is, improvisation. In that tactical sense, the improvisation of Blackness is purposeful. And that suggests a *strategy*. On that subject, Hungarian writer, sociologist, and former dissident György Konrád opines, "I find the concept of . . . 'strategy' more valid than that of . . . 'identity.' The latter is static, enigmatic, hard to pin down, while a strategy is visible in terms of action. We all have conscious or unconscious 'life strategies'; in other words, our actions are metaphorically interconnected" (167–68). Thus the errant protagonists, social associations, land biographies, and enclave communities discussed earlier, in their schemes to refashion territory, *insinuate* a strategy to overcome, or at the least ameliorate, the condition of uprootedness. More importantly, those metaphorically interconnected acts, whether coping mechanisms or survival techniques, whether seemingly the casual outcome of motherwit or the deliberate aim of intellectual investigation and disciplined studies, describe *how* such life-strategies have enabled those persons and communities to have constructed, and to continue to construct, their "own corner of reality" (Wynter "We Must Learn," 308).

Improvisation, terminology borrowed from the musical and oral spaces traditionally ceded to peoples of African descent, when successful, "puts you on good terms with life. It generates an atmosphere of well-being and celebration" (Murray 113) not reduced to the grinning jigaboo of Medieval Spanish Peninsular theatre, of minstrelsy in Cuba, the United States, or the River Plate region, nor to the "racy" caricatures in Brazilian film (for example, *Central Station* [Salles 1998], *Drought* [Felistoque and Cerdeira, 2000]).[3] Those derisive "scripted" antics, in their effort to represent celebration, distort the spontaneity of the contingent being, "the marginal man, who can be truly revolutionary because he is outside the prevailing social structure and its concomitant ideology" (Wynter "Eye," 15).[4] The contingent's "impromptu" interruptions, even when posed as caricature, communicate a disarming and astute lyricism. North American jazz critic Murray clarifies this point, writing, "By improvisation, of course, I most definitely do not mean 'winging it' or making things up out of thin air. The Jazz musician improvises within a very specific context and in terms of very specific idiomatic devices of composition" (112).

The view of improvisation proposed here does not, however, constrict itself to the narrower limits of musical or oral improvisation, a scheme that would continue to fragment the cultural realm and repeat the discourse of exceptional individuals who succeed one by one in a limited set of preordained fields. Rather, this analysis suggests the thought of cultural improvisation, wherein expressive strategy recognizes and celebrates all the communal bits and pieces, the small or sweeping gestures, reflected in or reflective of cosmology: a "síntesis de creencias y conocimientos, un saber integral sobre el universo natural y humano, una visión totalizadora del mundo que incluye tanto la superstición, como la ciencia" (Sogbossi 35) [synthesis of beliefs and knowledges, an integral understanding about the natural and human universe, a totalistic vision of the world that includes, in equal measure, superstition and science].[5]

The trajectory of Colombian author Manuel Zapata Olivella provides an example of the process of strategic cultural improvisation. The 1963 novel *Chambacú, corral de negros* centers opposition—multinational, geopolitical—and as such interrupts the context and devices of the master discourse by providing a hitherto ignored territory to its racially, socially, and economically disadvantaged cast of characters. Thus, the exemplary "insider-outsider" protagonist Máximo uses his formal education to uplift his community: "His articulation of that region's needs, long before the ghetto dwellers recognized what was lacking, fits neatly into the pattern of facilitator. Despite initial opposition among his own people, he is able to gradually raise the consciousness of the Chambacú citizens through the slow process of action and education" (Captain-Hidalgo 59, 60). The strategy here "answers back" in socialist realist dialectical fashion, highlighting the contradictions between metropolis and periphery, championing the common folk in day-to-day situations. Nevertheless, that instance of insurgency remains "boxed in" by the perimeters of that neighborhood and by the constrictions of the dominating discourse (although the metonymical extensions are infinite, as seen in the last chapter). While Zapata Olivella ably manipulates the "very specific context" of uprootedness, he has yet to resource the "very specific idiomatic devices of composition."

His 1983 tome *Changó, el gran putas*, which plays in the field of cosmology by contextualizing uprootedness, inventing an Africanized mythology as the explanatory model for New World Blackness, represents a significant departure. Captain-Hidalgo writes that "Zapata's emphasis on a vernacular expressive strategy sets him apart from most." She continues,

> Zapata departs from his peers in that for the first time in Spanish-American narrative, the African cultural element is successfully incorporated on its own terms as Spanish American. This claim of uniqueness is further affirmed by the fact that the work is profoundly Afrocentric while at the same time it is thoroughly New World. Even though it is outside the direct European influence, it simultaneously expands the notion of Western culture. *Shango* represents an intriguing and welcome challenge to its readers precisely because, in part, it belongs to all these categories without contradiction. (135)

Zapata Olivella's epic invents and records a cosmological "corner of reality" that "generates an atmosphere of well-being and celebration." That worldview gracefully conjoins uprootedness (context) and improvisation (devices), making sense of the full range of Black experience and expression in the Americas. The task is not an easy one, and other works, faced with the challenge to incorporate differences on their own terms, succumb to contradiction.

Guinean author María Nsue Angüe's *Ekomo* (1985) steeps itself in Fang tribal cosmology, taking great pains to describe beliefs, ceremonies, and rituals, in much the same way that Chinua Achebe's *Things Fall Apart* (1958) privileged Yoruba cultural systems and practices. Accordingly, Nsue Angüe's novel attempts to underscore the interdependence of cause and effect, sign and meaning, and the intimate tie between imminent and transcendent, between natural and supernatural. As had Achebe's narrative, the more recent African novel has at its disposal a ready cosmology and, in both, the outside intrudes in the form of colonialism, Christian missionaries, and Western medicine, reminiscent of the oppositional stance evident in Zapata Olivella's earlier novel. Nsue Angüe proposes another disjunction in a critique of the Fang worldview with her depiction of the prescriptive treatment of the female other, judged ontologically irresponsible in a case of adultery, yet as widow, cosmically liable for the death of the spouse. The contrary rigidity of the juxtaposed cosmologies—one patri-global and the other patri-local—accounts for the major distinction between Zapata Olivella's later epic and Nsue Angüe's first outing in the longer genre. Here, the clash within and between worldviews generates a disheartening atmosphere of infirmity, real and discursive. On the one hand, Nsue Angüe's choice to root her novel in Fang cosmology gives the impression that the narrative can withstand, up to a point, the incursions or contamination of other imaginaries. Such is not the case for the uprooted in the Americas, and Zapata Olivella's crisscrossed cosmology invention neatly attests to this, infiltrating and linking African and European master narratives. On the other hand, the announced "Fangness" in *Ekomo* finds itself in conflict with the westerly structured novel and its westerly modeled protagonist,[6] proposing "a divisive kind of integration" (Goveia 10)—set in Africa but not centered there—that never gets narratively resolved. Thus, this novel struggles between contexts (Fang-African, Iberian, and the author's own exile-immigrant perspective) and fails to find its own "expressive vernacular strategy," describing rather than exploiting those "very specific idiomatic devices of composition" at its author's disposal. While one might applaud the gutsiness of the novel's premise, these weaknesses distract from its exposition and conclusions. In Zapata Olivella, uprootedness dictated, pressured, in a lawlike fashion, improvisational strategies, which in Nsue Angüe, subverted by a too rigidly grounded universe and an oppositional challenge to it, cannot find expression.

Accordingly, improvisation's rule-governed rejoinders rely on a set of *possibilities*, practiced as part of a cultural system, which then guides the reaction—performance or interrogation—in a given situation. In his theory of culture, Hall argues the unconscious nature of such responses, asserting: "In informal activity the absence of awareness permits a high degree of patterning. . . . The informal is therefore made up of activities or mannerisms which we once learned but which are so much a part of our everyday life that they are done automatically" (*Silent Language* 73). Similarly, in a discussion of musical mannerisms, Murray declares: "To stylize is to conventionalize. It is to create a pattern which becomes a way of seeing things and doing things. Convention can function both as the container and the thing contained. It provides the structure as well as the content of human consciousness" (112). Thus as a part of musical culture, and by extension, cultural life-strategies, this out-of-awareness patterning can only function *gracefully* when it displays a sensitivity to cosmological context and to available devices. Amiri Baraka, when he was still LeRoi Jones, offered this example:

> Blues as an autonomous music had been in a sense inviolable. There was no clear way into it, i.e., the production, not its appreciation, except as concomitant with what seems to me to be the peculiar, social, cultural, economic, and emotional experience of a black man in America. . . . It was as if these materials were secret and obscure and blues a kind of ethno-historic rite as basic as blood. . . . That could not be got to, except as the casual expression of a whole culture. And for that reason, blues remained, and remains in its most moving manifestations, obscure to the mainstream of American culture. ("Swing" 37)

While some may want to argue that Baraka mystifies the blues (an assertion with which i do not agree), he quite "casually" demystifies cultural practices:

> Music, as paradoxical as it might seem, is the result of thought. It is the result of thought perfected at its most empirical, i.e., as attitude, or stance. Thought is largely conditioned by reference, it is the result of consideration or speculation against reference, which is largely arbitrary.
>
> There is no one way of thinking, since reference (hence value) is as scattered and dissimilar as men themselves. If Negro music can be seen to be the result of certain attitudes, certain specific ways of thinking about the world (and only ultimately about the *ways* in which music can be made), then the basic hypothesis . . . is understood. The Negro's music changed as he changed, reflecting shifting attitudes or (and this is equally important) *consistent attitudes within changed contexts*. And it

is why the music changed that seems most important to me. ("Swing" 40–41)

Likewise, *conditioned by uprootedness*, musicality and orality (and religiosity)—referenced to shifting conceptions of Blackness in the Latin American landscape—evinces "*consistent attitudes within changed contexts.*" *Refashioned by improvisation* (permutability and deculturation), the casual and informal patterning of Africana cultural production reflects life strategies: those "certain specific ways" in which Blackness references a "certain specific" worldview, without, however, degenerating into an essentialist or monolithic Blackness.

In spaces reconfigured and refashioned, such patterned stances represent the shared sum of common experiences—a "supply of standardized images, cultural icons, fads and fashions" (Immerfall 1)—involved in a complex, doubly conscious conversation. At the same time, a supply of evolving experiential and expressive strategies recalls, erodes, and parodies both the images favored by metropoly and those worshiped as a tradition apart. In this context, experience does not consist in know-how, joylessly amassed and hoarded,[7] rather "*Experience is something man projects upon the outside world as he gains it in its culturally determined form*" (Hall *Silent Language*, 119). A practitioner implicitly relies on this out-of-awareness strategy, predicated on "an intervening set of patterns which channel his senses and his thoughts, causing him to react in one way when someone else with different underlying patterns will react as *his* experience dictates" (121–22). In terms of communally bound artistic production, that experience also channels creation: "The artists in question are creatures of culture, their traditions are in them and inform their works" (Julien 25). In consequence, experience informs expression. Thus, the "casual expression of a whole culture" is not something that could be arranged or orchestrated to mute humbler origins, as was the jazz idiom and that of tango in the River Plate region, samba in Brazil, *vals* in Peru, and other miscegenated forms that bespoke, in their particular contexts, an "American" experience rather than the "Black American" experience implicit in their precursors: blues; candombe and milonga; *lando* and the so-called kitchen varieties of samba (for example, *lundu*, *maxixe*); and rumba, similar to the enclave jam session.

On the other hand, it is not impossible to learn or to adopt a means of expression, a practice that regularly took place in the Latin American context,[8] between slavers and slave, between denizens of posher neighborhoods and those in *favelas, terreiros,* or other marginal spaces, after dark, on the sly, on a lark (see Vianna, especially chapter 1: "The Encounter"). However, "slumming" too, has a cultural context wherein "actions are metaphorically interconnected" and, in the adoption (sometimes tantamount to cultural larceny) of Black cultural manifestations, a racial component as well. Echoing González's reading of the divergence between elite and popular cultural experience, Baraka suggests a versioned embrace of the artistic product where expressive strategies serve diverging ends that, referencing Hall, reflect the "different underlying patterns" and particular experiences that dictate reaction. In that context, Baraka asserts that "The white musician understood the blues first as music, but seldom as an attitude, since the attitude, or world-view, the white musician was responsible to was necessarily quite a different one" ("Swing" 41). Consequently, the uninitiated's approach, Baraka argues, "was based on the conscious or unconscious disapproval of the sacraments of his culture" that is to say "the 'official' or formal culture of North America" ("Swing" 41). Conversely, within "unofficial" or informal communities, a Black practitioner was more likely to be regarded "in terms of emotional archetypes, [as] an honored priest of his culture, one of the most impressive products of his society" ("Swing" 41).

Therefore a nuanced alienation from "official," "formal" culture asserts itself—in one case drawn in terms of rebelliousness or deviancy, and in the other, depicted in a belligerent stance toward an a priori social-historical-cultural estrangement from formal/dominant structures, an attitude celebrated and esteemed in "unofficial" cultural circles. From those differing alienations, diverging/converging versions of history result. For example, Dominican poet and essayist Aída Cartegena Portalatín, reflecting on her encounter with André Breton, Eugenio Fernández Granell, Aimé Césaire, and Leopoldo Sédar Senghor in France during Negritude's initial moment, echoes Baraka:

> Desde esta misma noche vi otro mundo dividido no en países sino en hombres blancos y hombres negros. Parecía bastante idealista admitir el hecho de que, en la comunidad de los negros, la función del poeta o del artista en general, es celebrar la existencia y permanencia de los valores y no su destrucción, como en el mundo de los blancos. (*Culturas africanas* 16)

[From that very night, I saw another world, divided not in countries but between whites and Blacks. It seemed fairly idealistic to admit the fact that, in the Black community, the function of the poet or of the artist in general is to celebrate the existence and permanence of values and not their destruction as in the white world.]

A misreading of these dynamics can lead to unnuanced conclusions. Based on a paradigm that spurns progenitors (where the dynamics of decultura-tion would better serve), Segal assumes that Black musicality "dismissed and defied the conventions of white music" (379) and Benítez-Rojo describes (an admittedly deracinated and deterritorialized) jazz improvisation as "a decentering of the canon" (19), without acknowledging "an-other" similarly exigent "ex officio" mastery to which the improviser pays homage. Chin-weizu would postulate that such cultural belligerency aims not to injure or recklessly reject, but rather

> . . . it simply means that we do not accept [an alien] authority. The cru-cial part of the entire hegemony business in culture is to get you to ac-cept without question, without doubt, the authority of alien traditions that are quite often in conflict with your interests and your well-being; and therefore, the crucial part of the liberation business is the disman-tling of the authority of all foreign traditions, especially those that are unsound or incompatible with one's survival, well-being and dignity. ("Deriding the Derridians" 241)

Tellingly, his observations echo the affect of improvisation—"well-being and celebration"—and signal the fundamental importance of stance or attitude in terms of the construction of a sui generis worldview. Thus the layered conclusions and the far-reaching effects of cosmology invention such as that practiced by Zapata Olivella and commented upon by Baraka and Cartegena Portalatín selectively embrace and continuously erode those versions of his-tory to which they simultaneously, if fitfully, pertain.

Certainly, other versions or differently interested conceptions of im-provisation run counter to that proposed here. Therefore Benítez-Rojo's description and Gilroy's positioning of the term bear examination. For his part, Benítez-Rojo attempts to elevate the concept (perhaps into more elite realms):

[I]mprovisation, if it has reached a level that I've been calling "a certain kind of way," has penetrated all of the percipient spaces of those present, and it is precisely this shifting "totality" that leads them to perceive the impossible unity, the absent locus, the center that has taken off and yet is still there, dominating and dominated by the soloist's performance. It is this "totality" that leads those present to another "totality": that of rhythm-flux, but not that of rhythms and fluxes that belong to in-dustrial production, to computers, to psychoanalysis, to synchronicity and diachronicity. The only useful thing about dancing or playing an instrument "in a certain kind of way" lies in the attempt to move an audience into a realm where the tensions that lead to confrontation are inoperative. (20)[9]

Areas of agreement exist. The penetration of improvisation into "all of the percipient spaces" suggests the visceral potential and extension of that prac-tice into all aspects of cultural production. The idea that one totality, say musicality or orality, is in sync, in "rhythm-flux," with another totality, for example a cultural or discursive cosmology, offers promising insight. In or-der to preserve the improvisation's culture boundedness, perhaps this project would append to the proffered definition, referencing Murray and Baraka, an italicized proviso: "a certain *very specific* kind of way."

Nonetheless, more profound differences arise. While seeming to recall the permutability of uprootedness, the advertised shifting totality raises—in the context of metaphorical interconnectedness—the issue of the perceived relationship between tenor (initial referent) and vehicle (the refigured-refashioned image that stands in its place). The "repeating" totality, itself a phantom akin to imaginary nations, has (deliberately) lost or forgotten—or never knew—its origins, inspiring the search for new explanatory models and abetting the continued cultural larceny evident in Ilie's model of de-culturation. The insistence on the sensual and spontaneous nature of im-provisation tacitly bars the production of peoples of African descent from the realm of materialities, that is, recordings. Unwittingly, such an asser-tion implies that Africa brought nothing material to the table of the hu-man family—no associative history or political organization—beyond those elements that needed to be exorcized or transculturated by self-replicating paternalistic institutions, slavery, and later, the nation. The present proposal suggests that an initial totality hints at (yea, grasps at, grabs at) origins, as

would the conception of cosmogony, while a second lays bare the cosmological "synthesis of beliefs and knowledges" achieved by Zapata Olivella;
the "integral understanding about the natural and human universe" inferred
in Cartegena Portalatín's idea of Negritude; and the "totalistic vision of the
world which includes in equal measure superstition and science" postulated
in tones heroic and casual by Murray and Baraka, respectively. Thus in terms
of Blackness in the Latin American landscape, the absent locus is the eclipsed
practitioners who, along with their innovative production, form the *absented*
locus, the center that has been taken *out* "and yet is still there," informing and
informed by the tenacious creativity of peoples of African descent and the
performance of Blackness and, through them, what many, including Carpentier and González, identify as Latin American popular culture.

Of course, to give any credence to this intentionally contentious assertion would necessarily interrupt that pleasantly sensual tensionless space
where only the miscegenated, "whitened" outcome matters, that is, racial
harmony or *mulatez*. Tellingly, Benítez-Rojo reiterates that "the only thing
that walking, dancing, playing an instrument, singing, or writing 'in certain
kinds of ways' are good for is to displace the participants toward a poetic
territory marked by an aesthetic of pleasure, or better, an aesthetic whose
desire is nonviolence" (21). The benefit of improvisation—"dominated by
the soloist's performance" (20)—is outwardly turned toward the audience
(20) and, here by explicit extension, toward society as a whole (21). As if in
answer, Chinweizu insists:

> The West's interest in keeping their opponents non-violent deserves to
> be understood. It is, after all, an ancient technique to saddle your oppo-
> nent with a reputation which inhibits him from using his most effective
> weapon. Because the West is determined not to concede to anything
> but superior violence, it endeavours, through propaganda, to shepherd
> resistance into the non-violent path. Using such emasculating honours,
> they can hold a leader captive within the futile options of non-violence.
> He, in turn, holds his followers in line, and prevents them from join-
> ing those who fight Western violence with a counter violence. Con-
> sequently, the armed opposition is smaller, and the Western system is
> safer. ("Pan-Africanism" 179)

In that light, the vision of the performance space as a place for letting off
steam on the nonviolent path toward the tensionless realm sounds suspi-

ciously similar to the practice during slavery when masters, faced with the circumvention of their authority, could make a display of largesse and gain an afternoon's entertainment by "encouraging" certain dance and drum performances on the Cuban *ingenio* as depicted in *Plácido* by Fulleda León, described by Esteban Montejo in *Biografía de un cimarrón* (Barnet), or recorded in the works of F. Ortiz in the urban setting for *cabildos* and *comparsas* on holy days or during carnival. However, the following Brazilian example shows how the benefit accrued to the system (*and* how tenuous that hold was in reality): "A double standard slowly evolved: local officials, as protectors of the public mores, arrested and punished Candomblé practitioners, while masters sought to safeguard the productivity of their workforce and the domestic tranquility of their households, which required tolerating Candomblé" (Wimberly 84). In *Rhythms of Resistance*, Peter Fryer offers the following commentary:

> For successful and prosperous colonists it was . . . a matter of prestige to have a slave orchestra—and often a slave choir in the chapel, too. Such possessions entertained not only the plantation-owner but also his or her family. They could be put on show to entertain, and impress, their guests and visitors, including visitors from overseas. And they could be sent to take part in festivals and processions in nearby towns, at first as a personal contribution showing how grand the owner was and what good taste he or she had, in the nineteenth century as a source of extra income. (134)

Conversely, the discussions of improvisation here emphasize the advantage for the practitioner, the improviser, whose most effective weapon—an attitude sometimes belligerent, sometimes playful that engenders well-being—transitorily neutralizes the effect of uprootedness.

Since Benítez-Rojo stresses the metamorphic aspect of live performance, he implicitly questions the authenticity and originality of what he terms *phantom improvisation* (19), the recorded jam, which "is not of much use if the scale of values . . . corresponds only with a technological machine coupled to an industrial machine coupled to a commercial machine" (19). Eileen Julien discusses the similar phenomenon of "feigned orality,"[10] a phrase coined by African Alioune Tine, that focuses "the discrepancy between the quality of performance and the quality of the tapes and transcriptions or oral narratives and poetry that bring them to readers or distant audiences"

(23). Her clarification, "orality on display" (21), argues the implicitly mandated use of empty gesture or devalued trope "as a measure of authenticity in contexts [for example, stylistic, political] where little else seems to emanate from traditional culture" (21). Accordingly, she asserts that artistic production does not strive for authenticity—a "zero degree"—but rather *accountability*,[11] which is not dependent on stability of form but on fealty to criteria and context: "Demands for authenticity are a prescription for mystification. I think that if we are attentive to the operations of narrative, its clarity and contradictions and its resonance with social reality, authenticity will take care of itself. . . . I would argue, moreover, that authenticity—even racists can be authentic—is less important than accountability" (154). Whatever the form of production, if "conditioned by reference" (to uprootedness), Afro-musicality and orality—live, recorded, or set down in print—reveal a predilection to improvisation based in a reciprocity between (communal and individual) experience and expression.[12] In other scenarios, a troubled relationship ensues between tenor and vehicle, between context and devices.

Reference also comes into play in Gilroy's proposed methodology that centers call and response as the dominant contribution of traditional, indigenous forms to the conversation with modernity—the sociologist's point of reference. Again, participants marginal to Western culture react to and are thus accountable to its stimulus in terms codified within its vocabulary.

> [I]dentity is fleetingly experienced in the most intensive ways and sometimes socially reproduced by means of neglected modes of signifying practice like mimesis, gesture, kinesis, and costume. Antiphony (call and response) is the principal formal feature of these musical traditions. It has come to be seen as a bridge from music into other modes of cultural expression, supplying, along with improvisation, montage, and dramaturgy, the hermeneutic keys to the full medley of black artistic practices. (78)

Posed in these terms, a resulting doubleness, the disjoining of call from response, produces an "unsteady location simultaneously inside and outside the conventions, assumptions, and aesthetic rules that distinguish and periodise modernity" (73). Jazz in the North Atlantic secularized, liberalized, Westernized aspect as an example of Black expressive culture then necessarily produces an unsteady critical site given to argument between binary oppositions where none exist. Yet, the so-called neglected modes remain as present as the absented locus. A conjoined term, call-response (rhythm-flux), rather expresses a distinct doubleness that consists of the reconfiguration of situated conventions, acted upon through erosion and parody. That refashioning by turns feeds on/feeds off (cannibalizes or in the specific context of Bahia "olodumarizes") those forms at its disposal in outlets acceptable (Gilroy 97) and unacceptable, cultures official and unofficial. Strategy is predicated not on a unitary "principal *formal* feature" (Gilroy's call and response) but rather on the varied "*casual* expression of a whole culture" (Baraka), an improvisation accountable to those values and circumstances that foster an attitude that stimulates life-strategies—here call–response, there off-timing or versioning, over there, indirection.

Consequently, the value of improvisation resides in stance and attitude; belligerence and contest; accountability and reference; and, well-being and dignity. Not coincidentally, those strategies in turn constitute the values celebrated and esteemed by peoples of African descent in specific cultural learning contexts, especially those of play, of joking relationships (Hall, *Silent Language,* 52–53), and of contest, which provide arenas for what Jon Michael Spencer terms the "mastery of form" following the paradigm suggested by literary critic Houston Baker Jr. Indeed, music critic Murray claims, "The convention of playful option-taking is what I call 'the blues idiom' and jazz music" (112). Metaphorically connecting the dots, he concludes:

> [P]lay . . . resides at the very center of all culture, and certainly therefore at the center of art. Play in the sense of competition or contest; play in the sense of chance-taking or gambling; play in the sense of make-believe; play also in the sense of vertigo, or getting high, or inducing exhilaration; play also in the direction of simple amusement or entertainment—as in children's games; and play in the direction of gratuitous difficulty—as in the increasing number of jacks one catches or the height or distance one jumps, or decreasing the time one runs a given course; gratuitous difficulty also in the sense of wordplay or play in the sense of sound—as in a Bach fugue. I submit that such play or playing around is precisely what is involved in the process André Malraux is referring to when he suggests that art is the means by which forms of raw experiences are transformed or rendered into style. (111–12)

Conversely, any dislocation—spatial, temporal, discursive, and cosmological—necessarily disrupts the coherency of experience and style. The functional accountability of songs, stories, and dances fades, and these and other cultural practices become objects of study, decontextualized fodder to be authenticated (or not), interpreted, dismissed (see Wynter "We Must Learn," 308), and manipulated by others to their own ends—local color, tourist attraction, career. Likewise, an official/formal conception of time (slavish fealty to a slavery-centered history) tends to stress its truth in the service of finality versus the veracity of process. If uprootedness reveals its importance in territoriality and has implications in spatial relations, improvisation accordingly emphasizes the dynamics of *temporality* or time relationships.

4

Temporality

Telling Times

Time talks. It speaks more plainly than words. The message it conveys comes through loud and clear. Because it is manipulated less consciously, it is subject to less distortion than spoken language. It can shout truth where words lie.
—Edward T. Hall, *The Silent Language*

At the beginning of the millennium, post-Marxian, postmodern theorist Fredric Jameson announced the end of temporality. Akin to territoriality, Hall's image of chatty-time is likely to resonate as quaint and out-of-date in the facile immediacy, simultaneity, and impermanence of the globalized world. However, the various "ends" announced by monopoly and now metropoly reflect a particular and localized version of history responding to a peculiar point of reference. Consequently, just as territoriality continues to be of concern for the landless and uprooted, so too does temporality for those dehistoricized beings typically depicted in timeless folkloric or mythic scenarios.

Again, Hall's bio-basic conceptualization of human culture explains the foundational/functional importance of time—in nature, conjoined to other primary cultural systems (for example, territoriality), or in relationship to events (timing): "Life is full of cycles and rhythms, some of them related directly to nature—the respiration rate, heartbeat, menstrual cycle, and so on. Such practices as age-grading (dividing society according to rather rigid age groups) combine both time and association. Mealtimes, of course, vary from culture to culture, as do tempos of speech. . . . [T]here can be no doubt that if you know the temporal relationships between events you know a tremendous amount" (*Silent Language* 46). In that light, in *The Rhythms of Black Folks*, Jon Michael Spencer proposes the idea of "rhythmic confidence," asserting that "through this lens, through this 'rhythmic hermeneutic,' I see our cultural reality as comprised of a dialectic between rhythmicity and

arhythmicity" (xi).[1] He suggests that the "mastery of form" and "the deformation of mastery" (x) represent those strategies that have enabled the survival
of temporal Africanisms into New World Blackness.[2] This attitude—similar
to the idea of stance described by Baraka and, in its workings faintly reminiscent of the deculturation paradigm proposed by Ilie, refashioned by change
and survival—represents "the result of neither design nor chance but the
dynamic interaction of a living substance with itself" (Hall *Silent Language*,
90).[3] The emphasis here falls not on the preservation of Africanisms nor
Europeanisms per se but rather on how the deformation of both pressures
the improvisation of Blackness (Americanisms) and the systems of mastery
that those imply.

Consequently, temporality broadly refers to the ordering of events, a process that, as it prioritizes one vision of history, distorts another. Time then
implies both poetic rhythmic relations *and* powerful narrative strategies.

> By scheduling, we compartmentalize; this makes it possible to concen-
> trate on one thing at a time, but it also denies us context. Since sched-
> uling by its very nature selects what will and will not be perceived and
> attended and permits only a limited number of events within a given
> period, what gets scheduled in or out constitutes a system for setting
> priorities for both people and functions. Important things are taken up
> first and allotted the most time; unimportant things are left to last or
> omitted if time runs out. (Hall *Beyond Culture*, 18)[4]

Despite promising claims of efficiency or of the benefits of prioritization
(or periodization), Hall confirms that monochronic time "is not inherent in
man's own rhythms and creative drives, nor is it existential in nature" (*Beyond Culture* 20). Instead, scheduling subordinates humanness to man-made
devices—be they machines (cotton gin, sugar mill); systems (chattel slavery); or relative or chaotic theories or ideologies:[5]

> The very history of Afro-Americans has always been dominated by a
> symbolic war against the social and artistic assembly line, especially
> since stereotypes are actually forms of intellectual and emotional auto-
> mation. In fact, slavery was a forerunner of the nation's social compart-
> mentalization, especially the sort upheld by the pieties of stereotypes.
> Those stereotypes maintained that certain people came off an assem-
> bly line in nature and one needn't assume them capable of the endless

possibilities of human revelation. They had a natural place, which was inferior, and they were sometimes to be pitied and guided, sometimes feared and controlled, but were never to be considered more than predictable primitives who functioned best in subservient positions. (Crouch 162)

Teasing the meaning suggested by Crouch, the announced death of temporality to which Jameson refers lays bare a congenital infirmity of Western timekeeping—its one-sightedness. The prosaic demise thus tardily acknowledges the challenge of another "rhythmic mode" (Carpentier) or an antagonistic "rhythmic confidence" (Spencer) beyond a stereotypical proclivity for dance and song. What seems the anecdotal concept of "Colored People's time" that skews those schedules that undergird official/formal history and culture, might better be seen as "off-timing," a strategy part and parcel of improvisation. Jazz critic Kirstin Hunter Lattany postulates "off-timing as a metaphor for subversion, for code, for ironic attitudes toward mainstream beliefs and behavior, for choosing a vantage point of distance from the majority, for coolness, for sly commentary on the master race, for riffing and improvising off the man's tune and making it fun" (qtd. in Spencer 138). Those mannerisms in consequence constitute both a conceptual approach and the "very specific devices" that fuel a peculiar code of mastery or "idiomatic orientation" (Malone 284).

While González juxtaposes "una visión histórica" against "otra visión histórica" (14) [one historical vision (against) another], Cuban Walterio Carbonell asserts that "contradicción es la esencia misma de la Historia" (60) [contradiction is the very essence of History]. In their converging treatments of the roots of national culture in the Caribbean, both aim to show that a foundational dissonance survives into the present. Carbonell, who mysteriously disappeared from the intellectual landscape of Cuba, stresses the "contradicciones de intereses" (64) [contradictions of interests], signaling the diverging points of view at work in colonial Cuba: on one hand, "las contradicciones entre la monarquia española y los 'criollos' esclavistas" (63) [the contradictions between the Spanish monarchy and the "creole" slaveholders] and, on the other, "los antagonismos entre esclavos y esclavistas que constituyen, dicho sea de paso, el eje de todas las contradicciones de la sociedad colonial" (63) [the antagonisms between slaves and slavers that constitute, however fleetingly, the axis of all of the contradictions of colonial society]. Likewise, shifting interests, contradictions, and antagonisms begin to describe the axis of a cultural divide.

Official temporality measures a world predicated on scheduled compartments, competition as winning, and serial deaths or, in some cases, premeditated homicides. Each succeeding manifestation dislodges the previous: B replaces A, C overshadows B, and so on, whether in art movement or ideology (for example, Gilroy's periodization of modernism). Hence, the smooth-running narrative (of artistic development, of cultural transculturation, of the nation) creates an illusory tensionless realm, often a replicate of machine-driven imagery, which cloaks interference. Alejandro Frigerio summarizes the periodization of River Plate *candombe comparsas* suggested by Lauro Ayestarán (1953) and perhaps based on an earlier historiography by Afro-Uruguayan Marcelino Bottaro (1934):

> Ayestarán distingue tres etapas en la evolución de la música afrouruguaya: 1) la primera sería secreta y estaría constituida por la danza ritual africana sólo conocida por los iniciados; habría desaparecido cuando muere el último esclavo africano; 2) la segunda sería pública, mezclaría características de origen africano con otras europeas y constituiría el candombe observado por los cronistas del siglo XIX; 3) la tercera sería la etapa de la comparsa de carnaval de las sociedades de negros desde 1870 hasta nuestros días. (415)

> [Ayestarán distinguishes three stages in the evolution of Afro-Uruguayan music: 1) the first would be secret and would be composed of ritual African dance only known to initiates; it would have disappeared when the last African slave died; 2) the second would be public, it would mix characteristics of African origin with others European and would constitute the *candombe* observed by chroniclers of the nineteenth century; 3) the third would be the stage of the carnival *comparsa* of the Black associations from 1870 until the present.]

Many, including Paulo Carvalho Neto,[6] followed this paradigm, asserting that "authentic" African music was only known, and then partially so, to *bozales*; it then entered a creolized stage, fitfully mixing African and European elements in raucous parades and "notorious" night spots; and then finally it produced a fully blended admixture, a deafricanized, nationalized product fit for elite and tourist consumption. Frigerio concludes that for Ayestarán and Carvalho Neto such temporal compartmentalization led to

> una preocupación excesiva por la reconstrucción de la[s] formas origi-
> nales, "verdaderas," del candombe y la identificación de sus elementos
> supérstites, y sobre todo, a dejar de lado en el estudio a los elementos
> que no formarían parte de estas supervivencias . . . (416)

> [an excessive preoccupation with the reconstruction of the original,
> "real" forms of candombe and the identification of their essential ele-
> ments and, above all, to omit from the study those elements that would
> not form a part of the surviving evidence . . .]

In the paradigm of rupture and substitution, artistic production, propelled by Social Darwinism, recalls a survival-of-the-fittest mentality wherein progress/modernity evolves from the simple to the complex.

Confirming a coherency with the periodized music paradigm proposed by Ayestarán and Carvalho Neto, Latin American Boom writers would con- sider themselves as without precedents:

> Para la mayoría de los escritores latinoamericanos el pasado es algo que
> hay que rechazar, un periodo que la presente generación debe denunciar
> y superar. Esta actitud se refleja notoriamente en el número de novelas
> modernas que tratan de las relaciones entre las distintas generaciones y
> la frecuencia en que la vieja generación se expone como ejemplo de in-
> eficacia, inescrupulosidad y fracaso. Frecuentemente se manifiesta esto
> en actitudes parricidas o casi parricidas. (J. Franco 245)

> [For the majority of Latin American writers, the past is something that
> one must reject, a period that the current generation should denounce
> and surpass. This attitude is notoriously reflected in the number of
> modern novels that deal with relations between the distinct genera-
> tions and the frequency with which the older is drawn as an example of
> inefficiency, unscrupulousness and failure. This often manifests itself in
> patricidal or almost patricidal attitudes.]

Here again, each moment has a determined frame and the appearance of each form must complete its life cycle in order for the ensuing manifestation to come to fruition, eliding the contradictions described by Carbonell. In the Latin American context, this same imaginary can pronounce the end of slavery and the birth of racial harmony as if no vestiges of the first impact the second. That same imaginary can also dispute the authenticity of subsequent forms, signaling their distance or progress from an extinct original, for example, the absented locus, neglected modes proposed by Benítez-Rojo and Gilroy.

Writing of popular traveling theater in Ghana, Catherine M. Cole sheds light on the conundrum that surfaces when off-timing meets compartmentalized histories and the impact of "smoothing" narrative:

> Concert parties [comic variety shows] occupy a nebulous position in Ghana's cultural hierarchy. Lacking the prestige of scripted dramas written in English and the "authenticity" of so-called traditional cultural practices . . . concert parties fall into that vast, amorphous terrain of African popular culture that has fallen outside the purview of dominant cultural paradigms (Barker 1987, 1997). The concert party's historical roots in cultural syncretism are in part responsible for its ambivalent status. Shows in the 1930s and 1940s . . . drew liberally upon Western sources. They featured plot scenarios from American films . . . foreign dance steps . . . and songs . . . . Some observers point to this history as evidence that the concert party began as a merely derivative performance, a pale imitation of Western vaudeville, far too hybrid to be considered genuinely African. (104)

Yet, Cole argues, this example of popular culture represented "a novel innovation of the twentieth century, [which] utilized techniques of creativity well established in traditional . . . performing arts such as festivals and storytelling" based on "key structural elements that are always repeated" (104). The argument here is much the same. For example, in the playful—yet still edgy—dynamic of improvised oral contest where tension spurs creativity (Hall), contestants riff and improvise off the contribution of the other and on a heritage of call and response. Tellingly, while the contest readies its practitioners to engage in battle—should they elect to do so—the exercise favors a prowess that showcases and requires not only grace under pressure but also graciousness in triumph. Likewise off-timing's contest with official tempo-

rality adroitly repeats historical strategies in its improvisation on uprootedness. Again referencing Murray, convention—here as pressured reiterated
innovation—"can function both as the container and the thing contained. It
provides the structure as well as the content of human consciousness" (112).

The overlapping continuum from traditional to popular to recorded music in Africa provides another version that confounds a closed progressive periodization;[7] instead, it signals the casual coexistence of "insular" traditional
styles, admixed patterns, and technologized "phantom" forms and better
describes the workings of cultural improvisation in the Americas. It must
be noted that the binding elements here are less stylistic per se and more em-
phatically functional—a reflection of a coherency, rather than a continuity,
between techniques of creativity.[8] Traditional music, a sometimes problematic intellectual designation, here refers to the use of ancestral "home-grown"
instruments and rhythms less influenced by foreign/Western elements (stylistics or materials) in particular ethnic communities. In the Latin American
landscape, *cabildos* in Cuba, *terreiros* and *candomblés* in Brazil, *canchas* in the
River Plate region and runaway communities, and *quilombos* and *palenques*
throughout the continent, exemplify similar cultural enclaves and supplied
the discursive basis of Abdias Nascimento's conception of *Quilombismo* and
of the later *Quilombhoje* artistic movement. As in Africa within a particular
ethnic community, music serves to educate listeners in appropriate morality
and compliance with social law or custom and to offer social commentary
and to entertain, although entertainment remains a felicitous by-product
since ritual rather than leisure defines the context. Accordingly, the culturally cloistered musical performance typically occurs at crucial passages in the
life cycle (for example, birth, maturation, coronation, death), and players
depend on the interactive response of the nonplaying fellow-worshipers who
join in with verbal encouragement or in dancing contests. This "casual" tie
between music, dance, and dramatization (ritual, spectacle) echoes the commentaries of Ruth Finnegan, Fernando Ortiz, and any number of folklorists
and anthropologists.

Fruit of the possibilities of contact and sociohistorical transformations
that result from migration within Africa and uprootedness in the Americas,
popular music signals the admixture of elements between ethnic- and racial-
cultural enclaves respectively and the insertion of these into the national and
international metropolis as pastime. In a process of deculturation, erosion

and parody work both on traditional sources and on the colonizers' Western stylistics and instruments. The French film *Noirs et blancs en couleur* (Annaud, 1976) provides a visual example of the admixture. The film illustrates the rise of national rivalries between colonists in Africa after they tardily learn of hostilities in World War I Europe. One sequence features a cacophonic contest between the German-trained and the French-trained marching bands, each sharply appointed in the exuberantly decorous uniforms of the respective combatants, armed with brass wind instruments, stepping sharply with bare feet down a dirt road. In the Latin American context, contact spurred by uprootedness also played an important part in the improvisation of popular forms, and there, too, new instruments appeared, while others disappeared or were transformed by the use of different materials or modes of manufacture—innovations often in response to restrictions that sought to muffle more strident tones.[9] Fryer reaches even further back in time: "The black contribution to the emergence of Brazilian popular music continued and deepened a process of acculturation in the Iberian peninsula which had begun in the eighth century with the arrival of Arab conquerors in Spain and Portugal and of African slaves in Spain, and had been reinforced from 1441 onwards by the arrival of African slaves in Portugal" (135).

Contact with European styles and between ethnic and racial groups— whether propelled by diaspora, urbanization, or migration—provided the setting and impetus for the amalgamation of varied cultural currents in dance clubs and nightclubs, social clubs, slave orchestras, and *orquestras de color* that entertained formerly cloistered or rural denizens, concomitantly encouraging a more secular culture of leisure.[10] In the backdrop of urbanization and industrialization, popular music existed in an atmosphere of perpetual innovation and conjoined tastes and styles. In comparison, traditional music was more formulaic and static. Confined to less public venues yet *parallel* to popular manifestations, traditional music continued to provide conventional ritual and social structures for a displaced population. Baraka offers a like case in the North American diaspora: for Mississippi migrants in Chicago, the chords and devices shared between spirituals and the blues inspired church goers on Sunday morning and entertained party goers on Saturday night.

The "transition" from popular to recorded music moves production from a local/national to a global/international context.[11] If autonomous music "had been in a sense inviolable" (Baraka "Swing," 37), popular musical forms become part of a decontextualized "culture" of entertainment, wherein performer and spectators need not share a common history or culture. Referencing the work of Hobsbawn (219), Robin Moore suggests: "The 1920s precipitated a crisis in European bourgeois art internationally. . . . This was a time of fundamental change in the commercial music of nearly all Western countries, driven partly by technological innovation in the form of radio broadcasting and sound recordings, partly by the nature of capitalism itself and a desire to expand markets into minority communities and overseas and partly as a result of growing wealth and increased numbers among the working classes" (3).[12] Technological innovations such as radio, long-play records, pirated tapes, and World Music CDs made more accessible, more immediately, to a more ample public the musical trends that before had moved slowly from one nightclub, neighborhood, or even hemisphere to the next. This sociohistorical transformation contributed to the construction of a consumer culture and the commodification of taste: a bourgeois model of an entertainment industry predicated on excess capital for leisure or luxury, be it in production or consumption, but often in conflict with non-Western economic circumstances.

In the Americas almost from the beginning, spheres both temporal and territorial intersected: private and public; traditional and popular; sacred and profane. Traditional music belonged to those "retreats" set aside for religious practices, yet also made strident appearances in *comparsas* on feast days and in carnival celebrations related to the Catholic religion. Work songs and calls that represented a more immanent example of traditional musicality— intoned a cappella with the accompaniment of task-related tools pressed into service as impromptu rhythm keepers—would provide a source of extra income on informal stages in bars and cabarets, embellished with guitar accompaniment. Similarly, the sight and sound of a Nigerian hairdresser in Salvador da Bahia listening to a "live" performance of daily prayers emitted from a compact disc player while braiding a client's recalcitrant locks does not represent sacrilege but novel convenience. Synchronicity—the possibility that traditional, popular, and "phantom" coexist—playfully "off-times" those temporalities that have favored compartmentalization and arbitrary periodization. Consequently, the negotiation of musical practices and policies often runs headlong into contradictory aims to erase the African roots of Latin culture and, when that failed, to "nationalize" Blackness within the terms of "official" culture. This effort hoped to legitimize, which is to say normalize, the image of harmonic national identities, smoothly transculturated and miscegenated in order to explain away or gloss over racial inequities. The historical timing of the reception of drums, a site of casual yet persistent belligerence, illustrates the implications for cultural improvisation, over time.

2

Coming to (Cultural) Consciousness

Talking Drums or Trying Times

The Off-Timed Tale

The focus on drums and timing is not purely a question of "rhythmicity"; it is ultimately a question of narrative necessity. In the 1977 tome *Oral Literature in Africa*, Ruth Finnegan includes a chapter specifically dedicated to "Drum Language and Literature" (481–99). She asserts that drums "communicate through direct representation of actual speech" and that "Such communication, unlike conventional signals, is intended as a *linguistic* one . . . and any musical effects are purely incidental" (481). If one takes her at her word, then the conventional narrative—that "official" version of history, of African entry into the West's "architecture of signs" (see Wynter, "Eye"), which underscores the loss of language as the loss of voice, agency, and independence—needs rethinking. This tabula rasa (in drum speak *tabla* rasa) tower-of-Babel conception of a cleaned or hopelessly muddled slate—further fogged by loss, forgetfulness, and lack of mutual communication—assumes a zero degree (or at least a degree in single digits) upon which European civilization or national culture can be writ in large letters. Structurally excluded from enunciation, the slave cannot frame, or only partially so, an identity or, in the sense intended here, a *strategy* outside of the dictates of that culture into which she or he was inserted.

Talking drums not only speak, they also tell stories. In Uruguay, *Las llamadas*, the distinct call-to-contest associated with particular neighborhoods, now serve by legalized and normalizing decree of 1956 as the official opening of carnival in Montevideo. Thus, if in colonial times displays of Africana culture were banned, hidden, and demeaned, the drum now "officially" symbolizes Uruguayan culture. Today, the calls show less differentiation one from another, and Tomás Olivera Chirimini stresses the difference between spontaneous and official, or one might say "phantom," manifestations (13) while Mario Pérez Colman alludes to their corruption as "un mero espectáculo para una sociedad que es mayoritariamente blanca y—dicen—racista y discriminadora" (58) [a mere spectacle for a society that is predominantly white and—they say—racist and discriminatory]. That official version often overshadows another.

Similar to spoken soul—the term employed by Claude Brown for informal vernacular Black talk—drums talk back in the "ceaselessly and relentlessly driving rhythm that flows from poignantly spent lives" (qtd. in Rickford and Rickford, 72), a speech act that "remains in its most moving manifestations, obscure to the mainstream of American culture" (Baraka "Swing," 37), north and south. In the sense of soulful Black enunciation, Pérez Colman writes of the *llamadas*: "Era tradición que cada barrio tuviera una llamada propia, caracterizada por su ritmo especial" (59) [It was tradition that each area had its own call, characterized by a special rhythm]. Master drummer Ángel Acosta Martínez elaborates: "[la llamada] es una forma de comunicación: llamar con el tambor, decir, tocar, dar un golpe . . . ese golpe puede ser un toque religioso, un toque de festejo o un mensaje" (15) [the call is a form of communication: to call, to say, to play, to give a beat . . . this beat can be a religious cadence, a festive cadence or a message]. Sociologist Chirimini describes the tonal and rhythmic quality of the diverse calls and troupes, observing:

[un grupo] practica un ritmo bien acompasado, inconfundible, en el que prevalecen los "bajos" o graves, mientras en las llamadas de [otro grupo] predominan los repiques por lo que el ritmo es más vivaz. (14)

[(one group) practices a very peculiar measured rhythm, in which the "lows" or deep tones prevail while in the calls of (another group) the higher tones of the smaller drums predominate, giving a livelier rhythm.]

He notes that "oídos profanos" [uninitiated ears] would fail to make the distinction while for those "entendidos en la materia" [knowledgeable on the subject],

hay un gran diferencia resultante de cómo, dónde y por qué se los toca. Tan es así que desde lejos ya saben quién viene tocando el tambor o por lo menos a qué grupo pertinence. (14)

[there is a great difference attendant on how, where and why the drums are played. The tone is so distinctive that from far away one knows who is playing the drum or at the least to which group it belongs.]

Thus the more central question no longer concerns whether drums beat out syllables but rather how their expressive function has developed within narrative as symbol, plot device, antagonist—or protagonist. Writes Bone on "pastoral inversion" in Fisher's "Arcadia," where the hero, through chicanery, is divested of his drums: "The superiority of blackness is the point: to be possessed of soul is precisely to be capable of improvising, of winning the contest *without* your drums. At bottom, Fisher is warning the black community to guard itself against a certain kind of spiritual loss. Don't abandon your ancestral ways when you move to the big city; don't discard the authentic blues idiom for the shallow, trivial, flashy, meretricious values of the urban world" (*Down Home* 156). While the overt point of reference is parochial (big city, urban world), metonymically, the tale conjures the adept diaspora denizen's negotiation of the universe, the cosmology created by monopoly and metropoly. In that light, drums, whether sacredly or profanely revered, form an important part of the cultural devices, and one could say strategies, available to peoples of African descent in Latin America as a "conduit for transmitting the *values* associated with [their] culture" (Graden 63; emphasis mine).

However, percussion's proverbial association with licentious behaviors in orchestra salons, dance halls, or street parades offers another version of history aimed at muting the values and deriding the contributions and participation of the darker kin.[1] For better and many times for worse, drums announce Blackness in a variety of contexts: neighborhoods in Montevideo and Buenos Aires, which carried the name *Barrio del Tambor*; movie soundtracks that beat out a familiar rhythm anticipating the on-screen appearance of the African or African-descended character; from bone-in-the-nose cannibals in Tarzan movies to the sacrificial lamb in the Spanish production, *Bwana* (Uribe 1996). In the 2000s, the Brazilian evangelical movement's televised condemnation of syncretic Africanized Candomblé features in its "re-creation of real events" a menacing drum track, forecasting the evils inherent in those practices for the true believer: spells, sorcery, ruination.

In much of the material—historical, anthropological, literary—drums also represent something akin to the anti-Christ: noise pollution that poses a threat to political order, social hierarchies (for example, Graden 63, 68) and Catholic morality; the nettlesome source of "potentially disruptive knowledge" (69), all clothed in the inflammatory vocabulary of cults, dens that appeal to debauchery and deviltry, enunciated in a nonsense or secret speech, impenetrable to official social orders. Alejo Carpentier, in his role as amateur musicologist, explains:

La repugnancia de Sánchez de Fuentes a admitir la presenia de los ritmos negroides en la música cubana, se explica como reflejo de un estado de ánimo muy generalizado en los primeros años de la República.
Hacía tiempo que los negros habían dejado de ser esclavos. Sin embargo, en país nuevo que aspiraba a ponerse a tono con las grandes
corrientes culturales del siglo, lo auténticamente negro—es decir: lo
que realmente entrañaba supervivenicas africanas al estado puro—era
mirado con disgusto, como un lastre de barbarie que solo podía toler-
arse a título de mal inevitable. (*La Música* 286)

[Sanchez de Fuentes's repugnance to admitting the presence of Black
rhythms in Cuban music can be understood as the reflection of a general outlook during the first years of the Republic. Years had transpired
since Blacks had been slaves. However, in a newly conceived country
that aspired to bring itself up to date with the cultural currents of the
day, the authentically Black cultural experience—that is, those deeply
rooted and surviving African elements that remained in a pure state—
was looked upon with disgust, as a kind of barbaric holdover from the
past, and could only be tolerated as a necessary evil.] (*Music* 256)

That generalized repugnance had a concrete effect as historian Robin Moore
observes:

Municipal decrees restricting drumming and related activities affected
both music making in the slave barracks and that of free blacks in the
street (Leal: 1980, 49). Police and legislators systematically suppressed
overtly African influenced genres such as the traditional *rumba yambú*
and *columbia* (Martínez 1977, 2). They concentrated most of their efforts on Afrocuban religious ritual and secret *ñañigo* societies because
they often served as clandestine centers of revolutionary activity. Police
records from the 1880s provide detailed descriptions of raids on *ñañigo*
meeting halls, as well as the confiscation and destruction of musical
instruments, dance costumes, and other ritual objects. (18)

One such decree published in the *Graceta de la Habana: Periódico oficial del
gobierno* (6 abril 1900) advises

1. Queda absolutamente prohibido el uso de *tambores*, de origen africano en toda clase de reuniones, ya se celebran éstas en a vía pública,

como en el interior de los edificios. Queda igualmente prohibido que transiten por las calles de esta ciudad las *agrupaciones, o comparsas,* conocidos con el nombre de *Tangos, Cabildos y Claves* cualquieras otras que conduzcan *símbolos, alegorías y objetos* que pugnan con la seriedad y cultura de los habitantes de este país. (Moore Appendix 1, 229)

[The use of drums of African origin is strictly prohibited in all types of meetings whether these are celebrated in public or inside buildings. It is also strictly forbidden that groups known as *Tangos, Cabildos* or *Claves* or others of that ilk parade through the street carrying symbols, allegories and objects that play havoc with the seriousness and culture of the inhabitants of this country.]

Blacks circumvented such prohibitions by moving to clandestine locations or employing less raucous instruments (see Wimberly, Moore, Fryer) and in consequence Africanisms "tardaron mucho tiempo todavía en salir de un confinamiento impuesto por el sistema social de la Colonia" (Carpentier 150) [took a long time to leave the confinement imposed upon them by the colonial social system]. Carpentier opines,

Habrá que esperar a fines del siglo [XIX] para que la música ancestral del Africa, oculta en los barracones, llevada en las mentes de los esclavos y libertos de reciente emancipación, salga de lo esotérico para insinuarse en la música de baile. (143)

[It was not until the end of the (nineteenth) century that the ancestral music of Africa, hidden in slave quarters, carried in the minds of slaves and of the recently liberated would leave the esoteric realm and insinuate itself into dance music.]

Those juridical restrictions would become a discursive snub in the epoch of the republic: "The occasional black and mulatto orchestras attempting to perform *danzones* with non-European hand percussion such as the *güiro* (gourd scraper) or *chéquere* were condemned for bringing 'savage' Africanisms into the ballroom" (Moore 24). Nevertheless,

Los jóvenes de calesa, chistera y leontina, que concurrían a las casas de baile, hallaban en el modo de tocar de las orquestas de negros, un carácter, un *pep*, una fuerza rítmica, que no tenían otras de mayores pretensiones. En numerosoas crónicas y artículos de periódicos coloniales no se habla de la creciente preferencia que se tenía por las "orquestas de color," en cuanto se refiriera al baile. Ciertas *contadanzas* "gustaban más," cuando las tocaban los pardos. Blancos y negros ejecutaban las mismas composiciones populares. Pero los negros les añadían un acento, una vitalidad, un algo no escrito, que "levantaba.". . . El negro se escurría, inventando, entre las notas impresas. El blanco se atenía a la solfa. (Carpentier *La música*, 141–42)

[It seems that the young bourgeois who rode in carriages and wore top hats and watch chains, who gathered at the dance halls, found an élan in the way black orchestras played, an intensity, a rhythmic force that was unpretentious. In numerous chronicles and articles of the colonial period a growing preference for "orchestras of color," when speaking of dances, is mentioned. Certain *contradanzas* "had greater appeal" when played by blacks. Blacks and whites performed the same popular songs. But blacks added an accent, a vitality, something unwritten that "perked things up.". . . The black musician was elusive, inventing between the written notes. White musicians stuck to the score.](*Music* 158)

Not surprisingly, Peter Fryer, writing in the Brazilian context, provides a similar commentary: "Black orchestras played 'classical' music with impressive skill. And when they were called on to play European dances, they tended to 'creolise' the rhythm, introducing a degree of syncopation, a 'beat' and 'swing' that Portuguese dancers, some at least of whom had already got used to such infectious [Africanized] rhythms in Portugal itself, found greatly to their taste. So far as popular music was concerned, this was the musical culture that their children were born into and took for granted" (136). Free to come and move between both cultural milieus, those whose birthright and color gave them automatic entry into elite culture had no need to defend its propositions and could (defiantly) risk an evening's entertainment in questionable settings. Baraka might suggest that "they could not help but do this with some sense of rebelliousness or separateness from the rest of white [society]" ("Swing" 40). Those who enjoyed no such guarantees took a very different—and dimmer—view.[2]

Carpentier had earlier noted the coexistence of "dos clases de negros, sometidos a muy distintos climas sociales" (143–44) [two classes of Blacks, constricted by very different social climates]. Of those "acknowledged as . . . valued servant[s] of Western hegemony" (Chinweizu "What the Nobel," 190), whom Baraka would derisively term *citizens* who had "moved away from the older lowdown forms" ("Swing" 46), Carpentier observes:

> Cuando las comparsas se sueltan por las calles, el 6 de enero, con sus diablitos, reyes y *culonas*, el "hombre político" se sesga, dejando pasar, como el blanco, aquel carnaval tolerado por las autoridades en virtud de una vieja costumbre. Si el tambor hace vibrar, por simpatía, las más secretas fibras de su corazón, no lo coniesa. Es posible que a veces asista a los *toques* del barrio de Carraguao. Pero en los bailes donde acúa por profesión, ejecuta el *Minué de Corte*. (*La música* 150)

> [When the comparsas are let loose on the streets on January 6, with their little devils, kings, and big bottomed women, the "political man" draws back, letting pass, just like whites, that carnival tolerated by the authorities, respecting an old custom. If the drum made the innermost fibers of his heart resonate in sympathy, he did not admit it. It is possible that at times (he) would attend the ritual drum beating of the Carraguao neighborhood. But in the dances where he performed his professional duties, he played the courtly minuet.] (*Music* 163–64)

In Brazil a similar situation existed: the confrontation of elite culture, to which mulattos—gatekeepers of dominant culture's paradigms—aspired, and Black popular culture that in the lighter brothers' estimation thwarted their own efforts to attain social mobility at every turn. Black popular culture made for an apt sacrificial prey, "[a]t a time when Brazil's small elite and middle class struggled to present a modern visage to international observers" and mulattos "desir[ed] acceptance into the educated bourgeoisie" (Graden 58).

> [The mulatto writers of *O Alabama*] painted a picture of debauchery and immorality spread by Candomble. Afro-Bahian words like *vodum* (*vodun*) and batucage (drumming) conjured up images of hidden dens and barbaric acts. Such words and phrases placed Afro-Bahian rituals in a negative light, as something licentious, uncontrollable, and foreign. Worse yet, the police had not acted with the determination and

force necessary to prevent the spread of subversion. The pounding of drums at night had disrupted neighborhoods composed of law-abiding citizens; uneducated blacks paying homage to unknown African gods and goddesses seemed to be overrunning the beleaguered European "civilization" to which elite Bahia aspired. (Graden 67)

Drawing upon the work of Martínez Furé, Moore offers a similarly motivated Cuban example:

Far from wholeheartedly accepting a diversity of Afrocuban-influenced music and dance for their own recreational activities, the *sociedades de color* [exclusive social organizations of the Afrocuban middle class] frequently forbade the use of drums or performance of genres such as *son*, *comparsa* and rumba. . . . The Club Atenas [*nota bene*, the Greek moniker], for instance, established a Comisión de Orden that monitored, among other things, the sorts of dance moves performed by guests and the instruments of the band. It specifically forbade conga drums well into the 1940s. (Moore 34)

So pervasive is this dynamic in the African-ancestored community that *Cabaré da RRRRRaça* (1997) [Race Cabaret], a play-ful collaboration between Márcio Meirelles and Bando de Teatro Olodum, pokes fun at such pretensions. In this work, business owner Rose Marie speaks in the affected tone and exaggerated accent of an elite wannabe, steadfastly denying that she has ever felt the sting of racism. Offering the fact that in her bank she always receives "tratamento VIP" [VIP treatment] because of her mimetic refinement, she interrupts the other players: "Não entendo isto que voces estão discutindo aqui: coisa de raça, de cor?. . . Eu, Rrrose Marie, nunca fui discriminada" (5) [I don't understand what you all are arguing about: a color thing, a race thing? . . . I, Rrrose Marie, have never been discriminated against]. When a drum sounds in the background, her body moves involuntarily to the beat, undergoing an instant metamorphosis in which she becomes a (stereotypically) loud, rough-talking, arms-akimbo *favela* woman who belligerently proclaims her dissatisfaction with her treatment as a Black woman, pounding her "bunda firme e redonda" [full-figured rear] to emphasize the point:

"Sou discrimminda quando pego o ônibus e criticam minha roupa, meu cabelo. Sou discriminda quando vou ao supermercado e o fiscal me segue como se eu estivesse roubando." (5)

["I am discriminated against when I ride the bus and they commence to yappin' 'bout my clothes, my hair. I am discriminated against when I go to the supermarket and the clerk follows me as if I was going to five-finger something."]

The reactive stance toward talking drums confirms the centrality of cultural context. Drums have become an essential part of Latin American culture, often ironically so. In the São Paulo International Airport, travelers can smother their cigarette butts or toss out their gum wrappers in the free-standing ashtrays/trash receptacles modeled on the form of a *batucage* drum painted in Rastafarian colors red, green, yellow, and black. In Buenos Aires, street demonstrations feature protestors who beat out monotonous rhythms to accompany their chants on the *piano*, the largest percussive instrument of the *candombe* traditional trio of drums. The deculturized treatment of the drum, in the first instance, seems to confirm a certain inherent disrespect—one would hardly think of a chalice being used in the same way—and, in the second, an association with noise makers, rebelliousness, and antisocial behavior (mob behavior). One might argue that these denatured pervasive presences represent a tribute to the persuasive persistence of Africanisms and New World Blackness. Doubtful. What such displays fail to consider—context, vernacular strategic devices, the drums' role as attitude, stance, worldview—they fail to consider precisely because "official" culture instinctively recognizes the threat, or one might better say, the challenge that Blackness—experience and expression—represents. In recognizing the drum, "official, national" cultures would also have to elevate African-descended practitioners and their practices—the absented locus—and thus give up racial harmony, the "official" conception of order and progress, and recognize the contradictory histories, diverging cultures, and the Blackness of its bottle-blond roots. The persistence of the drum connotes its strategic value, a "tabla rasa" [blank stage or, doubly, an inviting drum-head]. Upon it are writ peculiar notions of time and narrative and an invitation to the curi-

ous and the accomplished to appreciate the mastery of form and the meaning of contest. And the beat goes on.

Rhythmic Mode and Other Mysteries of Colored People's Time

When taught by a master, a young drummer carried away by a momentary
flash of Ricky Ricardo wildly slamming out his version of the rumba will
quickly be corrected in firm tones regarding appropriate stance, and the
proper care and carriage of the instrument.[3] Lessons emphasize a coherency
with tradition—prescribed drums calls, acute attentiveness to the teacher or
lead percussionist, the practical and historical role of each drum. Even "profane" players are as fanatical about their instrument as any concert pianist.
During a *candombe comparsa* in Uruguay or Argentina, the head drummer
taps out a syncopated beat on the drum's wooden rim, skillfully hesitating
over each note. The other percussionists, arrayed in either parade formation
or in an inward-facing circle, faithfully repeat the call and a rhythmic unison
takes hold, a balance between the three sections *piano, chico, repique*. Sonic-
visual interaction insures that each compliments (enhances) or complements
(completes) the timbre, intensity, duration, tone, movement, and force of
the other players, captured in their sight line or peripheral vision. What re-
sembles a state of trance disguises a heightened sensory-sonic-visual-tactile
awareness. And as the beats rain down in stylized syncopation, the effect on
the nonplaying participants can be overwhelming, breathtaking.

If diasporic percussive musical production connects peoples of African
descent, it is not because they share, in the narrow sense, a sense of rhythm.
Rather, each rhythmic manifestation consciously or unconsciously suspends,
or, to talk the talk, off-times the other's temporality. Given "the changing
means by which space and society are interrelated" (Immerfall 8), timely interruption necessarily refashions the other's territoriality. Thus in terms of
Blackness, rhythmicity—rhythmic confidence—improvises and refashions
a momentary space "back home," one's "own corner of reality," or "a retreat,
a homogeneous community where a collectivity of common experience
[finds] continuity and meaningful expression" (Ellison 454). And that's the
point. Just as narrative innovation reenergizes tradition in Zapata Olivella's
"vernacular expressive strategy" and in Ghana's Concert Theatre's use of
well-established "techniques of creativity," the drumming aesthetic reenacts
diverging/converging spaces and times without contradictions. It bears repeating that such displays of cultural improvisation represent "that which

both will enable contemporary man to be at home with his sometimes tolerable but never quite certain condition of not being at home in the world and will also dispose him to regard his obstacles and frustrations as well as his achievements in terms of adventure and romance" (Murray 277). Or again, as Bone has asserted, cultural strategies allow the uprooted to in-corporate/em-body/in-carnate the beat, "to be *possessed* of soul . . . capable of improvising, of winning the contest *without* your drums" (*Down Home* 156).

Accordingly, trained by the experience of uprootedness, marginalized peoples adeptly create their own retreats that suspend temporal, spatial, and linguistic distances that are the result of their dispersal and the disparities arising from that condition. And in "private" spaces other things happen. For example, in Seville, Spain, after the bars that cater to tourists in search of flamenco close down and the last waiter has gone home, outside the city's limits, in cramped and humble settings, the Romani (Gypsy) dancers and musicians gather informally. Only aficionados and the initiated know of these places, and the hour—beginning around three or four in the morning—and the location serve as barriers to the faint of heart. Much like jazz jam sessions or cutting contests, in this "different sphere of training" (Ellison 453), performers test their skills in casual contest with their companions.

> Here it is more meaningful to speak . . . of apprenticeship, ordeals, initiation ceremonies, of rebirth. For after the jazzman has learned the fundamentals of his instrument and the traditional techniques of jazz—the intonations, the mute work, manipulation of timbre, the body of traditional styles—he must then "find himself," must be reborn, must find, as it were, his soul. All this through achieving that subtle identification between his instrument and his deepest drives which will allow him to express his own unique ideas and his own unique voice. He must achieve, in short, his self-determined identity. (454–55)

Echoing fellow Briton Paul Gilroy's paradigm of Atlantic triangles, Fryer postulates the dissemination of musical forms amidst Brazil, Portugal, and Angola that resulted from similar impromptu sessions:

> [I]t was above all black seafarers, making music (giving "little concerts") in African, Brazilian and Portuguese ports in turn, and often putting in at that Lusophone "Crossroads of the Atlantic," the Cape Verde archipelago, where the ships of all nations were serviced . . .—it was black

seafarers who did more than anyone else to spread music and dance around the triangle. . . . We can be sure that any seafarer with musical skills would, on reaching port, seek out and participate in what today would be called jam sessions, in which tunes and dances, rhythms and riffs would be swapped, taught, learnt and passed on. (138)

Beyond empirical postulations or reasoned explanation, Alejo Carpentier writes euphorically of his attending such a "contest" jam session in Cuba:

Hay casos en que los tambores *batás* ayudados por la riqueza sonora de su afinación y el virtuosismo de los *tocadores*, ejecutan trozos completos a percusión sola, eliminando las voces humanas. En cierta oportunidad, en una fiesta de santería dada en la barriada de Regla, les oímos tocar una "marcha" y un "llanto" de considerable duración, que eran verdaderas piezas, completas, equilibradas, hechas sobre el desarrollo, dentro del *tempo*, de células rítmicas fundamentales. . . . Pero debe señalarse que, en muchos casos, ese toque fundamental cobra la amplitud de un *modo rítmico*. En efecto ¿cómo vamos a hablar de ritmo propiamente dicho, cuando nos encontramos con una verdadera frase, compuesta de valores y de grupos de valores, cuya anotación excede el límite de varios compases, antes de adquirir una función rítmica por proceso de repetición? Cuando esto se produce—y es frecuente—estamos en presencia de un *modo rítmico*, con acentos propios que nada tiene que ver con nuestras nociones habituales del tiempo fuerte y del tiempo débil. El *tocador* acentúa tal o cual nota, no por razones de tipo escancional, sino porque así lo exige "la expresión" tradicional del *modo rítmico* producido. ¡No por mera casualidad los negros suelen decir que "hacen hablar los tambores!" . . . ¡Piénsese ahora en el desconcertante efecto de movimiento, de palpitación interior, que se desprende de la marcha simultánea de varios *modos rítmicos*, que acaban por establecer misteriosas relaciones entre sí, conservando, sin embargo, una cierta independencia de planos, y se tendrá una remota idea del embrujo producido por ciertas expresiones de la percusión *batá*! (*La música* 300)

[There are cases where the *batás* drums, aided by their rich tuning and the virtuosity of their performers, play entire solo passages, eliminating the voices. Once, at a Santeria party in Regla, we heard the drummers play a "march" and a "call" of considerable duration, which were true pieces, complete, balanced, developed within the tempo, evolving from fundamental rhythmic cells. In many cases, this prime beat flowers into a *rhythmic mode*. Really, how can we properly speak of rhythm when faced with a true phrase, composed of notes and groups of notes, that outpaces all metrical limits before acquiring a rhythmic function through sheer repetition? When this happens—and it does so frequently—we are in the presence of a rhythmic mode, with its own accents that have nothing to do with accepted notions of a strong or weak beat. The player stresses this note or another, not for . . . scansional reasons, but because the traditional expression of the *rhythmic mode* demands it. It is not mere happenstance that blacks say that "they make the drums (talk)!" Now consider the disconcerting effect of movement, of internal palpitations given off by the simultaneous pacings of various rhythmic modes, which end up establishing mysterious relationships among themselves, conserving, however, a certain independence, and you will have a remote idea of the kind of bewitching effect produced by certain expressions of the *batá* drums!] (*Music* 264–65)

A similarly euphoric encounter took place in September 1997 in Bloomington, Indiana, during that city's annual World Music festival.

That impromptu contest of skill featured the Afro-Bahian group Olodum—the youthful Brazilian musical powerhouse who have performed with Paul Simon and Michael Jackson and throughout the world—and Los Muñequitos de Matanzas, an Afro-Cuban group of mostly mature drummers, singers, and dancers who enjoy a deserved fame and longevity. Slated to play the following evening, Olodum arrived to do a closing number with Los Muñequitos, already on stage. Despite a shared affinity for the drum, their styles vary greatly and the differing languages—Spanish and Portuguese—posed an added barrier. While the Brazilians are renowned for their inventive samba-reggae, the Cubans' presentation that evening carefully depicted first the African (specifically Yoruba) and then the Iberian (particularly flamenco) contributions toward what would become rumba in its varied forms: the house party style (for example, *calenda*), the ballroom mode, and one form accented with yet another borrowing, this time from their northern neighbors and costumed with Afro wigs and the bell-bottomed, powder-blue polyester of 1970s retro clothing. When Olodum exploded onto the stage, a rainbow of brown men and women attired in a cacophony of red, green, yellow, and black, the audience experienced "el virtuosismo de los *tocadores*," a unifying "*modo rítmico*," and a palpable "infinite alertness-become-dexterity." In an atmosphere of well-being and celebration, the unrehearsed coda provided a momentary interruption of diaspora dispersal and disparities and gave birth to a visual, visceral melting away of national borders, diverging styles, generational division, and linguistic constraints. Where words failed, drums spoke.

Admittedly, the tone of these observations betrays a mystical accent, an intonation similar to that of Baraka in his discussion of blues, the slightly embarrassed idealism evinced in Cartegena Portalatín's commentary on Negritude, and Carpentier's unabashed euphoria. The electrifying spontaneity of the performance or the jolting uniqueness of the manifestation contributes to this feeling, which indeed "penetrated all of the percipient spaces of those present" (Benítez-Rojo 20). The difficulty arises in a tongue-tied attempt to explain the sense of wonder produced in the presence of "the human imagination in motion" (Crouch 163). Yet, within a cultural context where drums serve a religious, or more broadly spiritual, function in ritual and pageantry (*Santería*, *Candomblé*, *Día de los Reyes*, *Misa Negra*, etc.), their ability to transform and transport seems only logical since musicality produced by peoples of African descent, even as secular spectacle, contains and is contained within a synchronic cultural cosmology.

For example, as "the casual expression of a whole culture" (Baraka "Swing," 37), the moving popular music of Cuban Celia Cruz, Peruvian Susana Baca, and North American Aretha Franklin, in their open evocation of the traditional and spiritual roots of Blackness, implicitly pays homage to the absented locus. Again, diverging historical versions and temporalities in contest provide a possible explanation:

> "Serious music" (a term that could only have extra-religious meaning in the West) has never been an integral part of the Westerner's life; no art has been since the Renaissance. Of course, before the Renaissance, art could find its way into the lives of almost all the people because all art issued from the Church and the Church was at the very center of Western man's life. But the discarding of the religious attitude for the "enlightenment" concepts of the Renaissance also created the schism between what was art and what was life. It was, and is, inconceivable

in the African culture to make a separation between music, dancing, song, the artifact and a man's life or his worship of his gods. Expression issued from life and was beauty. But in the West, the "triumph of the economic mind over the imaginative," as Brooks Adams said, made possible this dreadful split between life and art. ("African Slaves" 30)

In that sense, where culture *casually* represents a cosmological totality—an interwoven fabric that simultaneously affects and reflects every aspect of a life strategy—both the overlap between drums and spirituality and the corporeality of rhythm become redundant. Affinities and coherencies (for example, the marriage of dance and music) readily present themselves across ritual, pastime, and entertainment contexts with a casualness not overburdened by a belabored insistence on "authentic" roots. That casualness need not necessarily recognize the full force of the traditions or the traditional techniques it apes, but nevertheless remains accountable to its context because what the producer or participant "projects upon the outside world" in a new way reenacts an experience from which each "gains in its culturally determined form" (Hall *Silent Language*, 119).

That interconnectedness promotes the vision of "creatures of culture" formed and informed by a worldview predicated on tension and contest, in which values—belligerence, playfulness, esteem of honored priests and priestesses—reinforce that same view. While that philosophical incestuousness might bear closer examination in this and other cases, the more crucial complication arises when these "cultured" denizens find themselves at odds with acultural scenarios, for example, with mercantile models. That is, explanatory models built on contradiction and competition tend to posit and therefore to privilege closed periodizations and machine-driven imagery where one concept or action comes into being on the ashes or "completion" of another. In such conceptions, "Time is linear and segmented like a road or a ribbon extending forward into the future and backward to the past. It is also tangible; they speak of it as being saved, spent, wasted, lost, made up, accelerated, slowed down, crawling, and running out. These metaphors should be taken very seriously, because they express the basic manner in which time is conceived as an unconscious determinant or frame on which everything else is built" (Hall *Beyond Culture*, 19). This underlying estrangement of interests (expressed as resistance, deviations) recalls the antagonism commented on by Carbonell, an antagonism that has the potential to distort narrative, history, representation, and "empirical" theory. A reconsideration of the *meanings* framed by this troubled temporal construction necessarily allows other things to happen: the encouragement of other methodological approaches and the appearance of other, more layered, conclusions. In that light, one of Brazil's most important Cinema Novo directors, Nelson Pereira dos Santos, speaking of his own attitudinal shift, observed in an interview:

> [T]he deepest forms of cultural expression, those that come from the roots—like the expression of religious sentiment among the marginal sectors, for example—have always been suppressed and repressed within Brazilian culture. Religious expression has always had to conform to the needs of the colonizer. I proposed to use popular response to this repression of "deviant" spirituality as my point of departure, since it gave me a global vision, a way of thinking in relation to all of Brazilian society rather than to a small component. (136)

Thus to posit a temporal distortion is also to question the validity, value, and veracity of every aspect to which it refers.

Disturbingly, textbooks continue such distortion. In one instance, an otherwise unremarkable Portuguese language textbook detours from grammar and descends into culture. As is the practice these days, culture seems all the rage, no longer restricted to snippets of canonical literature or a description of this or that religious festival or alluring tourist destination. However, rather than initiate or educate the beginning or intermediate student of language in the intricacies of social traditions, history, politics, and the like, this window into the other world often presents a mere sound bite. In one such cultural reading, Indians warmly greeted the invaders, until a series of unfortunate and unpleasant misunderstandings strained further relations. For their part, Africans scurrying from hunger, intertribal warfare, and all the other standard markers of lack and underdevelopment typically applied to Africa to this day, pretty much throw themselves at slave ships in their effort to escape the evils of the Dark Continent. These especially desperate "immigrants" then willingly—it would seem— surrender themselves into the waiting chains of chattel slavery. To say the least, such approaches fail to offer a critical view of Latin American cultural terrains.[4]

In another case, *Relatos latinoamericanos: la herencia africana* [Latin American Stories: The African Heritage] edited by James H. Kennedy first offers a map of Latin America that gives percentages of the presence of peoples of African descent in the various countries of the continent. No accompanying explanation questions the arbitrary nature of such figures within discourses of racial harmony, *blanquecimiento* and *mestizaje* that devalue Blackness, or the fact, for example, that in Brazil and Argentina the census at various key moments did not include a category for those of African descent although the numbers of other "ethnic" groups, for example, those of Arab heritage (Lebanese, Syrian), were carefully recorded. The first chapter deals with carnival, always an intriguing topic for the foreigner, emphasizing the image of a couple of days of crazy abandon. Less titillating detail is elided: a long history of *Blocos de carnaval*, for example Ilê Ayê, Filhos de Ghandi, and Olodum in Salvador da Bahia Brazil; and the year-long careful planning that includes hiring a historian to research a selected theme, including personalities such as Zumbi and Negro Cosmos, and events such as the Buzios Rebellion. While the essays point out the "aportes culturales" [cultural contributions] of slaves to the European Catholic imaginary, this insight ignores that many of the rituals such as the *llamadas* that initiate Carnaval in Montevideo, Uruguay, present evidence of a parallel reality outside the European purview and demonstrate how Old World carnival succumbed, becoming transformed, transfigured, or, in a word Africanized by a tradition of Africana spectacle. The cultural supplement also ignores the juridical evidence of the many prohibitions meant to block Black contribution to and participation in this yearly event and repeats the historical, discursive error of presenting that contribution and participation as fragmented rather than fundamental.

Other essays focus on a who's who list of traditional heroes, for example, Chico Rey, tied to yet another religious festival, *Festa de Nossa Senhora de Rosario*, and Martin de Porres, the canonized Peruvian monk; yet there is no mention of the church's reluctance to admit Blacks into the priesthood, and there is no acknowledgment that Ricardo Palma, author of *Tradiciones Peruanas*, listed as a source of further reading, was himself of African descent. In the chapter on Zumbi, the reader learns almost nothing about the *quilombo*'s internal social, political, and cultural reality but receives precise information on the dates of armed conflicts with outside forces, tacitly revealing who, up to now, owns history: the conqueror. One notes, then, that the material is heavily weighted to Brazilian figures, forgetting or ignoring the admittedly smaller but no less vital populations in Ecuador, Peru, and Colombia, among others. Inevitably such approaches, however well intentioned, respond to a historical vision that always, already, narratively and necessarily, distorts the tardy inclusion to "fit" normalized dimensions. And the legitimation of those historiographies through sheer repetition cannot, however, obscure the idiosyncratic—or ideo-syncretic—effort to negate Africa, Blackness, peoples of African descent and, no less, the overarching cultural reality.

The value of improvisation—temporal or territorial—then resides in a number of factors: its real and metaphorical interconnectedness; its ability to cannibalize diverging/converging cosmologies and the forms they engender and still retain integrity; its ability, when faced with serial uprootings, to carve out a retreat, a space for creative endeavor, a unique and peculiar cosmology; its ability to construct vernacular expressive strategies coherent with one's experience; its ability to reference not only a stance, or an attitude, but more importantly the skill and serendipity, context and devices that make creating culture possible. The innovative religiosity of the protagonist of Barbara Neely's *Blanche Passes Go* (2000) offers a fitting example:

> So [Blanche had] made up her own ritual, just as she'd put together her own spiritual practice, including reverence for her Ancestors and the plants, and seeking energy from trees and healing from the sea. Some things she'd learned from African, Afro-Caribbean, Native American, and Asian ways of having a spiritual life, but she always added her personal twist. Until she'd come up with her own rituals she'd been hungry for ways to demonstrate her belief that there was more to life than she could see—ways that didn't require her being a member of the Christian or the Muslim or any other religion that had played a part in African slavery. She had no time for any religions that said she needed a priest or priestess to act as a go-between or worshiped a god called He. She was her own priest and goddess. (12)

Conversely, because of the emphasis on getting to a future or predetermined endpoint (civilization, modernity, progress), teleology tends to overlook past and present, or considers them only to attain a distant and clearly defined goal. Teleology locks itself into a predictable dynamic of the birth-climax-death of artistic or cultural movements, political systems, and the like that begin anew on the ashes of the previous manifestation. Such distorted time lines obscure the centrality—and cathartic affect—of *process*; Blanche's made-up, riffing spirituality rejects both an interested temporal authority and the implicit stranglehold of its underlying ideology.

Admittedly, peoples of African descent find themselves literally and figuratively embedded into Western scheduling, as Wynter writes, "in fact and fiction." Consequently, if and when monopoly, metropoly, or nation begin to believe their own press, the relationship between events becomes distorted, as in the case of peoples of African descent in the Americas, and a tremendous amount can be lost or, at the least, misinterpreted. In this light, the current embrace of drums belies contemporary disregard and current regard for the instrument, its creators, players, and public. And in this sense, "Colored People's time," in its antiphonic and synchronic aspect, steps to the beat of a different drummer.

Consequently, if taken narratively—in which "official" beginning, middle, and end coalesce to coherently prefigure and recall events and resolve conflicts within the narrative—the material and corporeal representations of peoples of African descent and no less the "contradictory" versions of their contribution and participation remain hopelessly at odds. One example of the standard narrative of African arrival to the New World illustrates:

> Arrancados compulsivamente de sus lugares de origen fueron arrojados en una sociedad extraña para la que simplemente eran la fuerza de trabajo. Donde no se les ofrecía la oportunidad de rehacer sus valores y sistemas de vida, su orden, su familia, su gobierno, sus lenguas y sus creencias y prácticas religiosas, sino que antes bien, se los aislaba, se los separaba, se buscaba quebrar los lazos comunes de coterraniedad y familia, para una más rápida y completa asimilación a sus nuevos lugares de destino. Este proceso radical de deculturación presentó diversas modalidades, según los lugares y sistemas de trabajo. (Chirimini and Varese 3–4)

> [Taken by force from their places of origin they were thrown into an alien society for which they were simply a work force. Where no opportunity was given to them to remake their values and lifestyles, their order, their family, their government, their languages and their beliefs and religious practices, but rather they were isolated, they were separated, ways to destroy the common ties of altruism and family were sought, for a more rapid and complete assimilation to their new destined places. This radical process of deculturation presented distinct modalities, according to the place and systems of work.]

Perhaps more poignant than other variations, the same narratively normalized conventions reappear: empty-handed arrival and the utter efficiency of the civilizing mission. Notably, the subtle modalities usually stressed in other paradigms between discreetly proscriptive South America and harshly seg-regationist North America here make little difference. Yet a complication inevitably arises, and the very same Chirimini notes the disparity—without, however, being able to explain it in the terms of the logic dictated by history or discipline or the narrative of nation:

> El caso uruguayo se da una paradoja. No obstante que el proceso de deculturación ha sido mayor, sin embargo, musicalmente hablando, el Candombe ha conservado a través de su ritmo de los instrumentos que lo crean, la más pura esencia de la música africana. (5)

> [The Uruguayan case gives rise to a paradox. Despite the thorough-going process of deculturation, musically speaking, the Candombe has nevertheless preserved, through the rhythm of the instruments that create it, the most pure essence of African music.]

While one could easily argue the problematic assertion of the essential purity or Africanness, it is indisputable that, as Carpentier had noted earlier, "un algo no escrito" and utterly non-European derails the official version.

In this instance, paradox signals that "the operations of narration" (Julien 154) remain out of sync, presenting a self-resonating, albeit not convincing, tale. The powerful sway of narrative—be it convention, necessity, or comple-tion—reveals itself. And this revelation gives a glimpse of narrative's inner workings and, more importantly, hints at what has been "edited" out and what gets inserted into the waiting slots. The traditional narrative of Black-ness conveniently backgrounds Africa, especially her cultural aspects; em-phasizes a skewed vision of slavery; and participates in the outright erasure of Black beings, that is, absented loci through miscegenation, transculturation, assimilation, syncreticism. Concomitantly, the "scheduled" appearances of peoples of African descent in Western narratives of empire, modernity, and progress consist of inventions to fill obvious voids—the use of local color, for example, to frame a peculiar "bucolic" vision of world events and human participation in and contribution to the scheme of things. In reality, such attempts to mask temporal dislocations instead signal the disjunctions and incoherence in "official" stories of the drum, contradicting, by extension, the cultural and social (and no less, the political) experience of Blackness. Indeed, drums talk.

6

Orality

A Word-Worldview

Faced with the nakedness of the natives who greeted him, Columbus quickly concluded that he had not come upon the one-eyed monsters that he had been led to expect—the deformed beings Marco Polo had feared—and that the lack of ostentatious costume signified the defenseless and faintly charming nature of these creatures who clearly posed no threat to his undertaking. One of the first orders of business called for reading the *Requerimiento*, a document, in Spanish, which advised the aborigines of the legitimacy of the Spanish endeavor and its endorsement by the church. The text instructed the assembled in the benefits to those who complied and detailed to the recalcitrant the dire consequences of real or perceived resistance to the master plan.[1]

While that particular scenario rings patently ridiculous in any other light than single-minded conquest, it also demonstrates the blinding power of a "*word*view," which attaches rightness and righteousness to the written document considered stable, fixed, and juridically binding. In a written universe meant to constrict variable, ambiguous, and unforeseen circumstance, there are valiant efforts to "pin down" orality's free-floating parole, to codify language in standard forms and grammar, to regulate even the figurative and lyric, and to confirm the authentic version. Supposedly stripped of language, kidnapped Africans later presented an equally "inoffensive" foil for empire's civilizing mission—without benefit of a pro forma document. Uprootedness would pose the issue of language faculty and fluency and make for intriguing improvisations.

Based on detailed travelers' accounts, Peter Fryer asserts that kidnapped Africans were encouraged to sing in their native language as they disembarked from slave ships along the Brazilian coast, in Bahia, Recife, Rio de Janeiro. He might also have noted that the types of work these bondspeople were required to perform quickly gave almost as immediate evidence of various displays of orality. Street vendors hawked their wares. Stevedores, miners, and porters—bent by the weight of coffee bags or the girth of distinguished *criollo* patrons or foreign guests—set the work pace with cadenced call and response as did cotton pickers and railroad workers in the United States. Wet nurses quieted their charges with narrations, both real and fantastic. To acquiesce to requests of slave owner, amateur and professional anthropologist or folklorist, or perhaps fellow bar patrons, these African-descended improvisers wove entertaining tales that provided off-timing opportunities "for sly commentary on the master race, for riffing and improvising off the man's tune and making it fun" (Hunter Lattany, qtd. in Spencer 138) or at least, momentarily tolerable, a strategy evident in the poetry of Nicolás Guillén, Obeso Candelario, Plácido (née Gabriel de la Concepción Valdés), and others. In more private or insulated moments, seeking solace, to amuse and no less to educate in the ways of culture, the African descended would hone oratorical skills in tale-telling and in contests with names as varied as the regions to which they belong.

Indeed, many suggest that such manifestations would plant the seed for later innovative scripted forms. Thus, orality, one of the few expressive territories ceded to those of African descent in the diaspora, traffics in those connections posed by Wynter and the metaphorical interconnectedness alluded to by Konrád. Analyzing the range, the accountability, and no less the textual transformation of expressive vernacular—the most compact of carry-on baggage—can reveal a great deal about the permutations propelled by uprootedness and improvisation. More than mere speech act, orality insinuates an effort to refashion a more amenable space and to off-time "official" history.

Underscoring orality's fundamental and formative importance, both Robert Bone and Richard L. Jackson consider it not only as a key step toward written text, but indeed toward a specifically Afrodiasporic, Afrocentric aesthetic. Accordingly, Jackson, in his foundational text *Black Writers in Latin America* (1979), begins his examination of Black artistic expression with a focus on oral production:

> The very first literary manifestation of the "true black experience" in Latin America is found in the folk literature that blacks cultivated orally before learning to write European languages. Whatever the "strata" of the folklore of black America, whether pure African, Negro (or Creole), or white folklore but absorbed by blacks, and regardless of origin, whether uniquely black American or from Africa, Europe, or even

Aesop's fables, folklore used by blacks in the New World tells us much about black survival [that is, transformations] reflecting as it does the unique New World experience. (16)

In the North American context, Robert Bone affirms that "the archetypal figure of Br'er Rabbit . . . is not only a major triumph of the Afro-American imagination, but also the most subversive hero this side of Stagolee" (*Down Home* 19). Thus the transposition of Br'er Rabbit (and no less that of Tío or Compay Conejo) has more importantly "kindled the imagination of black writers for almost a century," (19) serving a vital role in the history of their writerly approaches to Blackness. While specialists—folklorists, anthropologists, ethnologists, pan-Africanists, and others—debate the origins of this oral and literary body, Bone, like Jackson, astutely cuts to the heart of the matter:

What seems beyond dispute is that a very ancient African tradition survived the [Middle P]assage, and served as a basis of renewed creative efforts in the Western Hemisphere. At the same time we must insist that Br'er Rabbit tales were conceived not by Africans, but by Afro-Americans. For these tales reflect the social conditions and historical experience of black slaves [in the Americas]. They represent the first attempt of black Americans to define themselves through the art of storytelling; a heroic effort on the part of chattel slaves to transmute the raw materials of their experience into the [scripted] forms of fiction [they would encounter] there. (22)

More to the point, Bone believes that the tales' "internal evidence"—theme, tone, implied moral code, hidden motives—attests to the "unmistakable projection of the black imagination" (24) and he asks that the reader reconsider the often deforming overarching frame within which the tales are retold, collected, and disseminated. In other words, readerly reception depends on an astute understanding of characteristic tropes such as off-timing, indirection, ambivalence, and countering—*and* to which version of history one subscribes.

In the broader context of Latin American literary history, Jean Franco for her part recognizes oral literature as "an integral part of a living culture that as in medieval Europe provided an outlet for the unofficial activities and responses of the people" (5). Jackson comments: "Jean Franco is, of course, right, then, to conclude that oral literature can teach us much, particularly oral literature that under the cloak of anonymity escaped the censorship and control early written literature had to endure. It is not difficult, therefore, to trace in later print literature themes of freedom, injustice, humor, and pride in blackness back to early oral improvisations popular among blacks" (23). Bone echoes Jackson, observing that "The Afro-American oral tradition . . . functioned as a counterforce" that "was antipastoral in tendency. For the black slave's existence in America, while sylvan and agrarian, was something less than idyllic, and his earliest, preliterate attempts to fictionalize his experience were hardly governed by the white man's notion of Arcadia" (*Down Home* 18). Notwithstanding the dynamic and subversive potential of the improvised word—and world—orality in relation to the cultural production of peoples of African descent often finds itself confined to the quaint and inoffensive dimension of folklore, judged an entertaining but unoriginal exercise in rote memorization or inflexibly ritualized performance. The attendant subtext judges those of African descent as ontologically oral (mythical, sensual, and whimsical) rather than textual (historical, inherently rational, planned, and projected), the latter variously considered the terrain of more writerly inclined Europe, the white, elite culture, national chroniclers, and investigative collectors.

Not coincidentally then, the largest body of early Latin American studies of Blackness—anthropological texts and sociological tracts intrigued by the spontaneous folksy manifestations in their midst—offer descriptions of the native other's orality, musicality, and religiosity in tones more folkloric than scientific. In that light González notes parenthetically:

(Esa cultura, por cierto, sólo ha sido estudiada por los intelectuales de la clase dominante como *folklore*, ese invento de la burgesía europea que tan bien ha servido para escamotear la verdadera significación de la cultura popular.) (19)

[That culture, for certain, has been studied by intellectuals of the dominant class solely as *folklore*, that invention of the European bourgeoisie that has so well served to undermine the true significance of popular culture.]

Predictably, that subtext frames the entry and reception of Blackness into "official" elite culture. For instance, the better-known fancifully transcribed fables and local color digressions of canonical literature—replete with deformed language and childlike simplicity—represent what Bone describes as "a travel folder version of Negro life" (*Down Home* 140) or creations that Chinweizu suggests provide "enough Africanesque patina and inlays to satisfy the Western tourist taste for exotica. Such works become sophisticated versions of airport art" ("Pan-Africanism" 181). In the 1920s and 1930s, *Negrismo* (Negritude's inversely motivated poor relation) sought the validity of the autochthonous and, in so doing, recycled the tongue-tied or defective speech, onomatopoeic interludes, and a "tendencia a lo exótico-aborigen" (Hiriart "Prólogo," 17) [tendency toward the exotic nativeness] that also describe the seventeenth-century pseudo-Black poetry of Luís de Góngora and Francisco de Quevedo (who also authored an essay) and the prose of Miguel de Cervantes Saavedra.[2] Concomitantly, that folkloric focus reveals how the interested script has configured—and continues to reconfigure—the participation as well as the contribution of peoples of African descent.

That Bone and Jackson argue the foundational aspect of orality and each, with Franco, recalls its subversive potential, is itself an instance of discursive insurgency. Yet the emphasis on the idea that orality will become something else—scripted Black literature, a Black aesthetic—at times overshadows those instances of the oral's synchronic coexistence in traditional settings as well as in feigned or phantom or novel form, in techniques of creativity as well as a thematic seed. While the discursive indifference that those literary historians battled may be the main reason that orality often falls below the radar of literary criticism, disciplined territories may participate as well.[3]

A case helps explain. Not without its problems, Arturo Pizarroso Cuenca's text *La cultura negra en Bolivia* (1997) in the final three chapters highlights the artistic production of peoples of African descent in Bolivia—oral tradition, folklore, music—pointing toward untapped or insufficiently studied sources for possible investigation. Although tarnished with some rather flowery and stereotypic prose on the subject, Pizarroso Cuenca's work still offers openings that tacitly rethink the limits of other approaches. In the music chapter, moving past the mesmerizing drumbeat, he observes:

> En cuanto a canciones de trabajo, para los que no sólo nos interesamos por la músic, la literatura y el arte de los negros, sino también por sus condiciones de vida y labor, las canciones de trabajo que tanto abundan en su folklore poseen un doble interés, el estético y el social. (130–31)

[Regarding the work songs, for those of us that are interested not only in Black music, literature and art but also in the conditions of life and work, the work songs that are so abundant possess a double intrigue, the aesthetic and the social.]

Recalling the paradigm of North American Black poetry suggested by Martha Cobb (later adopted by Jackson) that suggests the necessary consideration of the relationship between expression and experience, the writer concludes "El antropólogo, el etnólogo, el sociólogo y aun el historiador tiene allí la mejor fuente de documentación para sus investigaciones" (131) [The anthropologist, the ethnologist, the sociologist and even the historian has there the best documentary source for their investigations]. One might wonder where the literary critic is in this line-up, especially in light of the following description of the material:

A menudo su expresión es solapada. Frases descriptivas ingeniosas, figuras de retórica, exclamaciones de penetrante intensidad dramática que revelan una acusada facultad imaginativa, de hondo contenido realista. Su música y su poesía nacida de la improvisación poseen un vigor y una vitalidad exquisitos. (131)

[Often their expression is sly. Ingenious descriptive sentences, rhetorical figures, exclamations of dramatic intensity that reveal an acute imaginative facility, of profound realist content. Their music and their poetry born of improvisation possess an exquisite vigor and vitality.]

The literariness is then apparent and even if it were not, the form deserves attention as a contribution to a Black artistic literacy—a hint of percussive soul *without the drums*, as earlier described by Bone.

The artistic production of peoples of African descent then pushes the limits of "literature" in the Western sense signaled by Franco. The focus on orality calls not (or not only) for trespass onto disciplined turfs, but for the recognition of how and where creativity happens within a cultural system that is an interwoven fabric. If "literary traditions are the beneficiaries of the oral genres," the cherished functions, themes, and techniques evident in the production of the Africana *word*view derive from the lively permutations characteristic of utterance performed, feigned, or displayed in "poetry, proverbs, riddles, narratives, epics articulated and performed orally—the so-called indigenous and authentic genres" (Julien 3, 4).[4] In the context of the Western Hemisphere, Robert Bone proposes: "The repertory includes animal fables, trickster tales . . . conjure stories, preacher tales, jokes, proverbs, anecdotes, and plantation lore of every description. Wonder tales, horror stories, voodoo legends, and what Zora Neale Hurston calls 'just plain lies' have passed from mouth to mouth in the black community for generations" (*Down Home* 20–21). Comfortable in simultaneity and the coexistence of forms, oral literatures tend not to assess fitness with the aim of displacement, but rather to cannibalize, in order to select out the juicy bits as it were (like *antropofagia* in Brazil). Despite—or perhaps because of—just that kind of "exquisite vigor and vitality," conceptions of orality as landless, timeless, folkloric production without identifiable or original creators persist especially in connection with Africa and her diasporic offspring (see Finnegan). Indeed, the ability of the "spontaneous" speech act to be everywhere presents a conundrum to discipline; its synchronicity defies progressive periodization, and its popularity elides facile categorization.

The mobility and permutability of oral forms, in variation or transcription, provide an enlightening instance of disciplinary trespass and cultural larceny. During the dinner sequence in the Cuban film *La última cena* (Gutiérrez Alea, 1976)—after the inebriated Conde drifts off to sleep in front of his "disciple" slaves and the elegant repast he had prepared in a mimetic re-creation of Christ's last meal with the apostles—recaptured runaway slave Sesbastian intones a parable about the Body of Truth crowned by the Head of Lie. In and of itself, the tale fascinates, and even more so when considered in the context of an earlier tale, "Lo que sucedió al árbol de la mentira" [What happened to the tree of lie], a significantly coherent variation on a theme in *El Conde Lucanor* (don Juan Manuel). That collection, based in North African oral antecedents, recalls the Socratic presentation of inquisitive novice and sage respondent.[5]

Each of the tales proffers a moral epilogue that, as enigmatic proverbs, have worked their way into the Hispanic imaginary. In "Eye of the Other," Sylvia Wynter examines a similarly liberal transcription-transformation: Hans Christian Andersen's "The Emperor's New Clothes," it, too, with roots to another Conde Lucanor tale, "The King and the Three Tricksters." The medieval tales and their intertextual offspring tacitly highlight the juxtaposition between "casual" oral performance on the one hand and on the other, scripted displays of orality. Here too the folk negro functions as a convenient literary device where the nameless skeptic, by virtue of his marginality, "escape[s] the censorship and control" of official society.

The mobility of the North African tales attests to their entertainment value as good stories, and their formal flexibility bears witness to the enduring truths encapsulated in their unassuming formats. In consequence, their affinities and intertextualities anticipate the encounter of Africa and Europe in the Americas, making twenty-first century end-of-millennium theorizing about postmodern globalization woefully old hat in light of those moving/morphing paradigms set in place as early as the eighth century and reactivated during the fifteenth and sixteenth centuries. An oral past, all but forgotten except by the odd specialist, bespeaks a connectedness often elided in Western conceptualizations of discontinuous artistic practices that rise phoenixlike from the pyres, or that disdain to feed on the "carcasses" of eclipsed aesthetic movements. In that moribund model, angry young men in post–World War I Europe would concur that "Experience, [as] quipped Oscar Wilde, is the name one gives to one's mistakes" (Shusterman 15).

Martha Cobb's brief discussion of the Lucanor tale suggests a differing generational relationship, a deference to both "emotional archetypes" and tradition (consider, for example, earlier discussion of Olodum and Los Muñequitos de Matanzas in chapter 5). She notes that "The author utilizes the framework of a storyteller—in this case a counselor named Patronio—who tells moral tales, usually with Moorish protagonist, to illustrate solutions to problems that his master, the Count Lucanor, presents to him" (25). Jackson, in the Latin American context; Bone, in the North American landscape; and, Cole in her specific examination of Ghana's Concert Theatre, each reiterate the centrality of storytelling in the cultural milieu of the Africana world and the importance of that oral practice as a springboard for later artistic production—not the least, the choice and characterization of the protagonist. Intriguingly the tale spinner in the Conde Lucanor text also acts as counselor, and his name intimates another avuncular function—a more layered version of Uncle Remus as patron. In the opening chapter of *Griots and Griottes*, the term usually employed to designate storytellers, historians, or praise singers, Thomas A. Hale attempts to catalogue the diverse and less remarked-upon functions of this figure. Hale compiles an impressive list including the roles of genealogist, advisor, spokesperson, diplomat, mediator, interpreter and translator, musician, composer, teacher, exhorter, warrior, witness, ceremony participant. Accordingly the project here focuses—along with the improvisations on orality as genre—the morphing function of the storyteller, a position continuously destabilized as a consequence of uprootedness.

Hale's later examination of the possible derivation of the term in vernacular Spanish and Portuguese provides evidence that, even as a borrowed term, the concept was current in Iberian imaginary and practice very early as a result of the 711 Moorish invasion, 1440s exploration of the African continent, and the presence of Arabs, Berbers, and Black Africans on the Iberian peninsula. The meaning behind the possible origins bears note. In the Portuguese case,

> travelers to the coast of Africa emphasized the noise that these performers made. There is an obvious link between noise and a Portuguese family of words based on the verb *gritar*, "to shout." It includes *grito*, "a shout," *gritalhao* [*sic*], "a person who shouts a lot," or *gritador*, "a person or place that is the source of much shouting or *gritaria* (many shouts at once). On the basis of the similarity of the first three letters plus some sound shifts, one could build a case for *gritar* as the origin. (359)

Though he will discount the likelihood of the *gritar/griot* connection, the tone of the Spanish case reveals a no-less-noteworthy pattern:

> [African] influence is evident in a variety of vocabulary, including the *guirgay*, a dance popular in Seville in the sixteenth century (Ortiz 1924: 246). Researchers know little about the dance, but *guirgay* . . . entered Spanish from this time as meaning something else: "obscure language, language that is difficult to understand." . . . [It] is quite possible that Spanish travelers invented this term to portray what they saw as the unintelligible song and bizarre dance of griots. (360)

Hale also remarks that a variation of the term *guirigaray* "is listed as an onomatopoeic word for 'confused speech, obscure speech, speech difficult to understand'" (360). (One cannot help but imagine the American aborigine's reaction to Columbus's reading of the *Requerimiento*.) These allusions to unintelligible noise mirror the reactions to drums examined in the previous chapter and the trope of deformed speech, suggesting the discursive location of and predisposition to Blackness and the African descended in Portuguese and Spanish imaginaries.

Dominique Loreau's film *Les noms n'habitent nulle part* (1994) [Names

Live Nowhere] offers a distinctly meaningful portrait of a soft-spoken modern-day Griot faced with the conundrum of how to locate expatriated members within local tribal-ethnic history. In consequence, the film presents an
example of how the condition of uprootedness provides the impulse for improvisation. In the opening sequence, the Griot, speaking directly into the
camera, introduces himself and explains his role/function as human archive:
"I am a griot. And no one can be a griot if he is not born a griot. That means
what it means. I am the master of the word . . . the memory, the preserver,
the store house . . . in short, the library of Africa. I am the depository and
the guarantor of the ancestral traditions. I am the historian, the poet, the
storyteller . . . I am the musician, the dancer, the singer, the actor . . ." Here he
pauses as drum patterns echo in the background. He cocks his ear to one side
and explains that they announce a baptism that "enter[s] [the child] in the
lineage to which he will belong forever and of which he is but the prolongation."

The Griot next appears in Brussels, clad in a heavy winter overcoat, where
he traces the steps of two émigrés, one recent, the other having wandered European paths for some ten years. The first is in the throes of a decision about
whether to remain or to return; the second enjoys a certain level of success,
still attempting to accommodate himself to Western modalities of time management and a ratiocentric world where tardiness and belief in magic are
likewise frowned upon by the enlightened. Fortuitously, the two meet and
manage a moment of reminiscence that allows them to relocate themselves,
as the shadowy figure of the Griot looks on, satisfied that a prolongation has
transpired.

Conversely, in the film's final sequence, the Griot tells the story of a dis-
placed/uprooted African woman who years before had been left pregnant
and stranded in Paris and whom he chanced to meet in a European train
station. In response to her assertion that she has no history—"as if," he notes,
"she had engendered herself"—the errant Griot is at first stymied, unable to
"place" her within a preset history, bothered that he cannot "say anything
more about her genealogy." "It's not normal. . . . It does not make sense," he
mutters confounded. The lanky tale spinner considers the case for a moment,
perhaps remembering a question he had earlier posed: "How do we tell the
story and genealogy of those who have left?" On second thought, he gathers
the meager details that he has about the woman—her approximate age, that

she spoke Malinke—and from these facts muses that she must have been born in such and such town and that her father might have worked at this or that trade or profession, and that her grandfather—"no, ancestors"—would have participated in the great fifteenth-century war between blacksmiths and nobles. Here, the Griot wonders aloud on which side the elder ancestor might have fought. In other words, he improvises a genealogy because, as he had noted earlier, "I love telling the story of all those I meet during my travels. . . . Each story and each face remains etched in me, and I always find the link, however remote, between them."

For better and sometimes worse, linkages to the griot figure present themselves or are calculatedly constructed. The archivist eyewitness of *testimonios* has this same linking aim, as with Cuban Miguel Barnet's contribution to the genre, which represents in some measure (given editorial input) another connection written, in fiction and nonfiction contexts—as does the protagonist who fulfills the function of counselor (often a feature in the novels of Zapata Olivella). As a secondary character in Adalberto Ortiz's *Juyungo*, the patriarch-mediator of the island where life begins to look up offers a temporary retreat that Lastre's abusive father could never have provided. However, in François Duvalier's Haiti the so-called Griots Group (associated with the publication of the journal *Les Griots* in the 1930s) improvised a more sinister function. Writes Michel Laguerre:

> In any dependency context, the elite play the role of brokers linking the center and the periphery. Although they are more often political and economic middlemen, they also play an ideological role because any system of domination, subjugation and exploitation tends to develop its own ideological apparatus to justify itself (Santos 1968). With their national philosophy and criticisms of the ideological practices of the traditional bourgeoisie, the members of the Griots group . . . aspired to become the new brokers of the nation. They purported to accomplish their goal by taking into account local customs and ways of life. (512)

In this improvisation, storyteller becomes power broker as a reminder that whoever tells the story shapes the discourse. And in various contexts and countries, writers of African descent ape these functions, some as cultural interpreter and translator or power broker, while others assume the roles of spokesperson, exhorter, or cultural mediator or diplomat. Caribbean poets

Nicolas Guillén (Cuba) and Luís Palos Matos (Puerto Rico), among others, employ fanciful transcription, as do prose writers Lydia Cabrera (Cuba) and Antonio Arráiz (Venezuela), in order to birth an authentic national identity or to resurrect a healthy polity in its most pastoral and idyllic—rural, indigenous, miscegenated—essence vis-à-vis Europe. Thus, the African descended writer-griot is uniquely positioned to be the library of the Afro-Americas.

Refashioning Spoken Souls

Street calls represent an instance of disciplinary trespass and literary larceny and make evident some of the considerations necessarily involved in the transfer of form into alien contexts, that is, oral into written. In one of his many texts on candombe, Rubén Carámbula takes up the subject of *Pregones del Montevideo Colonial* (1987),[1] which records street calls of *el aguatero, el panadero, las lavanderas, la vendedora de pollos y gallinas* [the waterman, the baker, the washerwomen, the female poultry seller] among others:

> ¡Aaaaguatero!... ¡Aaaaguatero!...
> Agüita fresquita
> en caneca de barro...
> Medio rial diez litros
>
> ...
>
> ¡Aaaaguatero!... ¡Aaaaguatero!... (34)
>
> [Waaaterman!... Waaaterman!...
> fresh water
> in clay containers
> ten litres, half a dollar
>
> ...
>
> Waaaterman!... Waaaterman!...]

The calls are posed in the quaint and inoffensive folkloric setting questioned by González, presenting "a travel folder version of Negro life" (Bone *Down Home*, 140), accompanied by Diego Ortiz's lithe illustrations and abbreviated musical notation.

Likewise, the Library of Congress Archive of Folk Culture has recently reissued several field recordings of calls and (prison) work songs collected in the North American South in the 1930s and 1940s, which the sales staff at Borders Books and Music tactfully suggested were perhaps most appropriate for a (ahem) scholarly audience. In Brazil, Lopes Bogéa and Antônio Viera released a compact disc, *Pregoneiros* (1999), based on an unpretentious book entitled *Pregões de São Luís* (1980) [Calls of São Luís]. There, the musical notation, while more complete, gives evidence of having been done by hand and the black-and-white line drawings by Elvas Rebeiro are less polished than those of the earlier Uruguayan collection by Carámbula. Yet, the Brazilian edition gathers offerings that possess a more playful tone that mixes marketing with a pithy narrative aimed at entertaining the potential client—and closing the deal:

¡Mamãe!
Lá vem o compra tudo
com sacos nas costas
gritando o pregão
Vou vender aquelas botas
que estão lá no porão.
Com o dinheiro vou comprar
Banana, farinha e pão;
essa vai ser a merenda
pra mim e Zeca meu irmão.
Mamãe! (22)

[Mamma!
There comes the junkman
with bags on his back
shouting his call.
I'm going to sell those boots
that are there in the doorway.
With the money I'm going to buy
Banana, flour and bread;
this will be the snack
for me and Zeca, my brother.
Mamma!]

These anonymous efforts hardly seem subversive. The second more than the first, at least extraliterarily, provides a glimpse of "true black experience," which Jackson associates with orality (16); but, as "an outlet for the unofficial activities and responses of the people" (J. Franco 5), neither song-poem proposes anything close to seditious revolt nor reveals any simmering resentment. The Blackness of the protagonist-performer remains conjecture: "Historically a large number of the street vendors have been blacks, and they were primarily responsible for the development of this art form in Uruguay [and Brazil]" (Lewis *Poetry* 19). Indeed, the reader must also extrapolate the idea of an unofficial economy, personal freedom, poverty, hunger, or oppression, the themes so evident—and critically celebrated—in the scripted calls of Afro-Uruguayan poet Virginia Brindis de Salas. Has too much been made of the continuity between experience and expression, oral tradition and written innovation?

Brindis de Salas (1908–1958),[2] generally acknowledged as Uruguay's leading Black female poet, collaborated in the publication of the journal *Nuestra Raza* in the 1930s and 1940s with other important figures of the Afro-Uruguay intelligentsia, such as Pilar Barrios and Juan Julio Arrascaeta. Brindis de Salas is also generally considered the most militant of the group. She favored "poetry of the people" (Jackson 161) written in *verso minor* or free verse that, whether the theme was militancy or the tone bitterly ironic, possessed a marked musicality. Considering her lyrical *pregones* [calls] and *baladas* [ballads] in relation to the "rhythmic and harmonic" poetry of Peruvian *decimista* Nicomedes Santa Cruz and the *son* inspired verse of Cuban Nicolás Guillén, Jackson postulates: "If we agree with Amiri Baraka who once said, I believe, that the best way to judge blackness in literature is to compare it to the richness and vitality of black music, then music should be the logical culmination of poetry rooted in the oral tradition" (161). Appropriately then, the first of Brindis de Salas's two published collections, *Pregón de Marimorena* (1946) [The Call of Mary Morena],[3] includes, in the last two of four sections, *tangos* and *cantos*. A second collection, *Cien cárceles de amor* [One Hundred Prisons of Love], appeared in 1949. Of her poetic style Mills-Young asserts:

> It is a poetry without elaborate metaphors and images, and the tone of her work ranges from anger to joy. As a poet, she frees herself from the bonds of the dominant discourse by taking "the shout" of the street vender Marimorena—her struggle, song, and joy—and moulds them into free verse. . . . Her leading characters are the poor and the oppressed, and, in their defense, she attacks those who ignore and reject them. In contrast, she praises those, like Marimorena, who manage to overcome misery, poverty, hunger, and prejudice. (12)

By "taking the shout," the "phantom" *pregones* ape the *function* of the traditional expression of orality, aiming to catch the attention of its public. By extension, the scripted improvisation calls attention to "the negro [as] the outsider, the 'lump' in the social structure," in "a social situation out of control" (Lewis *Poetry*, 19). Yet, similar to Spanish Medieval literature (without its pejorative cynicism), the folk negro serves Brindis de Salas as a "literary device . . . by which the writer—who exists in a dual relation to the official reality of his society (i.e., part of it, yet marginal to it)—poses the *ideology* of [her] society as a problematic" (Wynter "Eye," 15). Concomitantly, as an African-descended woman, Brindis de Salas is part of, yet still marginal to, a slightly more elite official reality. In this sense, the poetic voice, robed in Marimorena's "cloak of anonymity" (Jackson 23) and "seeking catharsis with Mary Morena in which the agony will be symbolically transferred to herself" (Lewis *Poetry*, 19), becomes militant—and orality achieves its militant potential—entering into a verbal contest with the spectre of power:

> Toma mi verso
> Marimorena
> yo sé que lo has de beber
> como una copa de alcohol
> a cambio de él
> quiero tu angustia
> Marimorena
> Quiero tu angustia,
> quiero tu pena,
> toda tu pena
> y el tajo de tu boca
> cuando ríes
> como una loca
> Marimorena,
> toda ebria
> más que de vino,
> de miseria. . . . (34)

> [Take my verses
> Marimorena
> I know that you have to drink them

like a shot of rum,
but as a fair exchange
I want your anguish,
Marimorena.
I want your anguish,
I want your suffering,
all of your suffering
and the tilt of your mouth
when you laugh
like a crazy woman,
Marimorena,
drunk
not so much on wine
as on misery. . . . (Translation Mills-Young, 5)

This strategic transformation—the stylized re-presentation, the diverging thematic—then reiterates the function and extends the potential of the folk form, "lumping" together the folk negro and the citizen Black.

However, the characteristics of mobility, flexibility, affinity, and intertextuality signal/signaled to some that oral traditions (and no less, their creators) could be and needed to be corrected/edited and displaced/replaced by a "progressive" metropolis or nation in "modern" printed textual formats. In that light, the transplanted, trans-scripted utterance captured in such works as Lydia Cabrera's *Cuentos Negros de Cuba* (1940),[4] Antonio Arráiz's *Tío Tigre y Tío Conejo* (1946),[5] and Julia Cristina Ortiz Lugo's *De Arañas, Conejos y Tortugas* (1995) reveals a great deal in terms of implicitly dueling discourses or historical visions. Even as they "trespass" into a terrain outside "official" culture, the two phantom tale spinners and one researcher often offer interpretations of the tales that reflect not the internal evidence so crucial in the focus proposed by Bone, but rather a distinctly disciplined worldview. If the prohibitions against drums in part revealed the slave owner's fear that the telegraphed beats communicated seditious intents—a planned escape, an imminent uprising—likewise in terms of the oral tales, the reiterated interpretive emphasis on aspects of trickery (engaño) and ingenuity (ingenio) as a kind of passive-aggressive resistance or on the weaponry "del débil en su lucha contra el fuerte" (Stampp 389) [of the weak in his struggle against the strong] also projects the fears embedded in masterly discourse. Logically, if the tales could be restricted to the realm of entertainment—amusing anecdote, a release valve that, at least momentarily, distracted from less pleasant realities—those narratives could be assigned what Chinweizu terms the "emasculating honours" of nonviolence, a necessary explanatory element of the justificatory narrative of slavery. Thus the conflict that ensues from transplantation-transcription becomes evident in the tension between the internal evidence and the overarching frame into which the uprooted and improvised stories have been inserted. Pushed toward a successfully de-Africanized (that is, decontextualized), nationalized product, the denuded tales and the "aventuras maliciosas" (Roger Bastide 54) [malicious adventures] contained therein become inoffensive, stripped along the way of implicit reference to cultural—or strategic—functions. Conversely, in the sense proposed by Konrád, the identifying attributes of agility, astuteness, and dexterity need be read as improvised strategies, similar to Cole's description of "techniques of creativity well-established in traditional . . . performing arts" based on "key structural elements that are always repeated" (104).

Problematically, Fernando Ortiz's comments in the Cabrera prologue suggest a framing that dislocates the teller and the oral text and smoothly de-Africanizes *los cuentos*:

> No hay que olvidar que estos cuentos *vienen a las prensas* por una colaboración, la del folklore negro con *su traductora blanca*. . . . Quizás la anciana morena que se las narró a Lydia ya las recibió de sus antepasados en lenguaje acriollado. Y de esta habla tuvo la coleccionista que pasarlas a cada *una forma legible en castellano*, tal como ahora se estamparán. La autora ha hecho tarea difícil pero leal y, por tanto, muy meritoria. Conservando a los cuentos su fuerte carácter exótico de fondo y de forma. Y su colección abre un *nuevo capítulo folklórico en la literatura cubana*. (10; emphasis mine)

> [One must not forget that these stories *come into print* thanks to a collaboration, that between Black folklore and its *white translator*. . . . Perhaps the old negress who told them to Lydia had already heard them from her ancestors in creolized language. And from this language, the collector had to put each of them into an *understandable standard Spanish form*, such as that with which they will now be stamped (immortalized). The author has done the hard but faithful—and as such

very meritorious—work. Preserving in the stories, their marked exotic character, in form and content. And her collection opens a *new folk-loric chapter in Cuban literature.*]

Here, Cabrera's transformation from collaborator/*coleccionista* into research-er/*traductora* into creator/*autora* neatly displaces those nameless, faceless, yet authenticating griots and griottes: "antepasados" and "la anciana morena." Raising the same question of language faculty and fluency that greeted African entry into the European imaginary from the eighth century forward, the metonymical convergence of press, whiteness, legibility, Spanish language, and national literature displaces "yoruba, ewe y bantú" or "[e]l idioma ames-tizado y dialectal de los negros criollos"(10) [native West African languages or the admixed and dialectical speech of New World Blacks], and with them, orality and Blackness.

Ironically, the work of "phantom" griots often receives high praise for originality. Yet, to paraphrase a Wynterian proposal, the critical reception of these lyrical transcriptions that seizes upon *lo africano* [an Africanness] shows that oral tradition as the product of *writers* has a function within the national imaginary, though the eclipsed oral storytellers—the absented lo-cus and their "neglected" forms—do not.[6] Even as word becomes text, dis-played orality (but not so much oral tradition) has a function as evidence of a non-European artistic liveliness and tenacity, the exquisite vigor and vitality noted by Arturo Pizarroso Cuenca—a reminder of a troubled racial separateness (through slavery, racism). As Benedict Anderson suggests, the nation celebrates the universal and unifying myth often at the expense of the particularities and divisiveness of its own reality.

Even while Ortiz Lugo as researcher underscores the tie to Africa and Ca-brera in her role as *colecionista* recognizes the African debt, the critical reading emphasizes the American-ness—a subtly deracinated Cuban-ness or Puerto Rican–ness—of the tales, a position further bolstered by Fernando Ortiz's critical reading and a reflection of his own work. Note that in the overarch-ing frame suggested by Jackson and Bone, it is the *Afro*-American-ness that reveals the import of the tales (an additive, inclusive-versus-subtractive, exclusive vision). For his part, Arraíz's *Tío Tigre y Tío Conejo* eclipses the African and Afro- connection, and Juan Liscano's critical reading of the text furthers the origin erasure, deracinating the source, placing it vaguely within "el folklore agrario venezolano" (12) [rural Venezuelan folklore], although the titular figures are unmistakably African descended (see Alegria, Bastide, Frobenius). Likewise the critic reconfigures the New World conflicts, based in the contentious relationship between kidnapped and interloper, slave and master, Black and white (themselves reconfigured from the theoretically more pacific Old World intraethnic/tribal context):

> El interminable pleito entre Tío Tigre—más que el mal o la maldad es la inconsciencia de la fuerza bruta, más que la voluntad agresiva la simplicidad brutal, incapaz de pensar un plan, de elaborar una venganza, en cierta forma, la inocencia del bruto—y Tío Conejo—alegre estoicismo, cálculo, pensamiento, ardides, viveza con su pieza de cinismo y picardia . . . decimos, pues, esa interminable disputa culmina con una posible revolución contra el dominio de Tío Tigre. (Liscano 12)

> [The unending argument between Tío Tigre—more than a question of badness or evil is the unconsciousness of brute force, more than aggressive will, the utter simplicity, the incapacity of forming a plan or to devise a revenge is, in a certain way, the innocence of the brute—and Tío Conejo—happy stoicism, calculation, thought, passion, vivacity with a touch of the cynical and the picaresque which is to say that . . . unending dispute culminates with a possible revolution against the dominance of Tío Tigre.]

Liscano goes on to assert that "Aquí Arraíz se deja ir a la moraleja pacifista. Le invade . . . la tradición intelectual venezolana de condenar la violencia como forma de ascenso político-social" (12) [Here Arraíz gives himself over to pacifist moralizing. The . . . Venezuelan intellectual tradition which condemns violence as a path to political-social ascension takes over]. This echoes Benítez-Rojo's idea of tensionless totality and concomitantly reactivates Chinweizu's disparaging commentary on nonviolence. What it means in this case is that the stories become inoffensive or infinitely less offensive if compared with the acute cruelty of field transcriptions. Within such dynamics, this posture reflects the rebelliousness and deviancy of select members of the dominant group against the constrictions of "official" culture, rather than the belligerent attitude that better characterizes the stance adopted by peoples of African descent.

Even though that wily rabbit Tío Conejo possesses characteristics indistinguishable from those that describe African, Cuban, and North American manifestations such as Br'er Rabbit and Compay Conejo, his reputed malfeasance is tranquilized. However, the collected version of the ever-ready bunny offered by Juan García paints a different picture. After the tiger eats his parents, the rabbit exacts a macabre vengeance, killing members of the tiger clan and then offering their smoked meat to Tiger's unsuspecting starving widow; the tale concludes:

> Así es que la tigra se jue desconsolada y no lo pudo coge' al conejo. . . .
> Y el conejo le mató al marido y a los cinco hijos grandes y él se quedó
> tranquilo en su montaña. (116)

> [Thus Aunt Tiger was inconsolable and incapable of capturing the rabbit. . . . And the rabbit killed her husband and her five oldest offspring and he remained tranquil in his mountain.]

The tiger world could find little peace in this resolution, especially if "mountain" conjured the impenetrable terrains of *palenques* or *quilombos* of times past or later burrow-like enclaves.

Akin to the discomfiture caused by the Haitian Rebellion or unintelligible talking drums, the omnipresence of the stories—and no less the belligerent attitude they foster in this form—might represent another concern. Writes Juan García: "Los verdaderos autores son todos nuestros informantes . . . : pescadores, agricultores, carboneros, artesanos" (7) [the true authors are all of our informants . . . : fishermen, farmers, coal miners, artisans]. He continues, "Los cuentos y las demás informaciones no son de una persona, sino la suma de aportes de todos los miembros del grupo Afroecuatoriano" (7) [The stories and the other information are not from one person, but rather the sum contribution of all members of the Afro-Ecuadorian community]. Accordingly, in dialogue with those sources, his goal resides in challenging "los nuevos modelos de cultura llamada 'universal' [que imponen] entre nuestra gente una falsa generación de mitos y costumbres que nada tiene que ver con nuestra vida ni con nuestra herencia cultural" (8) [the so-called 'universal' cultural models (that impose) on our people a false generation of myths and customs that have nothing to do with our life, nor with our cultural heritage].

The equivocation to which García refers involves not a question of authenticity, but rather raises the issue of the normalizing distortion that seeks to tame the tale. Hence the "telling" difference between Brindis de Salas's and García's improvisational efforts (despite other problems they might present) and the renarrated "translations" of Cabrera and Arraíz resides in their accountability first to their anonymous sources and by extension to the cultural context of Blackness. In other words, re-writers, not content to simply clean up the grammar, attempt to clear away the threat of a historical vision at odds with the implicit ends of a universalizing nation-discourse.

Almost ironically then, as the titles indicate, the cited texts tacitly or explicitly conjure orality in metonymical relationship to Africanness/Blackness. *Cuentos* are to *negros* as *cuentística oral* is to *presencia africana* as Tío Conejo is to Latin American (conceptualizations of) Blackness rooted in Africa. The supposition affirms that "al hablar de astucia y habilidad en los cuentos de animales hay que pensar en el 'Compay Conejo' o en el 'conejo africano'" [speaking of astuteness and ability in animal stories, one has to think of "Compay Conejo" or of the "African equivalent"], reasoning:

> Si tanto en América como en Africa el conejo encarna la agilidad, la astucia y la destreza, si sus armas son el engaño y la farsa, el conejo puertorriqueño entonces no debe ser la excepción. (Ortiz Lugo 24–25)

> [If as much in America as in Africa the rabbit embodies agility, astuteness and dexterity, if his weapons are trickery and farce, the Puerto Rican rabbit should not be the exception.]

In that light, however, to feign or display orality in direct or fanciful transcriptions would seem to problematically appropriate the raw material of the Other (spoken word or other creative enunciation) into the final product of another. The practice becomes even more convoluted. The attempt to self-decolonize Cuba, Venezuela, or Puerto Rico vis-à-vis Europe by asserting orality/*presencia Africana* as a measure of national authenticity (for example, *cubanidad*) paradoxically would seem to colonize the inventiveness of peoples of African descent, placing them at the disposal of "alien" discourses from which they do not profit (see Zenón Cruz, t1:21–74)—a move not so unlike the profit made from the physical labor of enslaved nation builders.

Consequently, again extending Wynterian logic—since oral traditions are there to be collected, transcribed, feigned, and displayed—the re-writer replaces the speaker, that is, the intermediary (transcriber, interpreter, critic) displaces the creative source (the informant's version of the tale).[7] Yet even identifying the source does not in and of itself resolve the quandary. In those texts that acknowledge their sources the focus turns from the literariness of the offerings to the drier sociological context in which they were created. It is therefore noteworthy that Ortiz Lugo in *De Arañas, Conejos y Tortugas* lists the names of informants with a bit of information as to race, age, education, work, and location. She also includes an appendix that contains the original performance of the transcribed texts featured in the main (and central) part of the text. These concessions insinuate that the pressures of authenticity have become differently rigorous. While it was sufficient to signal the nameless, faceless Blackness of the stories "written" by Cabrera or to rely on the oblique titular reference by Arraíz in the forties, such is not so in the nineties. Accountability demands more: identifying the *context* of both informant and tale.

Therefore, as Julien proposes in *African Novels and the Question of Orality*, "We must consider how the category of 'African orality' permeates literary criticism, how it is subject to ideological pressures, and how it has come to define and confine the scope of our interest in and perception of African writing" (7). Her African-centered discussion applies as well to the diaspora context:

> The dominance of oral language in Africa is obviously a matter of material conditions and not of an "African nature," but more than a few literary critics take this accidental fact for an essential one and assume almost invariably that there is something ontologically oral about Africa and that the act of writing is therefore disjunctive and alien for Africans [and conversely that Europe is ontologically scripted]. . . .
>
> What seems to be overlooked in such assessments of African music and poetry, however, is the consideration of their context and material conditions and reference to *traditions* of poetic practice. Presented abstractly, with no reference to their context, "accidental" attributes take on the force of essentialist, ontological truths. Just as it has seemed not only plausible but altogether *natural* that African-Americans should express themselves in music—spirituals, blues and jazz—it has seemed inevitable (and, perhaps, even reassuring) that Africans and their descendants should express themselves in poetry. Apart from questions of "God-given talent," African Americans' musical expressions may seem singularly prominent because of the lesser participation of [B]lack Americans in other *less accessible* realms—political, scientific, or otherwise. (8)

(That "natural" musicality might also embrace, in the Latin American context, Brazilian samba, Jamaican reggae, calypso, Argentine milonga, Uruguayan/Southern Cone candombe, Puerto Rican bomba, Cuban rumba.) In that explanatory light, the metonymical relation between Africanness/Blackness and orality describes the *situation*—not the essence, nor the nature—of peoples contextually barred by law and custom from writing history and nation (for example, citizenship) or writing a history of their participation in and contribution to the nation.

Decontextualized from world history, Black orality represents national treasures based on state affiliation rather than also diasporic gems that recognize an altruistic racial identity that transcends polities. As such, the oral genres can be pressed/pressured into the service of discourses not of their own invention or improvisation, just as Hans Christian Andersen's reinscribed "Emperor's New Clothes" speaks to hubris rather than to caste earlier emphasized in Don Juan Manuel's *El Conde Lucanor*. Ironically, the nation paradigm pleads for a coherency with "Old World" Africa dating back to time immemorial while fragmenting New World affiliations and techniques of creativity. That view, which under-props the immigrant narrative, cynically elides the commonalities in the peculiar, shared experience between peoples of African descent in the diaspora. Thus outside the context and the material reality of uprootedness, slavery and racism can be made to seem individual aberrations—here soft, there harsh; in one instance, overt, in another, quietly proscriptive—rather than systematic, systemic, institutional, and ideological efforts to annihilate, dehumanize, and debase a racially marked other.

As Julien suggests, the effort to blend Africa/Blackness and orality both hides and reveals two conflicting biases: "the first . . . holds oral societies (and traditions) to be impoverished. The second . . . holds them to be exemplary" (10–11), "equating . . . voice with purity, the natural, and the good" (17).[8] Summarizing Paul Zumthor's argument, she observes, "Orality/Africa (passive and female) is the victim of writing/Europe (virile, aggressive, and male). Zumthor thus bemoans the plight of orality: suffocated virgin voices, pure defenseless memory, suppressed by literature that has prospered at orality's expense" (Julien 13).[9] This impoverished view assumes a poverty of spirit and ability, conventionally narrated in the Americas as empty-handed arrival, the inability to eloquently navigate written European languages and genres (for example, the novel), and the incapacity to negotiate (that is, participate in or

contribute to) European civilization and its gifts and discourses. That framing implies the necessity of a translating intermediary and an ever-watchful
eye to combat a predisposition to immorality and "lujuria" [lustfulness].[10]
The centrality of language in the praxis of conquest and the construction of
colonial hierarchies needs no comment (see Todorov and any and all texts
by Wynter).

On the other hand, the exemplary bias juxtaposes decadence and mor-
bidity on the one side with wholesomeness and liveliness on the other (for
example, Rousseau's *buen salvaje/bom salvagem*, Disney's Pocahontas). The
presentation of Black orality and its belligerent survival despite horrendous
mistreatment or misuse becomes a convenient metaphor for the victimization
and perseverance of a deracinated Latin America vis-à-vis its colonial—and
neocolonial—interlopers. Clearly, this attitude has less to do with Africa/
Blackness and more to do with the myths and realities of the metropolis:
"The cultural myth under-props the economic and political power of Europe
based on its exploitation of non-Europeans; the cultural reality of Europe
consistently attacked and opposed this dominance, this concept of Europe
as a super-culture, as the end product of Man's glorious march towards 'humanity.' The cultural reality of Europe sees the ambivalence of its own power
and glory" (Wynter "We Must Learn," 311–12). This ambivalence finds an
echo in the works of Cabrera and Arraíz, which encapsulate the gap between
the cultural myth and the cultural reality of the Americas—racial harmony,
smooth racial and cultural *mestizaje* [mixture] and transculturation—which
do not recognize that despite egalitarian pretensions, a hierarchical order exists, based in long-held ordering paradigms of race, class, and caste (Goveia).
Their texts also evince a discrepancy between their mythical claims—to orality and to authenticity—and the stylistic reality of writerly exercise; thus
certain dissonances result. That is to say, the body of the stories, evincing
studiously mediated rewriting, do not and cannot orient themselves toward
performance nor as the *casual* expression of a whole culture. While readerly
response might vary, neither can the texts respond "in-the-act" to the reac-
tions/needs of their audience, as might renditions accountable to source,
context, and public.

Regarding the confusion of cultural myths and realities—of Europe or
of the Americas—in the sociopolitical context of the Caribbean, Wynter
would astutely anticipate "the swing of the pendulum . . . towards the *myth
of Africa*" (312; emphasis mine). In their misguided search for authenticity,

the Griot Group in Haiti chose this course in reaction to that Eurocentric cultural myth that sees Africa as the Dark Continent, impoverished, lacking, backward, sensual rather than rational, and a pathetic detour on the glorious march toward modernity and progress. Conversely, the cultural reality of Africa acknowledges a diverse scene, an admixture of modernities and traditions, allegiances and animosities (toward tribe, nation, foreign metropolis), and great material riches that contrast with poignant material poverty. Nevertheless, many approach the reality framed by the myth, expecting an unchanging, un-evolving, static space—or quagmire, depending on the perspective—where a singular, nebulous African identity and tradition ever awaits the next harvest: to validate religious practices of Voodoo in Haiti, Santería in Cuba, Candomblé in Brazil; to leaven Black nationalism's embrace of Pan-Africanism; to locate a Rastafarian system of thought; to "locate" narrative sources; or, to gauge the authenticity of ritual drum rhythms.

All of these attempts to represent the improvisation of uprootedness react to the myth of the fixity of dominant paradigms. The implication is that for change, progress, and modernity, look to Europe—even when that continent is in the midst of upheaval or at battle with its own decadence.

> It is no coincidence that a particular reverence for the "oral character" of Africa should mark the writing of the negritude writers and other pan-Africanists who have looked to cultural origins as a way of differentiating and shoring up the identity of Africa vis-à-vis Europe. Thus adherence to a view of orality as distinctively African complements the tenets of negritude ... the view that emotion, spontaneity, nature (and orality) will serve "to leaven" rationality, artifice, culture (and writing). (Julien 18)

Writing from surrealist Paris, Aída Cartegena Portalatín seemingly exemplifies this stance when she comments on her move toward

> una revalorización de los elementos culturales rítmicos frente al intelectualismo occidental y la supremacia del dinamismo cultural sobre las formas occidentales tecnificadas. (25)

> [a revalorization of rhythmic cultural elements in comparison with Western intellectualism and the superiority of cultural dynamism over the technicalities of Western forms.]

Responding to the paradigm of rupture and substitution, the Dominican writer color codes the participants. While the validity of her sweeping assertion may give pause, she makes an important point in signaling "la existencia y permanencia de los valores" (25) [the existence and permanence of values] *if* that indicates the necessity to contextualize the value of orality: to consider accountability, within history, intellectual traditions, material conditions, and cultural contexts, both mythical and real.

Accountability then represents the crucial difference between the creative transcriptions compiled by Cabrera and Arraíz and the lyrical borrowing evident in the poetry of Brindis de Salas. Although the Uruguayan's use of the folk negro device does raise questions, in her function as storyteller, the poet employs techniques of creativity that strive to validate "rhythmic cultural elements" of the community that surrounds her, marking out a territory denied by the dynamics of uprootedness.

Conversely, in Cabrera and Arraíz, the folk negro is eclipsed in favor of a nebulous national imaginary, a frame that responds to the concerns of the intelligentsia for their own decultured territory as distinct from both Europe and the national underclass. Cabrera's and Arraíz's supposed deviations from "official" culture are soon enough accepted as canonical but leave no opening for the prototypes upon which they were based. Thus their efforts reflect the contrived need of a homogenizing national discourse to "enrich" impoverished genres through rewriting. Pushing the very definition of literature, Brindis de Salas exemplifies the possibilities of experimentation on an already-rich literary tradition.

Jackson writes that "Blacks have also put their humor to good use in verbal battles with white opponents. In these literary contests, the black improviser could protest his state and ridicule whites, and sometimes do both things at the same time" (21). For example, Valaurez B. Spratlin explains that for the Cuban poet Plácido (née Gabriel de la Concepción Valdés), "the spontaneity of his muse compensated in part for the discipline for formal studies. His gift for improvisation was remarkable, and he wandered over the island reciting and composing occasional verses in the manner of a medieval troubadour" (52). In the film version of Gerardo Fulleda León's play *Plácido*, the renowned poet's censure, telescoped by the disapproving look of the Black orchestra conductor, subtly admonishes him that the posh white gathering is neither the proper place nor the proper time for the poet's playfully irreverent posture.[11] This correction allows the bard later in the film to respond more graciously to a poetic opponent, a mulatto who affects Grecian airs, in a barroom verbal contest. According to Stanley J. Stein, *jongo*, a Brazilian riddle form, provided opportunities for similar surreptitious commentary:

> Slave gangs often worked within singing distance of each other and to give rhythm to their hoe strokes and pass comment on the circumscribed world in which they lived and worked—their own foibles, and those of their masters, overseers, and the slave drivers—the master-singer (*mestre cantor*) of one gang would break into the first "verse" of a song in riddle form, a *jongo*. His gang would chorus the second line of the verse, then weed rhythmically while the master-singer of the nearby gang tried to decipher . . . the riddle presented. . . . *Jongos* sung in African tongues were called *quimzumba*; those in Portuguese, more common as older Africans diminished in the labor force, *visaría*. (163)

Stein confirms that the genre, with its thinly disguised cast of animal or in-animate characters, "lent itself well in phrasing the slaves' reactions, for, as with all riddles, the purpose was to conceal meaning with words, expressions, or situations of more than one possible interpretation" (137), the same trope of indirection mentioned by Bone. Likewise, within the transcribed story-telling tradition, Jackson notes, "Even the folklore of Pai João, the legend-ary Brazilian Uncle Remus, who was popular among whites because of his resignation, managed to reflect the true black experience in the New World" (20).

The tradition of *décimas*, *jongos*, and *payadas* in Latin America, and the dozens and rap music in the United States, provide additional diasporic ex-amples of gracious, if sometimes raucous, contest and Blackness. In the short story "Triumph," Trinidadian C.L.R. James describes another such contest:

> No longer do the barrack-yarders live the picturesque life of twenty-five years ago. Then, practising for the carnival, rival singers, Will, Jean, and Freddie, porter, wharf-man, or loafer, in ordinary life but for that season ennobled by some such striking sobriquet as The Duke of Nor-mandy or The Lord Invincible, and carrying with dignity homage such as young aspirants to literature would pay to Mr. Kipling or Mr. Shaw. . . . They sang in competition from seven in the evening until far into the early morning, stimulated by the applause of their listeners and the

excellence and copiousness of the rum; night after night the stick-men practised their dangerous and skillful game; the "pierrots," after elaborate preface of complimentary speech, belaboured each other with riding whips; while around the performers the spectators pressed thick and good-humoured, until mimic warfare was transformed into real, and stones . . . flew thick. (85)

Likewise, in the testimonial biography of Peruvian Erasmo, the elder reports a similar occurrence in a bar where patrons have gathered to enjoy "décimas de historias, a lo divino, de insultos, de amores, de plantas y otras cosas" (Matos Mar and Carbajal 67) [verses about history, to the divine, of insults, about love, appearances, or other things]:

> Estaban dos días sin parar, cantando décimas y siempre tomando licor. Ganaba el que cantaba más décimas y ese era respetado y admirado por todos. A veces el ánimo se caldeaba y los rivales decían décimas con lisuras y el desafío terminaba a golpes. (67)

> [They were there two days without stop, singing verses and always drinking. Whoever sang more verses won and was respected and admired by all. Sometimes the high spirits boiled over and the contestants recited verses with honey-tongued insults and the match ended in blows.]

Such melees likely account for, in addition to the negativity always already attached to Blackness, official culture's efforts to sanitize and decontextualize the contest, thus disassociating itself from the rawest forms of Black creativity.

Yet, in another historical vision, the eloquent word *jockey* became an "emotional archetype" or "honored priest of his culture" (Baraka "Swing," 41). In *Pasado y presente de los Negros en Buenos Aires* (1997), Juan Carlos Coria asserts that the tradition of oral contest represents a stage between candombe and tango in which dueling singers, "generalmente en contrapunto con otro, improvisa sobre temas variados" (95) [generally in counterpoint with another, improvise various themes]. In this way,

> [s]e establece en el confrontamiento entre los cantores-payadores una competencia poético [*sic*] musical, en la que ambos tratan de superarse logrando de ese [*sic*] manera el apoyo y la adhesión popular. (95)

[in the confrontation between the singers, a musical poetic competition is established in which both attempt to outdo themselves in order to win public acclaim and popularity.]

George Reid Andrews suggests, "the art form was almost purely African in its derivation. . . . A vocal variation of the tapadas [denial contest], the drum duels, the *payada* was the lineal descendant of the African tradition of musical contests of skill, a tradition that has produced similar phenomena in every American country where there is a large black population" (170).

Certainly the phenomenon is widespread: oral contests, challenge songs, and instrumental dueling include decimistas in the Caribbean corridor; the *concurso* in Brazil; *las llamadas*, drum duels between neighborhood groups in Uruguay; *décimas* and *argumentos* in Ecuador; and in the United States, playing the dozens or "*impromptu countermelodies*" in the jazz context of featured soloist and orchestra (Baraka "Swing," 43) and the East-West rap duel between Tupak Shakur and The Notorious B.I.G. (also known as Christopher Wallace). However, the claim of "lineal" descent eclipses, in the slightly hyperbolic style of the same contestants, similar decultured traditions from the Iberian peninsula, the presence of the genre in countries with even small Black populations (for example, Peru), the rural-urban differences in the form, and not the least, the questions of orality on display and the "enlightened" secularization of artistic production. Recalling that "It was, and is, inconceivable in the African culture to make a separation between music, dancing, song, the artifact, and a man's life or his worship of his gods" (Baraka "African Slaves," 30), context, intent, and function must become part of the conversation. Something of that African sense of indivisibility marks the uniquely American flavor of such oral displays, creating a refashioned territory equal to that which Bone and Jackson stress in terms of folkloric protagonists and to that realm of spiritual transport commented upon by Carpentier in his observations on the display of "profane" drumming.

In the Argentine case, there are telling distinctions between the traditional rural contest and the urban manifestation. Social commentator Domingo Sarmiento had earlier remarked on another function of the type of gaucho he simply labeled "the singer" who "está haciendo candorosamente el mismo trabajo de crónica, costumbres, historia, biografía, que el bardo de la Edad Media" (228) [is doing the same work of chronicle, customs, history, biography as the bard of the Middle Ages]—and, one might add, that of the

African griot. The Argentine further asserted that "sus versos serían recogidos más tarde como los documentos y datos en que habrá de apoyarse el historiador futuro" (228) [his verses would later be collected as the documents and evidence on which the future historian will rely]. Notwithstanding, the fervent champion of "la civilización europea" [European civilization]—and hence not the most unbiased source—disparages the contamination of this feudal influence and minimizes the "pesada, monótona, irregular" [heavy, monotonous, irregular] original poetry of the lawless, landless singer. Although Sarmiento grudgingly admits that some of the efforts have merit, the father of Argentine formal education writes:

> Cuando refiere sus proezas o las de algún afamado malévolo, parécese al improvisador napolitano, desarreglado, prosaico de ordinario, elevándose a la altura poética por momentos, para caer de nuevo al recitado insípido y casi sin versificación. (229)

[When (the singer) refers to his prowess or to that of some famous no-account, he makes himself seem the Napoleon improvisor elevating himself for moments only to fall again to insipid recitation, almost without versification.]

One will no doubt notice a certain *word*view that judges (Black) orality harshly, associating it with asocial behaviors—a worldview repeated in various guises in the discussion of the rustic origins of blues, jazz (an explicit theme in the play [1975] and movie [2002] *Chicago*), rumba, tango, samba, fables, and folk tales.

Coria concentrates on the urban Black *payador* in the nineteenth and early twentieth century (97–106), among them, Gabino Ezeiza "considerado como el último payador" (102) [the last/best of the contest singers]. In *Afro-Argentine Discourse* (1996), Marvin Lewis concurs but stresses the fact that Ezeiza also labored as a journalist and poet, with several publications to his credit, including original collections, compilations, and anthologies. That the *payador* could move smoothly between the oral and writerly worlds posits him as an apt example of cultural synchronicity.

The writerly use of orality continues in various experiments. Dialogue is one, contest another. Certainly both share a long history of interplay, coexistence, and improvisation. The concern here is twofold: one of approach and one of posture. On the one hand, the adulation or condemnation of the uses to which orality has been put must be tempered by the layered consideration of the historical paradigms at work. On the other, what position the writer adopts and what interpretation the critic proposes needs to be seen in the context of a complex challenge to the overlooked metonymical meanings that they suggest.

The first-person narrative "La llamaban Aurora (Pasión por Donna Summer)" [They Called her Aurora (Passion for Donna Summer)] by Aída Cartegena Portalatín (1975) favors an in-your-face dialogue, punctuated on the rhythmic refrain "No. Noo. ¡Y Noo!" which eschews the introverted reflexivity of polite bourgeois autobiography. Similar to the deliberate choice for self-reflective icons evident in storyteller Patronio's preference in *Conde Lucanor* for Moorish protagonists, she evokes the belligerent image of disco queen Donna Summer. Weighted by a dissonant identity, Colita/Aurora, the narrator lives a bifurcated existence:

> No. No voy a quedarme triste, cabizbaja, como las hojas golpeadas por vendavales y lluvias con tronadas, dentro de estas paredes rodeadas de un césped siempre verde y de algunos arbustos frutales. Ni acepto aquello, dale que dale de su Aurora es una negrita inteligente, ni de que me diviertan los negros, ni que los negros con su jazz y su ritmo, o que los negros alegran el mundo, y vete a la tienda y tráeme el último disco de Donna Summer, y que algo deben hacer los negros, que está bien que diviertan a los blancos. No. Noo. Y noo. Me complace esa música sinfin de la Donna Summer, garrapateando, aullando sin cesar, o cayendo como una cascadita vibrante y excitante. Pero no es cierto que Doña Sarah me va a guardar para siempre dentro de su caja de música excitante, qué el ragtieme o los beguín, etc. (14)

> [No. No, I am not going to remain sad, head bowed like the leaves beaten down by the wind and the rain, inside these walls surrounded by an ever green lawn and robust fruit trees. Neither do I accept—not again!—that Aurora is an intelligent little Black girl, neither that stuff about how Blacks amuse them, nor that trash about Blacks and their Jazz and their rhythm nor that Blacks make the world a happy place and go to the store and bring me the latest Donna Summer record and that Blacks ought to do something, that it's good that they entertain white folks. No. Noo. And noo. That Donna Summer music pleases me no

end, scatting and howling without stop or crashing down like a vibrant and stimulating waterfall. But it's not a given that Miss Sarah is going to keep me locked up forever inside her "exciting" music box, ohh the jazz, ahh the boogaloo, ohh the ragtime or that 1970s style, etc.]

As a figure of iconic identification, within the context of the story, Donna Summer represents belligerence. Even in the hyperbolic world of 1970s disco, Summer—on matters of style—presented a larger-than-life persona: nose-bleed platform shoes, big (no, *really* big) hair, a luxuriously false, voluptuous cascade of ebony curls, shimmery psychedelic sequined gowns, and a lust-ily commanding voice, enhanced by the hypnotic, insistent backbeat that so characterized her disco anthems "Last Dance," "Hot Stuff," and "She Works Hard for the Money." Certainly, the same exoticism and mystic hypersexuality that has always characterized the reception of Black music and Blackness in general and Black women in particular was at play in the popularity of this ebony chanteuse, but Summer seemed to take her own advantage of these proverbial and constricting stereotypes, willfully parodying to the hilt puritan prudishness and segregationist squeamishness, the not-yet-fully ex-orcized inheritance of earlier discourses. Yet, even as Summer-as-icon oozes liberation, Aurora/Colita senses that it is the music box, rather than the gilded cage, that constrains.

Aída Cartegena Portalatín juxtaposes the protagonist's plaintive voice and the overproduced music, cleverly conjuring the synchronicity of tra-ditional and technological. In Brindis de Salas's *Marimorena* the poetic voice attempts to speak *for* the folk negro, and in so doing usurps the caller and makes her an object of pity, an issue forced to await the intervention of writerly discourse. In contrast, Cartegena Portalatín's equally fictitious figure manages to impose herself, proving herself capable of an equally ef-fective—and more direct—battle against the demons that haunted both the vendor and the poetic voice. Aurora/Colita is immersed in the context, the monologue-become-dialogue engaging the reader as sounding board and contesting the employer's racism and disregard and the discursive mytholo-gization inherent in the representation of her race and sex, with no promise of a magical deus ex machina transposition that would symbolically lift her burden. Akin to rap, she does not need the answer-back. If Marimorena is a device, Colita/Aurora is a character.

In the tradition of folk tales from Cuban Compay Conejo to his Puerto

Rican equivalent and from his Venezuelan cousin Tío Conejo to his northern relation Br'er Rabbit, the mouthy Aurora represents "ironic attitudes."
Effectively, while the monologue, seeming to present no outward challenge,
constrains the "no," the format provides "a vantage point of distance" allowing the frustrated narrator/speaker to mumble under her breath or shout
under the timbre of the blaring disco her uncensored thoughts.[12] And her
humorous yet poignant plaints provide an opportunity for off-timing, making fun of the master—or, here, mistress—mimicking their bossy and effusive tones. Notably, her allusion to a white preference for Black music allows
her to employ off-timing to more seditious ends, what Robert Bone terms
indirection:

> Afro-American animal tales belong to the genre of the beast fable
> which is a species of satiric allegory. They are allegorical by virtue of
> their veiled presentation of the slave's situation through images drawn
> from the animal world. They are satirical by virtue of their veiled at
> tack on ole Massa. To attribute human traits to animals is one of those
> devices of indirection which are the trademark of the satirist. This in
> direction springs, in all literature, from the fear of censorship, suppres
> sion, or retaliation of the high and mighty. (*Down Home* 25)[13]

The passion for crossover artist Summer, which supposedly can be shared by
all comers—the demanding mistress, the put-upon servant, chiding school
chums, and the "bodeguero, el italiano hijo de su mamma" (15) [the shopkeeper, that Italian son of his mother] who lavished unwanted attention on
the girl—does not celebrate sameness and unity but underscores the social
and historical fissures that separate Summer's fans. Aurora also notes the
fickle regard for *lo negro*:

> Me revienta ver cómo tantos millones de blancos se deleitan ahora con
> la Donna Summer, la negrita que canta excitante. Una vez llegaban al
> delirio con Armstrooung, después con Makeba. Qué el jazz y todo rit
> mo que nace tan alegre. ¡Felicidades! No, si yo fuera la Donna Summer
> recogiera todos los discos que se encuentran en las tiendas, en los danc
> ing, cabaretes, hoteles y moteles y en las casas high. (15)

> [It turns my stomach to see how so many millions of whites now take
> such delight in Donna Summer, the Black girl who sings sexy. Once
> they were delirious about Armstrong, and then Makeba. Jazz and all

that natural born happy rhythm! Congratulations! No, if I were Donna Summer, I would gather up all the records to be found in the stores, in the dance clubs and cabarets, hotels and motels and high class houses.]

Akin to Caliban's prompting the drunken sailors to pilfer Prospero's prized books, Colita/Aurora incites the disco queen to repossess her lyric. Additionally, Donna Summer represents an attainable aural refuge, again Ellison's retreat, in which Aurora can drown out all the "white" noise: "Donna Summer, mi negrita querida, llena con su voz y excita con su ritmo la casa de la señora Sarah" (17) [Donna Summer, my dear Black girl, fill Miss Sarah's house with your voice and animate it with your rhythm]. If a unity is established it is between Black women, especially those real and fictional young girls sent out to service, who, no matter their station, visibility, invisibility, or fame embody what they always already represented: drone, sexual object, entertaining commodity.

Not coincidentally, double naming as indicative of double consciousness—the ability or the necessity of being conversant in official and unofficial discourses at one and the same time—represents a reiterated strategy in the writing of peoples of African descent. Consider Lastre Asunción/Juyungo in Adalberto Ortiz's novel; Nay/Feliciana the romanticized African mammy in Jorge Isaacs's novel *María* (1867); and Argentine writer Nené Lorriaga's *Carimba*, which reenacts the nominal transformation of kidnapped Africans to renamed American slaves. Consider also the real-life, nominally Christian titular transformations depicted in the film *Amistad* (Steven Spielberg, 1997); the morphing identity of Malcolm Little to Red to Malcolm X; and the memoirs of Enrique López Albújar, *De mi casona* (1924), which recount the travails of a child left with relatives unable to wholly accept his maternal Black heritage. These represent just a handful of examples. This identificatory tension in some cases speaks to the nostalgic effort to safeguard a stolen past and in others to the bridge between rightfully given names and imposed identities. All employ psychic bifurcation or duplicity to evoke complication, oppositions within and around the protagonist that insinuate or underscore conflicted allegiances attendant in this perplexing upheaval. Colita/Aurora gains from that double vision, seeing in the divided self the layered historical versions—one over which she exercises some mastery, another that would demand adherence to rules that promise her no benefit.

Colita/Aurora also becomes a replaceable predicate term within the larger project of narrating Caribbean realities of Blackness. Accordingly, Puerto Rican Mayra Santos Febres will pen her own version of yet another tale of yet another young Black girl sent out to service in "Marina y su olor." Marina has much in common with Colita/Aurora: a precocious intelligence, the separation from the family, the disagreeable work conditions, the meanness of her white female employer, and the unwanted attentions, in this case, of the employer's son. Each girl faces alone prepubescent questions of identity and sexuality and attempts to muster the inner (bodily) forces with which to defend and develop her own space. Intriguingly, that refashioned territory results from a sensory sensuality motif: in the case of Cartegena Portalatín's protagonist, the ability to find an aural refuge in Summer's disco music; for Marina, her unique ability to produce smells that in an olfactory way reshape her world.[14] From slavery to Summer, from Colita/Aurora to Marina, each improvisation transforms the official historical version, and deciphers what is at stake by returning to the absented locus. Santos Febres puts the writing exercise in the following terms:

> [E]xiste una intención por recontar hechos históricos vistos desde la muy irreverente imaginación (nunca se está quieta la condenada) como punto de partida para la elucubración de lo que pudo haber pasado y jamás se narró, por pena, vergüenza, decoro o censura oficial. (*Pez de vidrio* 9)

> [(T)here exists an intention to recount historic events seen from the very irreverent imagination (the condemned is never quiet) as a point of departure for the elaboration of that which could have occurred and was never narrated, for pain, shame, decorum or official censure.]

Another innovative use of orality can be found in an oral novel by Ecuadorian Nelson Estupiñán Bass, *Toque de Queda* (1978) [*Curfew*] (1992). Less well known than his poetry and narrative novels, the prose work employs and refines many of the techniques of creativity evident in those: for example, the singing contest in the poetry collection *Timarán y Cuabú* (1956). The action takes place in "real" time, divided into hourly sections that contribute to the mounting tension of the chaotic events that follow the military coup d'etat that is the motivating event of the novel. Although never made explicit, the captured snippets of conversation taking place, over radio waves and perhaps telephone wires, throughout the city give an impression similar to that of accelerated MTV editing (a more rapid innovation on Soviet Montage) of the cacophonic aural simultaneity of malfunctioning or hopelessly crisscrossed listening devices. The reader must exert some effort to discern the speakers and their location since the format eschews establishing narration. One can only imagine the physical appearance of the speakers, but accent, vocabulary, and topics of conversation do furnish a reliable sketch. Eventually, the reader comes to "recognize" the voices, and the exercise does not become tiresome or overworked (as it tends to do in the more limited use of this device in Cabrera Infante's *Tres Triste Tigres*, [1965]). Similar to other prose inclusions of written orality—for example, Black Eubonics in Hurston's *Their Eyes Were Watching God* (1937)—the reading of the novel benefits from a "theatrical" reading (out loud) rather than silent meditation.

Estupiñán Bass's approach and posture to orality uniquely illustrates a cultural synchronicity that smoothly moves between written and oral universes and echoes experiments undertaken throughout the Black Diaspora. Similar to the jazz novel envisioned by Langston Hughes and other writers of the Harlem Renaissance, Estupiñán Bass manages to master the rhythmicity suggested by Spencer. Akin to the cadenced flow of Guillén's 1930 poetry collection *Motivos de son*, the Ecuadorian captures the vitality and musicality of the speech act. Juxtaposing oral genres such as jokes, proverbs, and anecdotes, the text also colonizes the written word. Official communiqués from the newly formed military government, perhaps faintly reminiscent of the juridical tone of the *Requerimiento*, drip irony and ring false in comparison to the other smoother, more natural enunciations and exchanges between the other characters: the wife of the incoming general; the rebellious students; their worried parents; the police and military; and the variously politically positioned members of the community. Consequently, the ensemble cast of unseen faces interrupts the ordered monologue by answering back—versioning, recoding, off-timing, riffing—to the formal scripted message. What better challenge? What better tribute?

Blackness Unbound

A Tale of One's Own

*We have only gradually come to recognize not merely the sheer complexity of the question
of origins but also its irrelevancy for an understanding of consciousness. It is not necessary
for a people to originate or invent all or even most of the elements of their culture. It is
necessary only that these components become their own, embedded in their traditions,
expressive of their world view and life style.*

—Lawrence Levine, *Black Culture and Black Consciousness*

In *Amistad*, the 1997 Steven Spielberg movie fancifully based on true events,
John Quincy Adams (Anthony Hopkins) counsels Baldwin, the inexperi-
enced advocate (Matthew McConaughey), "It has been my experience that
in a courtroom whoever tells the best story wins." The elder goes on to ob-
serve that while the ragtag legal team of the uprooted captives has managed
to determine "*what* they are—Africans," it has failed to ascertain "*who* they
are." Thus the young lawyer and the ex-slave abolitionist Joadson (Morgan
Freeman) who aids him set about attempting to unlock the story of revolt
leader Cinque (Djimon Hounsou): his migration from juridical object to
fully human subject. Further underscoring the potency of narrative, the
prosecutor attempts to discredit Cinque's testimony by derisively contend-
ing that "like all good works of fiction, it's entertaining" while citing "logical"
paradoxes and impossibilities in order to undercut its veracity and dissuade
susceptible soft-hearted listeners.

Contextualized within his own story, Cinque stands as griot-guide in a
richly woven narrative. His tale is that of a man who killed a lion with a rock,
and he concludes, "I'm not a big man, just a lucky one." His story is also that
of the Middle Passage, the revolt, perhaps ironically insinuating that he is
indeed a big man, but not a lucky one. Within the Judeo-Christian tradition, this Daniel facing the lion or David overshadowed by the giant Goli-
ath ascends mythical heights. One of the other prisoners who, fascinated by
the illustrations in a purloined Bible, invents a narrative to link the draw-

ings, thus reasons that Cinque's—and by extension, their collective—story parallels that of Christ: celebration, capture, accusation, punishment. The Black Adonis's story within the more contemporary North American imaginary also recalls the Rambo, Rocky, or Diehard Hollywood plot: lone man against overwhelming odds triumphs in the end. His narrow escape from chattel slavery makes him in dominant discourse the perfect poster boy for the "forced immigrant" narrative that pretends to paint all comers to the Americas—and even those resident "first immigrants" indigenous natives— as part of one cynically universalizing narrative. As the archetypical hero in a quest tale, the kidnapped African likewise endures a series of tasks—as trying physically as they are mentally—which he must complete satisfactorily in order to eventually return to his—decimated—native village in Africa. Within his aboriginal system of meaning, Cinque would have remained simply a lucky man. Alienated from that context, sequestered into a distinct worldview—winners, losers, leader, followers, master, slaves—he emerges as a big man and a griot-guide, who is trying to get lucky.

Similar to the mouthy Colita-Aurora, protagonist in the Cartagena Portalatín short story "La llamaban Aurora," Cinque effects and participates in his own liberation by telling his tale, a tale discursively at odds with official history and culture. That storytelling permits metonymical substitutions or improvisations: Colita to Aurora to the icon of recaptured belligerence, crossover artist Donna Summer; and Cinque from folkloric figure to tragic hero to "universally" human. Every emotionally and psychically draining setback forces each to invent strategies that prove the wisdom of irascible John Quincy Adams who advised the utility of an advocate "whose inspiration blossoms the more you lose"—akin to oral contestants, *payadores*, *decimistas*, and rappers whose spontaneous or studied repartee, in its most moving manifestations, gains eloquence and proficiency with each succeeding round.

Conde Lucanor's Patronio's preference for a Moorish protagonist who could spin a yarn sympathetic to that worldview proves instructive as well. Although Cinque and Colita/Aurora manage to get their version on the record, they remain ultimately susceptible to "the operations of narration" (Julien 154), be it fanciful, critical, or otherwise disciplined. More crucially then, their stories continue to be malleable to the operations of *discourse*, akin to the most remembered tale about Prometheus, that disobedient Titan who gave fire to mankind and for his trouble was chained by the miffed rulers of the universe to a rock and beset by daily humiliations. Few remember, however, that—before the fire incident—the same Titan also instructed mankind in various arts and captured the world's ills in a box (later unwisely unleashed by the curious Pandora). That history, largely unremarked, is no less remarkable. Likewise, African-ancestored peoples and personae are bound by the narrative necessity of a myriad of institutions—ecclesiastical, juridical, and, not the least, the institution of chattel slavery. Thus they are bound to grapple tirelessly with the reiterated *meconnaissance* or misreading of a distinctly versioned worldview. The thoughtful (in the sense proposed by C.L.R. James) improvisation on uprootedness allows for a more thoroughgoing challenge. Prometheus had to await the largess of Hercules.

Staging Blackness: Race as (High) Drama

> All the world's a stage
> And all men and women, merely players
> Each has his entrance and his exit
> And one man, in his time, plays many parts
>
> —Shakespeare, *Hamlet*

A wealth of theatrical vehicles express the experience of uprootedness, both cosmological and concrete, through the improvisation of imagined or, as it were, staged communities.[1] Although the details vary, responding to nationally or politically specific contexts, the reiterated thematic of lack of territoriality, and the attendant effort to privilege a proper place within which to rehearse Old World Africanisms and to enunciate a New World Blackness, suggest a unifying intuited diasporic consciousness. Just as Greek chorus and Brechtian ensemble describe a certain worldview, so too do the conception, preproduction, and performance of works by African-descended dramatists that stage the issue of race as a discursive and theoretical position, a position generally "overlooked" or overshadowed in other explanatory models (for example, gender, class, nation). Hence, clever riposte set in a call-and-response form or imbedded in a slyly doubled perceptiveness serves as celebration of a peculiarly Africanized orality and speech rhythm. More profoundly, reaching beyond the boundaries of the traditional proscenium, the ready improvisation on uprootedness recalls the "inherent antagonism between the consciousness of the Black masses and the reality of their lives" (C.L.R. James, *Jacobins*, 407). Both tradition and invention foster intriguing performances of diasporic Blackness in such works as those by Cuba's

Gerardo Fulleda León (1942) and Teatro Rita Montañer, Uruguayan Jorge Cardoso, the Brazilian troupes Bando de Teatro Olodum based in Salvador da Bahia, and Companhia dos Comuns in Rio de Janeiro, among others.

A first question concerns the standard representations of Blackness. On the one hand, this reading recognizes that—in the eyes of others—phenotypical features negatively mark the African descended as bad, alien, irrational, superstitious, salaciously sensual, or perhaps just folklorically quaint. The most obvious theatrical cases include the foolish caricature in Spanish medieval theatre, a figure that reappears in *El tigre* (1955) [The tiger], a one-act play by Ecuadorian Demetrio Aguilera-Malta; the black-faced "negro" and the sensual mulata (alongside the equally hackneyed *gallego* [Spaniard]) in Cuban Alhambra; and in the Southern Cone, the soot-faced carnival revelers of Uruguayan *comparsa*, beset by mimetic desire, no doubt. Notwithstanding the reputed entertainment value of those derisive caricatures, such traditional representations in large part reflect the condition of uprootedness and spring from the lack of territoriality, be it narrative, discursive, historical, or cosmic. In consequence, staging Blackness requires reordering, or more appropriately, refashioning the narrative of lack—empty-handed arrival, sluggish participation, limited contribution—by rewriting the discursively precarious relationship to territory that serves as a basis for such typically disparaging representations. While racial harmony might promise a place for all comers (openness and fluidity with the implicit promise of upward mobility), place—and certainly, its lack—has consequences in representation.

Indeed, the antagonism between consciousness and reality motivates the theatrical conception of territoriality—real, symbolic, imagined, or psychological. The dilemma of place resides not in a question of center-margin-periphery (a là bell hooks), but rather in taking, using, and defending a territory, that is to say, constructing one's "own corner of reality" when others have been constructing it for you. For example, Jorge Cardoso's *El desalojo de la calle de los negros* [The eviction on the Black folks' street] and the early work of Márcio Meirelles/Bando de Teatro Olodum (BTO), *Essa é nossa praia* [This is our 'hood], the first installment in the *Trilogia do Pelô* [Pelorinho Trilogy] (first performed January 25, 1991),[2] grow out of a challenge to the explicit deterritorialization of urban renewal strategies; these works belligerently confront both dispossession and deculturation—and the modernity of the moment.

Cardoso's play dramatizes the real event under the military dictatorship in Uruguay that razed apartment buildings within sight of the sea with the idea of replacing those admittedly decaying structures with lucrative tourist hotels or exclusive condominiums—the fiction portrayed in Zapata Olivella's *Chambucú, corral de negros*—and resettling the ousted occupants into diverse outlying areas of the capital. In the play, the Afrocentric university student Kaulicoro comforts Doña Coca, the woman who adopted him after the death of his parents, pointing out optimistically: "Ya pronto va a tener su casita. . . . Una casita nueva con un jardin grande" (15) [Pretty soon you're going to have your house. . . . A new house with a big yard]. Doubtful of the reality of that cheery vision, Doña Coca remains understandably dismayed as she reminisces on her life in the neighborhood, reasoning, "Sí, [é]ste ha sido mi mundo y no puedo abandonarlo de pronto y decir que me da lo mismo" (15) [Yes, this has been my world and I cannot abandon it just like that and say that it doesn't matter]. The threat of dispossession moves various members of the community to attempt to find the benefit of portable territory, emphasizing the psychic profit. Accordingly, a song later in the play affirms:

Vivimos en la misma ciudad
pero también nos sucede algo más:
vivimos en el mismo corazón
reír podemos, cantar podemos
crear universos de ilusión. (20)

[We live in the same city
but more than that,
we live in the same heart (where)
laughing we can, singing we can
create visionary universes.]

Near the very end of the play, Fausto celebrates "La solidaridad" [solidarity], observing "Acá en este momento hay una comunidad dejando su barrio, sacando sus aperos con amargura, pero con la fe del apoyo mutuo" (26) [Here and now there's a community leaving its neighborhood, bitterly gathering their belongings, but with a belief in altruism].

Others, less willing to go quietly into the uprooted night, express exasperation. Anselmo, Kaulicoro's adoptive father and biological uncle, counters the solidarity argument saying,

> "¡Y de qué sirve la honra si cuando sos viejo te echan como a un perro y no podés decir ni jota porque si no te arrastran a punta de bayoneta!" (26)

> [And what good is honor if, when you are old, they evict you like a dog and you can't say a word because if you do they skewer you on the end of a bayonet!]

In another instance, the quarter's matrons reprove the young street drummers for their seeming disregard of the impending eviction: "Este desalojo es un crimen" (21) [This eviction is a crime] and in a still sharper tone

> "¿No entienden nuestra situación? ¿qué estamos desamparados? . . . ¿qué nos arrancan de nuestros hogares por culpa de algún mandamás, que no quiere negros en el barrio?" (21)

> [Don't you understand our situation? That we're homeless? . . . That they're kicking us out of our homes because of some officious bureaucrat who doesn't want Blacks in the area?]

One participant in the percussive scene, the bookish militant Kaulicoro,[3] addresses their concerns:

> "Cuando nos trajeron a América . . . En los trapiches en las plantaciones, en las grandes mansiones, ¿qué hicimos? . . . a pesar del cansancio cantábamos. Y ese canto, fue una oración que nos mantuvo vivos. Por eso, en este triste momento, pensábamos hacer lo . . . mismo al son de aquellos tambores . . . Elevar una oración de fe." (23)

> [When they brought us to America . . . in the barracks on the plantation, in the big houses, what did we do? . . . in spite of the exhaustion, we sang. And that song, was a prayer that kept us alive. That's why, in this sad moment, we thought that we'd do the same to the sound of those drums . . . to raise a prayer of faith.]

Aping the griot's role as cultural mediator, and implicitly indicating the intelligentsia's accountability to the community, Kaulicoro manages to "find the link, however remote, between" the two events—the Middle Passage and the eviction—and lays bare the interconnectedness between the two improvised cultural strategies.

Similarly, Brazil's BTO *Essa é nossa* deals with the threatened uprooting of the sizable Black community amidst rumors of urban renewal plans for Pelourinho, historic center of Salvador, site of the slave auction in the then-colonial capital. Riffing on the master discourse, the title plays on that of the popular and long-running television show *Essa é nossa praia* [This is our plaza] that features humorous sketches centered on serendipitous encounters of community members in a common park or plaza. Likewise featuring everyday characters in everyday situations, the collectively written BTO script presents an African-descended community that faces the same neighborhood decay and municipal bureaucracy as in Cardoso's play, but—making for a more layered discourse—the area's denizens are also beset by corruption and moral decline within the community itself. In that light, the *favela* dweller's thinking man, Marcelo, reprovingly confronts the local policeman's corruption—bribery and drug use—making the link with the ills of an earlier uprooting:

> "É por causa de coisas desse tipo que a gente continua sendo oprimido, discriminado. Precisamos descolonizar-nos desses males que ainda perduram dos tempos da escravidão. Precisamos conhecer a nossa verdadeira face, deste país que os negros construíram às custas de muito sangue, suor, lágrimas e muito sofrimento. Nós somos considerados cidadãos de segunda classe por causa de um racismo perverso. E a gente tem que procurar ter consciência desses coisas e não maltratar o nosso semelhante. Somos negros, somos importantes e somos iguais a todo mundo." (85)

> [It's because of things like this that we continue to be oppressed and discriminated against. We need to decolonize ourselves from these evils that still persist from slavery times. We need to know our true countenance, of this country that Blacks built at the cost of a lot of blood, sweat, tears, and much suffering. We are considered second-class citizens as the result of a perverse racism. And we have to find a way to be conscious of these things and not mistreat our own. We are Blacks, we are important, and we are equal to all.]

Here Marcelo, a now-familiar personality, reprises the figures of Máximo in Zapata's *Chambacú, corral de negros* and Cardoso's Kaulicoro. As a similar "insider-outsider" facilitator (Captain-Hidalgo 59) undertaking the griot's roles as historian, interpreter, and exhorter, his optimistic words and favored position echo theirs, but their roadmap to cultural consciousness represents only one of many options available to the community.

Other strategies reflect earlier responses to uprootedness. In one instance, Baiana [street vendor of food typical of the region and African-based cuisine] invites newcomer Maria de Bonfim [a city in the interior city and patron "saint" of Bahia] to join the latest in a long line of fugitive retreats:

"Nós criou essa Associação pro mode da gente ir na Prefeitura revindicar as coisas daqui da comunidade. E graças a essa Associação, a gente já conseguiu muitas coisas: creches, os cursos para as mães aprenderem costurar, trançar cabelo e outras coisas." (79)

[We created this Association in order for us to approach the city government and repair things here in the community. And thanks to this Association, we have managed to get a lot of things: childcare classes for the mothers to learn how to sew, braid hair and other things.]

Reminiscent of the *cabildos, candombles, candombes, tangos* and *tanchas, quilombos* and *palenques*—social, cultural and political territories established for mutual aid—the association serves an important function, especially for women in the community. Other strategies reveal a more individualistic bent, yet are no less typical. For his part, the character of Lord Black recalls the figure of the *malandro*, a streetwise trickster, a neighborhood power broker, both respected—even loved—and feared (akin to orisha Exu). His complaint concerns the empty promises of official culture, especially those of the church:

". . . eu não preciso ler o livro dos homens pra poder falar palavras bonitas e assim enganar. Não pense que sou igual a vocês que tomam o dinheiro do povo. Eu não invento óleos sagrados, lenços ungidos e digo ao povo que passando na enfermidade eles vão ficar bom. Não tomo óculos, muletas e digo ao povo que eles já estão curados, não. Agora digo uma coisa a vocês, os falsos profetas estão chegando, cabe a vocês acreditar ou não acreditar neles. O meu recado já está dado." (89)

[... I don't have to read the bible to be able to speak with pretty words and to fool (people). Don't think that I'm the same as you who take people's money. I don't invent holy oils, anointed cloth, and say to sick people that they'll get better. I don't take eyeglasses and crutches and say to people that they're cured, no. No, I'll tell you something, the false prophets are coming, it's up to you to believe or not. I've said my piece.]

An antihero in other contexts, Lord Black retains an air of honor, and it is his savvy if untutored voice that closes the play. He adroitly connects the neighborhood's history of traffic in human flesh: the slavery auction block, the bordellos, and the impending "renewal" and displacement of the most recent "galera bonita" (94) [lovely collection] of variously belligerent community members.

These more recent examples contrast with an earlier strategy wherein those bad students, encouraged by Aristotle to question premise and paradigm, insinuate themselves and their communities *into* dominating discourses by recoding canonical works. Demetrio Aguilera-Malta, member of the innovative Grupo Guayaquil in 1930s Ecuador, transfigures Greek tragedy in *Infierno negro.*

Negro I.   Pero no es cierto que la obra del hombre está concluida, que basta con adaptarnos al paso del mundo.
Negro II.   La obra del hombre acaba de comenzar.
Negro III.   y el hombre tiene todavía que conquistar toda prohibición
Negro IV.   Inmovilizada en los rincones de su fervor.
Negro I.   Y ninguna raza tiene el monopolio
Negro II.   de la belleza,
Negro III.   de la inteligenica,
Negro IV.   de la fuerza.
Coro.   (Lentamente) Para todos hay lugar en la cita de la victoria.
    (343)

[Black I.   But it is not true that the work of man is done, that it is enough to adapt ourselves to the ways of the world.
Black II.   Man's work is just beginning.
Black III.   and man has yet to conquer every taboo
Black IV.   Paralyzed in the corners of his fear.
Black I.   And no one race has the monopoly

Black II.   over beauty,
Black III.   over intelligence,
Black IV.   over power.
Chorus.   (Slowly) There is a place for all at the date with victory.][4]

Here, the playwright cleverly manipulates the operations of Greek classical drama (for example, the answering chorus) in order to address the fluidity of uniquely American, Hispanic, and Black issues and tropes, not the least the device of call and response. Likewise, Aimé Césaire's *A Tempest* upends Shakespeare's Elizabethan drama *The Tempest*, featuring a clench-fisted, Uhuru-shouting Caliban, also known as "X." In another instance, Trinidad-born Rosa Guy recasts Hans Christian Andersen's "Little Mermaid" into the novel *My Love, My Love, or, The Peasant Girl* (1985), the basis for the play *Once on This Island* (a musical by Lynn Ahrens and Stephen Flaherty), the impossible love story of Ti Moune, Black peasant girl, and Daniel, landed white. For his part, Derrick Walcott (Santa Lucia/United States) also occasionally favors the adaptation of theatre classics. His *The Joker of Seville* (1978), set to calypso music, recodes Spanish playwright Tirso de Molino's *Burlador de Sevilla*, itself a variation of the Don Juan legend. Even the Brazilian group Bando de Teatro Olodum, who typically create their works using a process of improvisation, have also experimented with rescripted endeavors such as *Ópera de três reais*, a cannibalized tribute to Brecht, which served as prelude to further recoded experiments like *Um sonho de verão* (based on William Shakespeare's *A Midsummer's Night Dream*). A production of *Dom Quixote*—similarly "olodumarizado" translated into the troupe's peculiar expressive vernacular—enjoyed varying success from the standpoint of audience, actors, and critics, each wondering if the group had strayed too far afield from the Bahian landscape (and by extension, textual territories) so much a part of their original works. In Rio de Janeiro, director Antônio Abujamara took advantage of a growing number of Black actors of big and small screen in the metropolis for a 2002 production of *Hamlet É Negro* that continued the recoding tradition.

Not unexpectedly, within the calculated striving for universality in the cited re-creations, the difference between original and improvisation stands hauntingly apparent, a reminder of the "contradictory relationship of . . . orthodoxy and heresy" (Wynter "Meanings," 479). On the one hand, the apt use of theatrical irony—in deed and speech—insists that both original and improvisation represent the norm. Nonetheless, even while modeled on the gems of Western discourse, the off-timing strategy of these plays specifically underscores the conflicted relationship to "ostensibly 'universally' applicable meaning and discourse-complex" (Wynter "Meanings," 479). Similar to Trinidadian thinker C.L.R. James who "set out to master the literature, philosophy, and ideas of Western civilisation" ("Discovering" 163), playwrights take on the classical stage and as a result localize—that is, resituate—a "universality" that has "lost" its locus. Thus in the mold of the feudal romantic Don Quixote, their protagonists or collectives lampoon the reigning political order, its icons, and conventions: chivalry, warrior mentality, distressed damsels—the commodification of what once constituted a moral code.[5] These playwrights—and the directors, companies, and actors who breathe life into the writers' words—construct a properly unorthodox and contestatory historical space. Yet, by mirroring the dominant discourse or even by inverting the "official" text, examining its soft underbelly, they actually integrate themselves into it and assimilate its paradigms. Since the plays necessarily reflect a particular cultural context and the peculiar discourse within which the work was created (and with which it remains in dialogue), the simple "blackening" of the players (literally in the case of *Hamlet É Negro*) represents in many cases a half measure at best. The players may only fleetingly find entry into a discursively weighted context never meant to acknowledge or to comfortably accommodate their presence.

Ilie suggests that "[t]he contrary event is insulation" (26), an option largely unavailable at the porous American crossroads. Yet, accessing sources largely ignored by or obscure to mainstream culture, Cuban Gerardo Fulleda León borrows African legend and Black experience and biography to create his plays *Ruandi* (1977), *Patakin*, and *Plácido* (1967–75). Each drama conjoins self-awareness and discourse-awareness in order to refashion a territoriality and envisions a temporal dimension in which narrative necessity argues for the centrality of the Black presence. In *Chago de Guisa* (1989), set in 1865–68 Cuba, Fulleda León offers a coming-of-age quest narrative (for knowledge, riches, and power) "[i]nspirada en una leyenda (Patakin) de procedencia sudanesa (yoruba) y con elementos bantu (congo)" (cover blurb) [inspired by a legend (Patakin) of Sudanese (Yoruba) providence with Bantu (Congo) elements]. Recipient of the Premio Casa de las Americas (a Cuban literary prize of continental importance), the play's story is as compelling and entertaining as *Popul Vuh*, complete with trickster guide, irascible deities, strong magic, and human foibles. Thus, alongside Oloffi, "amo del cielo y de la tierra" [master of the sky and land], his secretary, Orumbila, and ancestral "egguns" [deceased ancestor spirits], other fantastic figures in the play recall Greek personalities: the sirens who tempt the sailors in the *Iliad* and the one-eyed Cyclops, here the alluring river being "de piel blanquecina y rubio pelo" (79) [with translucent white skin and blonde hair] whose initial visage hides "una mascara de ojos muy grandes y rojos como de vaca y grandes colmillos" (94) [a mask with very cow-like large red eyes and large teeth]. Themes include *espejismo* [the play of mirror images] as in the case of the love interest whose identity metamorphoses through the clever use of anagram: Ibis, Sibi and Bisi melding African, mythical, and indigenous aspects. This play then is less about a head-on binary confrontation with or assimilation into dominant Western white discourses that devalue Blackness—although this thematic is subtly at play—than about the insulation of the *palenque* and a particular conceptualization of manhood and, certainly, more broadly, humanness. The play reenacts the response to uprootedness: the impulse to create and celebrate the improvised retreat described earlier by Ellison.

Circularity also constitutes a central theme of Fulleda León's work. Clearly significant in the structure of the play, the errant protagonist, after having passed each successive test, finds himself at a crossroads where the trickster announces "al final o al regreso que es el comienzo, te encuentro" [at the end or at the return that is the beginning, I will find you]. Accordingly, the young hero repeatedly sets out toward a goal, participates in the assigned adventure, and captures the prize. Then, rather than completing the cycle and returning to his home, he bequeaths his prize to fellow initiates. Only after his peregrinations allow him to realize the importance of the privileged space of the *palenque* will Chago recognize it as the ultimate prize; the comfortable rhythmic redundancy of the quest phases and the reiterated temporal suspension make that realization possible.

The straightforward attempt to "Africanize" drama by the application of vernacular terms recalls experiments with privileging race characters in essentially bourgeois guise in Fulleda León's earlier works. The play *La querida de Enramada* (1981) dramatizes the events after the death of a wealthy man in the arms, in the bed, in the house of his lover. The extended family who shares the abode must determine how to move the body to a more licit location before polite society learns of the man's demise and the questionable circumstances surrounding the entire liaison. Complications multiply, and at one point the legitimate spouse does indeed put in an appearance, causing predictable consternation. Admittedly, this narrative represents fairly standard fare (for example, Lydia Cabrera's transcribed tales or García Márquez's *El amor en los tiempos de cólera*, [1980]).

Also the fact that the lover is a *mulata* reenergizes a circumstance that enjoys a long history in Latin American literature, elevated to the level of a rhetorical device, the trope of the tragic *mulata*, which fueled Villaverde's romantic epic *Cecilia Valdés* (and several plays, movies, and soap operas in its wake, including Estorino's *Parece blanca* [1995]). *Vejigantes*, one of the plays in Francisco Arriví's well-known trilogy *Máscara puertorriqueña*—a triptych that dramatically laid bare the dynamics of race in Puerto Rico—offered a novel and thus discomfiting take on this trope. Similar to a recoding, more direct structural borrowing of a specific text is a strategy that experiments with genre conventions while continuing to reflect the Western discourse that provides its initial motivation: class and racial hierarchies, social mores, melodrama or chamber drama, and so on. Nevertheless, Arriví's *Vejigantes* and Fulleda León's *La querida de Enramada* do manage to look at the familiar in a fresh way by privileging life's secondary characters who are sharply and sympathetically drawn and ably supported by smart and rhythmic dialogue reminiscent of Estupiñán Bass's mastery with "oral" parley.

Through strategies of inversion and insertion, these and other plays by Fulleda León attempt to interrupt and destabilize the weightiness of official, formal culture. *Chago de Guisa* explored popular and traditional sources, for example, the convention of the quest narrative, common to European and African contexts. However, the improvisation remains limited to interchangeable themes, a replaceable predicate, and conventions that do not suffer in translation with the addition of a female rather than male lead, a Black or a white protagonist, or centering attention on formerly overlooked bit parts. Absent the renovation or innovation on *strategic techniques* of creativity, the novelty of insertion and inversion threatens to wear thin. Recognizing this, the Cuban playwright attempts to do more.

Based on Fulleda León's desire to conjoin his theatrical avocation with his childhood memories of spectacle and religiosity in his native Santiago de Cuba on the eastern extreme of the island, his more recent project moves to improvise on cultural practices, for example, orality and ritual, as a means of reintegrating life and art and sacred and secular communities. Discussing one such practice in the so-called teatro ritual caribeño, a theatre "in dialogue with ritual forms" (137), the playwright emphasizes

> la elaboración de una dramaturgia que recoja de forma contemporánea y novedosa las fiestas populares y religiosas de procendencia católica sincretizadas, los carnavales como los patakines (cuentos con proyecciones oblicuas que acompañan a cada letra Oddum o predicción de los caracoles), como las otras predicciones oraculares, las danzas y cantos rituales, la gestualidad y sobre todo la energía y la trascendencia otra de los manifestantes en las sesiones de santería o regla ocha (de procendencia yoruba), el palo monte (bantú), o regla arará (de la cultura fon), la sociedad secreta abakuá (del Calabar), o el espiritismo donde el actuante cumple un rol primodial. ("El rito" 134)

> [the elaboration of a dramaturgy that gathers in contemporary and inventive/novel form syncretic Catholic popular and religious festivals, carnivals such as patakines (stories with oblique projections that literally follow rituals of Oddum or adivination) like the other oracular predictions, ritual dances and songs, the movement and above all the energy and the altered transcendence of the participants in the sessions of Santería or the order of Ocha (Yoruba custom), palo monte (Bantu) or the order of Arara (from the Fon culture), the secret Abacua society (Calabar), or spiritualism where the actor fulfills his primordial role.]

Similar to the "scripted" space for exchanges with audience members in *Cabaré de RRRRRaça*, part of the repertoire of Bando de Teatro Olodum, interactivity represents another aim of the Cuban's ongoing project. He muses, "Potencialmente, pues, actuantes somos todos los que nos podemos reunir en una sesión llevados por el fanatismo, la necesidad, la fe, la curiosidad, la convicción, la moda o por el simple 'por si acaso' ("El rito" 134). [Potentially, then, actors are all of us who can come together in a session carried by fanaticism, need, faith, curiosity, conviction, fashion or for the simple "just in case."] In this conception, improvisation resists a slavishly mimetic impulse and approaches traditional practices tempered by the spirit of "la reflexión, la crítica y la transgresión" (134) [reflection, critique, and transgression]. In this spirit, one of Fulleda León's protégés led a workshop (Salvador da Bahia, August 1997) that attempted to induce the state of religious trance as a strategy for actor training. Independently, Bando de Teatro Olodum and Companhia dos Comuns in Brazil embed elements of communal spectacle—carnival, *capoeira*, and *candomblé*—in their process of theatrical creation.

Clearly, the limitations and possibilities for this type of experimentation need to be addressed as a part of preproduction concerns. At least some or a part of the enterprise relies on structural considerations. The relative stability offered by the resident theater company can to some extent ameliorate the uncertainties attendant in a "spontaneous" endeavor. Two companies still extant at this writing that have sufficient history, ideological coherency, and success are, in Cuba, Teatro Rita Montañer and, in Brazil, Bando de Teatro Olodum, which enjoys residency in Teatro Vila Velha, a performance space with its own impressive history. Such is not the case with Uruguayan novelist and occasional playwright Jorge Cardoso, whose desire to stage the play *El desalojo de la calle de los negros* required that he press into service community members who generally reserve dramatic and theatrical energies for *candombe comparsas* during carnival. Such was also not the case with Aguilera-Malta, whose physical deterritorialization—emigration to Mexico—would have consequences in terms of casting, audience, and surely content.

Refashioning a theatrical territory, whether physical or discursive, has the potential to disrupt the applicable historical text, the race aesthetic. Beyond simple cancellation or inverse paralleling of the overarching discursive script, all aspects and personalities of the theatrical enterprise mount a fundamental challenge to the master narrative through the production of their own communal lexicon. Thus the choice of *patakin* or call-and-response works well to embrace Africanness and to express multiple and sometimes contentious views of New World Blackness without overtly dismissing conflicting enunciations or collapsing individual experiences into a monolithic—and false—universal. The *perceived* spontaneity, immediacy, and collectivity of theatre—the scenic reincarnation of orality—would seem to elude the writerly novel. Such is not the case.

Novel Performances of Caliban's Blackness

Akin to Fulleda León's Ibis, Caliban—"that freckled whelp on whose nature, nurture would not stick"—began his existence as little more than a clever anagram.[6] Throughout his twentieth-century discursive travels and travails, the Shakespearean buffoon has acquired the trappings of the short-sighted inversion of José Enrique Rodó's sainted *Ariel* (1900), a mouthy rebel in Aimé Césaire's *A Tempest* (1985), and a stalwart revolutionary and ideologue in Roberto Fernández Retamar's *Calibán: Apuntes sobre la cultura en nuestra América* (1971) [Caliban: Notes on the culture in our America]. From negation to celebration, the malfeasant's metaphorical course in the intellectual history of Latin America and the Caribbean represents a crucial axis of "staged" identity. The many parts played by the Caliban myth as subtext, whether unwitting or acknowledged, in the writing of peoples of African descent in the New World follow the dramatic character from troubled youth to maturity. His belligerent trajectory—learning to curse and inciting rebellion and criminality, including an alleged rape and attempted petty larceny ("seize but his books")—provides a key to deciphering the maturation of the Black protagonist in Latin America, beginning here with Adalberto Ortiz's *Juyungo* (1943) whose picaresque barbarian Lastre Asunción "acts up," framing his rebelliousness as poorly as did his spiritual progenitor. Cathartic cursing aside, Gregorio Martínez's *Crónica de músicos y diablos* [Chronicle of musicians and devils] and Manuel Zapata Olivella's *Changó el gran putas* (1983) "thief" Prospero's dominating discourse. Both novels seek to "correct" the historical scenario of victimized or thankless/ungrateful/humbled entities in order to "act out" a distinct identity of contribution and participation for peoples of African descent in Latin America and the Caribbean.

Two propositions motivate the representations that typically describe the sojourn of peoples of African descent in the Hispanic New World: one (inhospitable) material, the other (the beneficial) corporeal. The first emphasizes enslavement, offering a picture of catatonic beings dumped into an alien and hostile environment where these *piezas de india* would endure unspeakable horrors and humiliations. Naturally, according to this point of departure, slavery necessarily impeded the meaningful, that is to say material, contribution and participation of these put-upon, pitiable, empty-handed drones in constructing the New World and its systems. Largely elided in this conceptualization is Africa, the sequester of Africans, and the Middle Passage. Within canonical literature, Jorge Isaacs's text stands in stark contrast to the Cuban antislavery/abolitionist novels such as *Sab* (1841) by Gertudis Gómez de Avellaneda and *Cecilia Valdes* (1882) by Cirilo Villaverde, in which both Africa and the Middle Passage are tellingly absent—Benítez-Rojo's "absent locus, the center that has taken off and yet is still there, dominating and dominated by the soloist's performance" (20).

The second proposition, to some extent a correction of the first, holds that, despite material lack, kidnapped Africans and their New World progeny inexplicably managed to retain a collective, corporeal memory (see the earlier discussion of Chirimini's discomfited musical history in chapter 5). An extension (or corruption) of Aristotelian thought, the Enlightenment emphasized the rational and, later, the classically based explications of las Casas, which allowed kidnapped Africans and peoples of African descent, by dint of rote memorization, to reenact songs, ceremonies, tales, and practices that would then be inserted into and remade in the new environment through various processes of adaptation: assimilation, racial and/or cultural mestizaje (for example, mulatez), transcription, transculturation or acculturation. Both insertion and omission insinuate a narrative convenience where such inclusions or absences "confirm the world of the worldview" (Godzich 363). Here too, the absented locus becomes noteworthy. The emphasis on the Europeanness and the nationality (for example, *cubanidad*) of these societies implies that Africa brought nothing material to the table—no associative history or political organization beyond those elements that needed to be exorcized or transculturated by self-replicating paternalistic institutions, slavery, and later, the nation.

Whatever the point of departure of the two propositions, dominant narratives, more often than not, have portrayed as prey or victims those who suffered the cruelties of the cosmological shift from Africa to the New World. Predictably then, the physically grotesque, morally backward, or laughably simple Caliban signals the negation, the lack of the righteous qualities with which New World society sought to assign itself, as in celebratory master narratives (for example, Domingo Sarmiento's *Facundo* [1845]) or in polemical treatises (for example, Esteban Echeverria's short story "El matadero" [1840] or Isabel Allende's novel *Eva Luna* [1987]). The proverbial paternalistic and maternalistic treatment of Black characters typically shows the African descended as the downside of civilization, that is to say, barbarity. Their association with the wild side of drums, the disrespect they incurred as a result of their uprooting, and the dismissal of their cultural production illustrate the effects of this view. In fact, in the Latin American imaginary, those of African descent virtually sweat lack from every pore: they lack rationality and are therefore trapped in a sensuous, superstitious existence; they lack maturity and hence are playful and forgetful possessors of a child-like retardation in the social, educational, political, and cultural arenas; foolish and childish, they lack context in progressive historical time and consequently are locked in the immediate and the tangible present or remain imprisoned in the repetitions of a mythical past.

Now and again, the exceptional "Afrocitizen" can escape the weight of his race. Cuban works such as Anselmo Suárez y Romero's *Francisco: El ingenio o Las delicias del campo* (1838) and even Juan Francisco Manzano's *Autobiografía de un esclavo* (1841)—which celebrate a being able to overcome his surroundings (and racial heritage)—partake in this narrative dynamic. Notably these protagonists all seem gentle, sensitive to the extreme, and docile, although all (mostly inwardly) rail against their compromised freedom and individuality, but seldom appear overly sympathetic with the plight of their own darker brothers. Intriguingly canonical literature consistently pairs these freedom seekers with a desperately and hopelessly expressed desire for female whiteness. Just as predictably, these unions never work out, as either one or the other meets a violent end or tragically sigh themselves to death.

Cuba did not, however, corner the market on "exceptionalism."[7] A more vexed representation contained in other texts would, with Prospero, chide an ungrateful Caliban for not showing proper appreciation for the training received: the attempt to sully Miranda's virginal purity and the failed plan to usurp the throne with the inebriated tars, Stephano and Trinculo. This portrait of a thankless Caliban motivates the Cuban so-called antislavery novels. In those works, the dark-skinned protagonist comes into intimate contact with the ideal world of the dominant through a civilizing apprenticeship or *transculturación*, *blanquecimiento-mulatez* and, not uninvited, trespasses the sanctity of white femininity. The idea of bounded territories and proper behaviors in turn dictate narrative permissibility, in such works as *Matalaché: novela retaguardista* (1928) by Afro-Peruvian Enrique López Albújar, whose arrogant title character ends his prosaic trajectory fried in oil for his transgressions; and in the real-life travails of Cuban poets Plácido and Juan Francisco Manzano, both implicated in the so-called Conspiración de la Escalera (1844) and whose perceived "ungratefulness" had fatal effect in one case and chilling consequences in the other.

In the final scenes of the Shakespearean drama, Caliban establishes his "nobility" when the knave accepts his inferiority to Prospero and in the "order of things." Likewise, this treatment finds its echo in Jorge Isaacs's romantic novel *María* (1867) in the portrayal of Nay-Feliciana, whose humility and gratitude to protagonist Esteban's family indeed represent the very mark of her nobility as does the self-effacing indebtedness of Natividad to childhood companion Don Federico in the 1950 Venezuelan novel *Cumboto* by Ramón Díaz Sánchez. Despite the seeming variety, these figures share a level of passivity based in the assumption that they needed to be "acted upon": civilized, restrained, and/or pitied whilst being instructed in the rules of civilization, the mores of society, and the laws of culture. The culture-bringers, of course, are others.

Nevertheless, certain novels contest this vision of the negated, passive, inferior folk *negro*. Much like North American Black male artistic production, the first texts that articulate the Black male reality in Latin America are marked by the anger of their tone. In the northern context offerings include Richard Wright's *Native Son* (1940), Eldridge Cleaver's *Soul on Ice* (1967), James Baldwin's *Notes of a Native Son* (1955), and *Autobiography of Malcolm X* (certainly the book coauthored with Alex Haley [1964] and secondarily the later inspired film by Spike Lee [1992]). In the context of the Spanish-speaking deep South, examples include *Canal Zone* (1935) by Demetrio Aguilera-Malta, Arnoldo Palacios's *Las estrellas son negras* (1949), *Juyungo* (1943) by Adalberto Ortiz, and Isabelo Zenón Cruz's dissertation-turned-two-tome-treatise *Narciso descubre su trasero* (1974–75), texts that Jackson writes "startled the Puerto Rican reading public" (217). The anger in *Canal Zone* and *Las estrellas son negras* is of a spent type; the sensitive protagonists, disillusioned by hard knocks—hunger, poverty, discrimination, criminality—have tired of the unattainable promises of upward mobility through education and hard work. Their rancor is contained, and this will prove their end. Conversely, the central figure in *Juyungo* throughout most of the novel openly professes his hatred of whites, an inheritance from his war-hero relative. Although he lives with María de los Ángeles, a white woman, he badly mistreats her in a mix of what Franz Fanon might diagnose as attraction/repulsion to a world, an existence, that could never be rightly his within the terms of the reigning discourse—which if it cannot recognize his existence can also then refuse to acknowledge his pain. His rancor narratively contained, he too dies, signaling the fatal consequences for Blacks with a bad attitude.

Recent efforts to represent the sojourn of peoples of African descent into and in the Americas present a nonfiction challenge on various fronts to the image of passivity. Unearthed histories include *La insurrección de los negros de la serranía coriana: 10 de mayo de 1795 (Notas para una discusión)* (1996) by Pedro A. G. Rivas, Luis Dovale Prado and Lidia Lusmila Bello;[8] *El ci-*

marrón 1845: Sumaria formada en averiguación de la muerte de un negro que se encontró ahogado en el río de Bayaon (1979) by Benjamin Nistal Moet;[9] and, *Caetana Says No: Women's Stories From a Brazilian Slave Society* (2001) by Sandra Lauderdal Graham.[10] Movies, as well, seem newly interested in the theme: *Amistad* (United States), *Plácido* (Cuba), *La última cena* (Cuba), and *A Soldier's Story* (United States), to name a few. In these narratives, an exceptional Afrocitizen performs as a hero acting upon his environment in the backsliding midst of his variously victimized and (slavishly) grateful fellows.

However, lest such approaches seem a mere flip-flop, the performance of (anachronistic) agency then comes as an afterthought largely predetermined by other exigencies: principally the angst to record "an-other" historical version. Admittedly, as a result of the weighty inheritance of limiting characterizations, the Afro-Hispanic writer has several implicit challenges to confront. The first consists of witnessing to the very existence of peoples of African descent, as the prolongation signaled by the filmic Griot, in the Caribbean and Latin American diasporic imaginary and reality. This representation goes beyond local color or shadowy stereotypical flat background filler, reaching toward a complex rounded echo of the peculiar experience of Latin Blackness. In that light the use of Black-speak in Nicolás Guillén's 1930 *Motivos de son* (for example, the poems "Negro bembón" and "Mulata") raises troubling questions, indicating that just talking the phantom talk does not the Black persona make.

Puerto Rican literary critic Zenón Cruz's sometimes shrill *Narciso descubre su trasero* alleges that the status of Africana peoples in the Americas is predicated on the willful invisibility that degrades and invalidates their cultural contributions. Off-putting for its strident tone, many of the work's salient points have been lost to posterity; it has been accused of offending everything from sensibilities to stylistics. Nevertheless, the breadth of the project—querying the literary and sociohistorical representations of Blackness in the Puerto Rican context, complete with a laundry list of quaint racist practices as formative/deformative of Black identity—suggests the gap between the consciousness and the cultural reality of diasporic Blacks everywhere. The provocative title upends, as it were, the favored image of progress and "moons" the interested dream of modernity. Here the mix of corporeality and the implied serviceability of the hind quarters seem particularly apt since those meanings mapped onto the body compound negation in order to structure and drive the hegemonic discourse. Consequently Zenón Cruz interrogates the rush to utopian visions and teleological futures, which he suggests do not have a heinie upon which to rest from the arduous labor of empire, nation, or discourse building. This corporeal imagery proves that the premised lack does not exist outside the system of meaning, nor is it marginal, but rather "essential." Overall the project moves beyond the binary opposition of Narcissus and his *trasero* [backside] to signal a Prometheus unbound, and by extension, Blackness unbound.

Many of the improvisational strategies explored there—riffing, call-response, answer back, indirection, recoding, off-timing, parody, erosion—reflect the strategies of the analyses of other thinkers who likewise pose a series of interruptions that sometimes give pause to and other times challenge the order of things in an attempt to change the course of thinking. An earlier critique offered in Cuban historian Walterio Carbonell's *Como surgió la cultura cubana* remains largely forgotten, save for the few translated pages that appear in *AfroCuba* (Sarduy and Stubbs, 1993). The book-length project took to task the historical discipline and cogently signaled the fundamental, foundational antagonism of interests that impacts the present Cuban—and one could suggest diasporic—imaginary. The late Brazilian geographer Milton Santos, in a collection of essays, *O País Distorcido* (1999)[The Distorted Country] (and an impressive series of books and articles), examined the ways in which the "body" politic is mapped onto local, national, and global geographies, each the expression of an interested distortion of territory, temporality (for example, the unreflective celebration of the quincentennial), and identity (for example, citizenship). As important as what such thinkers propose is the manner in which the debates unfold. Each announces, as had the Griot in Loreau's film *Les noms n'habitent nulle part* [Names Live Nowhere], "the lineage to which he will belong forever and of which he is but the prolongation." The path remains open for more to "find the link, however remote, between them" and the stories that connect peoples of African descent, over time, through space. The more profound challenge consists in deciphering and deconstructing those traditional canonical representations. Thus the central focus of this inquiry into performance resides in the question of staging.

Staging sets up expectations, establishes the tone of a work, and contains a thick set of working premises: point of view, setting, organization. Framing the cultural myth of European superiority, the year 1492 reads as triumph and expansion, while the cultural reality remembers that same year as the moment of the expulsion of Jews and Moors, the tragedy of inquisition and incursion, intolerance and consolidation. If narrative assumes a beginning, middle, and end (in whatever order), the tendency to start with the victim view—for example, the thankless/grateful Caliban scenario—always, already constricts the outcome and the telling of the story. Consequently, if the stories of peoples of African descent always start in the New World, that narrative posture elides a fundamental/foundational beginning, proclaiming that these characters remain always already displaced within a time-story-plot line to which they are tangential—for example, as local color, touristic diversion—be it within a narrative of imperialism, nation, or immigration.

By framing the cultural reality in 1444, the year of Portuguese exploration in West Africa, a differing historiography reveals itself. A return to the eighth century, the moment of African incursion into Europe, represents perhaps an even more destabilizing point of reference, as would a beginning that predates European contact or one that initiates its narrative with cosmological stirrings: precisely the premise of Zapata Olivella's *Changó, el gran putas* and Nsue Angüe's *Ekomo*. These narrative strategies (textual approaches) necessarily rewrite the participation and contributions of peoples of African descent in stark contrast to canonical tales that infer that peoples of African descent constitute tardy and tangential additions to the American mix (for example, José Carlos Mariátegui). Moreover, the choice of genre carries within it certain a priori assumptions as far as context, organization, and emphasis. Just as a comedy unequivocally moves toward a happy ending after a series of humorous false steps or complications, tragedy forebodes an unhappy result (for example, death, metaphorical or literal, ensuing from the gradual unraveling of a flawed hero), and, the tragicomedy promises a bittersweet outcome, lessons valuable, albeit hard-learned. More centrally, in the novels examined here, staging also refers to thematic framing whether by the rightfully suspect authorial intention or by the sometimes overzealous intervention of the critical gaze.

In contrast to the comatose and empty-handed victim, two elements—uprootedness and improvisation—stage the performance of Blackness in Latin America and, by extension, in other parts of the African Diaspora in the length and breadth of the Americas. Both elements provide the thematic framing—the much-needed historical and conceptual backdrops—within which to read the performance of a novel's actors. Uprootedness has variously personal (Adalberto Ortiz) and cosmological (Zapata Olivella) consequences. For example, Lastre Asunción's picaresque peregrinations echo those of the prototypical Lazarillo de Tormes. However, in neither case does the break with family simply read as a reaction to a "wicked" stepparent or a strange or abusive guardian. The rootlessness in the earlier tale and the uprootedness of the more recent narrative reflect a particular historical reality and, within that context, each circumstance forces the protagonist to "make do" with a host of duplicitous bosses and religious authority figures. In Lazarillo's case, the absence of the father, the resulting poverty, and the ensuing illicit relationship between his mother and the Moor respond to and criticize the senselessness of those contemporary juridical (for example, debt laws) and ecclesiastical (for example, moral laws with regard to "shacking up") sanctions at work in monarchical Spain. In juxtaposition, Lastre's situation in *Juyungo* underscores the dialectic of freedom/unfreedom (Wynter) within his liberal-national context—what Elsa Goveia describes as "a divisive kind of integration" (10)—which highlights "the conflict of directly opposed integrating factors, the particularism and the ascription of race and wealth on the one hand and the universalist, the democratic ideas of one man one vote on the other" (15).

Consequently, eliding the slave-centric version of history, Zapata Olivella's *Changó, el gran putas* draws uprootedness as part of a divine plan rather than a horrible deviation/disruption along a plotline. Accordingly, the massive tome's first of five parts centers on Africa—the land, the cosmology, the discourse. The Colombian author cleverly apes the cosmological reaccommodations practiced earlier by flat-earth skeptics and the India-dreaming Columbus, which retrospectively inserted the New World into Old World systems of meaning. If the Christian God was all-knowing and the supreme deity of all men, how did one explain heathens: the infidel Moors; the invincibly ignorant American aborigines who had heard the word but forgotten it; and the invincibly ignorant kidnapped Africans who having heard the word refused to accept it? Likewise, in this instance, the Americas—"la olvidada tierra donde Olofi dejo su huella" (83) [the forgotten land where the supreme deity Olofi left his mark]—form part of *African* Old World imaginings: "la ciega maldición de Changó" (74) [the blind curse of Changó].

Fue después, hoy, momentos no muertos
de la divina venganza

cuando [Changó] a sus súbitos
sus ekobios
sus hijos
sus hermanos
condenó al destierro en país lejano.
La risa de los niños
los pájaros sueños de los jóvenes
la heredada sabiduría de los Modimos
los huesos
los músculos
los gritos por los siglos encadenados. (80–81)

[It was afterwards, today, in undead moments
of the divine vengeance
when (Changó) condemned his subjects
his minions
his children
his siblings
to exile in a distant country.
The laughter of children,
the winged dreams of the young,
the heralded knowledge of the fully human,
their bones,
their muscles,
their shouts, chained over the centuries.]

Blending and collapsing temporal distinctions between past, present, and future—synchronicity—Zapata Olivella underscores the utter completeness, and, no less, the seeming arbitrariness of the condemnation. Capricious it is not, however, since the reprobation remains accountable to the system of knowledge akin to the Old Testament harshness of the Christian deity who likewise expelled his favored creations from Eden and later imprisoned his chosen people in Egypt. Encapsulated in a primal scream, expulsion and bondage have repercussions, both concrete—deterritorialization of the flesh-and-bone human—and intangible—the erosion of laughter, dreams, knowledge. Accordingly, a cosmic justification explicates the African presence—and experience—in the Americas where they are left

la tarea de liberarse por sí mismo
contra el verdugo, las crueles
Lobas de roja cabellera. (81)

[the task of freeing themselves by themselves
against the shame, the cruel
red haired wolves.]

The newcomers's desperation becomes as palpable as that expressed during a 1524 confrontation between an Aztec priest and Spanish missionaries where the shaman begs to be put to death "puesto que se han muerto nuestros dioses" [since our gods have died].[11] In both instances, the cosmological surety assumed in one's "own corner of reality"—extending even to sacrificial candidates or subjugated captives of intertribal warfare—evaporates. One who is banished needs to improvise.

The use of the structuring premise of uprootedness in Martínez's *Crónica de músicos y diablos* appears on a variety of levels. Here the kidnapped Africans and their heirs were neither comatose nor thankful and consequently can be shown to have been everywhere apparent in the formation of the nation. Two parallel story lines that trace assimilation and isolation (Ilie 1) provide evidence: the first as direct multiracial descendants of Pedro Guzmán, "hijodalgo español tangible y de legítima estripe" (Martínez 21) [the Spanish son of somebody of tangible and legitimate lineage], and the second as progeny of "esclavos y cimarrones" (21) [slaves and runaways]. Tellingly the opening lines of the novel proffer a mythical veracity that echoes the insistent surety of Zapata Olivella's cosmological staging: "Muchos años atrás, en el oscurecido tiempo de las antiguas leyes, cuando se hacía torres de vidrio y los conquistadores oficiaban como los empinados señorones de la existencia terrenal . . ." (21) [Many years ago, in the misty time of ancient laws, when towers were made of glass and the conquerors ruled as the grand masters of landed existence. . . .] Nonetheless, while the world drawn in Zapata Olivella's work emphasizes the divine hand in the affairs of men and women, Martínez's chronicle stresses the triumph of the man-made or the self-made as befits the secular insinuation of progress and modernity in liberal-humanist imagining. Accordingly, the thankless rebel leaves aside the passivity of earlier representations; it is a strategy reminiscent of carnival groups in 1970s Salvador da Bahia who rejected the image of the acquiescent *bom salvagem/buen salvaje*/self-effacing Caliban of the national historical narrative and opted instead to mimic the (admittedly just as problematic) Hollywood caricature of the warring Apache. In both manifestations of a brave new world, profanely secular men and women create themselves and their new circumstances and its discourses.

In this scenario, improvisation constitutes a response to the cosmological shift set in action by the Middle Passage: uprootedness and the lack of a proper course. The thematic staging assumes, first, the necessity to artfully historicize the roots of antagonism and belligerence that describe and motivate the actions of Lastre Asunción (for example, his combative relations with his father, his "brusque" treatment of women) and the retaliation of the "esclavos y cimarrones" featured in the parallel chapters in Martínez's chronicle. Second, staging poses the question of what uprootedness makes happen: the picaresque roving in the one case, the distrustful distancing in the other. Without this attention to discourse formation, the chafing against the dominant grain seems meaningless, absurd, a simple inversion of power. Rather, the historicized framing of narrative within a larger discursive tale goes hand in hand with the contextualization of narrative elements within the range of cultural practices employed to uniquely express the experience of Blackness. For example, the idea of learning to curse, suggested from the title of Stephen Greenblatt's book, insinuates that these Latin American authors of African descent have metaphorically stolen Prospero's tomes by having grasped the "idiom"—not only what narrative says, but what narrative *does*—to such an extent that these writers can then improvise, "riffing on the man's tune," turning to their own ends the conventions, formulae, and tropes typical of the style. Hence, the question of style—and concomitantly, tonal treatment, for example paradox—also represents an implicit premise of staging, as here with the bourgeois novel *Juyungo*; the chronicle of conquest, *Crónica de músicos y diablos*; and the mythical epic, *Changó, el gran putas*.

Juyungo is representative of a period of writing that follows the moment of Black awareness in the United States—the Harlem Renaissance—and in the Caribbean, Europe and Africa—Negritude—in the first third of the twentieth century, but which did not find root or wide acceptance in the Latin American world. As Lemuel Johnson observes, Black consciousness comes about "when one realizes that not only are they black, but also that they are non-white," (65) a logical leap blocked by the myth of racial harmony. This has particular resonance in the cynical paradigms of *mestizaje* and racial harmony that shape or deform the harsher reality of race relations in that region. While the Harlem Renaissance and Negritude actively sought to value Blackness, sometimes by overly essentializing its dimensions, *mestizaje* on the other hand tacitly or openly sought to erase and dilute Blackness, most often by blurring its features within the nationalistic soup, salad, or market stew of the reigning discursive moment. Nevertheless, the Ortiz novel's fundamental question remains one of racial identity staged in individual, almost autobiographical, terms.

Thus, much of the Afro-Hispanic literature written during the 1940s and 1950s is definitely angry in tone and strident in its method and denunciation of proscriptive racial practices reminiscent of the challenge to whiteness—a confrontation launched as directly if more frontally in Leroi Jones's *Dutchman* (1964) and August Wilson's *Ma Rainey's Black Bottom* (1985) as in the nonfiction of James Baldwin, Eldridge Cleaver, and Malcolm X—and evocative of the simmering discontent so much a part of the embattled perspective of Lastre Asunción. This response exemplifies the justified and predictable outcome of a coming-to-conscious visibility of the dynamics of Blackness in Latin America and a growing frustration with Latin American narratives of racial harmony and national unity based in nonproblematized *blanquecimiento* and/or *mestizaje*. However, the overwhelmingly male histories of the period remain decidedly polemical, deadly serious, and distressingly didactic, their treatise often obscuring a more rounded vision of Black community. Part of the reason for such flat characterizations and humorless plot schemes is precisely the weightiness of the thematic. Nevertheless, this staging seemingly has more to do with the effort to adapt a narrative of Blackness to the discomfited demands of the traditional canonical genres. For example, novels such as Adalberto Ortiz's *Juyungo* functioned—intentionally or unwittingly—to "color" the bourgeois novel by bronzing the brow of the protagonist: including scenes of local color that featured the bucolic descendants of field slaves, replete with shaded references to syncretic religious practices or more often superstitions (vodun, trance-inducing drums late into the night) and color-coding language to reflect the peculiarities of various Afro-Hispanic dialects (idioms) by changing "l" to "r," dropping a final "s" and sometimes even entire syllables (for example, Guillen's "pa' na'" [para nada] in the poem "Mulata"). The chromatic transformation—"just white people with deep tans" (Neely 265)—recalls that of television's father figure Robert

Young from *Father Knows Best* into Bill Cosby's Cliff Huxtabel in the *Cosby Show*.

Much like Rómulo Gallegos's *Dona Barbara* (1929)—itself a feminine recoding of the actively dominant male narrative—*Juyungo* transformed nature, in both its human and maternal configurations, into determinant protagonist: ever-threatening chaos and irrationality. The beleaguered central figure had to gather force of will and destiny in order to wage war against both philosophical and environmental demons while facing defeat from the multifaceted arbitrariness of human, natural, and supernatural nemeses. The struggle was individual, unique, even when it pretended toward universality. Lastre stood out among his fellows for exceptional strength and drive in a slim-pickings pool—disdained, envied, sometimes admired albeit grudgingly (but never dismissed), recalling the exceptionalism of Du Bois's talented tenth.

Yet, however engaging the narrative, the tale it told remained an adaptation. And the relationship between source and secondary creation, however loyal or irreverent, sets up an opposition between an orthodoxy and its "heretical" offspring. Thus *Juyungo* follows the conventions of the bourgeois novel, particularly its notions of individualism and romanticism, and akin to the theatrical recodings discussed earlier, both original and improvisation, here absent irony or parody, pose themselves as the norm. In the dialectic of man versus nature—the lush and long-winded descriptions of garden and jungle so typical of Romanticism—the central motivating conflict becomes whether the subject will conquer or atavistically succumb to the environmental forces arrayed against a teleological vision of progress and modernity. Conversely, the resulting challenge then lies in the invention of a narrative that creates its own genre, which in other words sets the stage for an expressive performance more "formulaically" consistent with the experience of the community it seeks to represent and replicate, again raising the issue of accountability stressed by Julien. In that experimental, improvisational trajectory, *Juyungo* represents a tentative first step.

As the title suggests, *Crónica de músicos y diablos* by Gregorio Martínez improvises on the chronicle, again a European narrative form traditionally apt for glorious accounts of conquest—a system of myths to justify the triumphs, and predicaments, of imperialism. Typically then, chronicles record history through the human eye, and while not histories of Olympian deities, their tone is equally as celebratory, under-propping the cultural myth of Europe based in the exploitation of the non-European. In this narrative form, an arguably interested eyewitness describes for the greater glory of church or state benefactor, and/or that of the conqueror, events deemed central in the teleological completion of narrative expectation. That is to say, all the bits and pieces are not arbitrarily chosen but indeed must seem to confirm the "rightness," the righteousness, of the final outcome, be it the victory of the warrior in battle or in the triumph of civilization among the miscreants. These sagas of winners and losers, conquerors and vanquished then provided a fitting vehicle for representations of Europeans as culture-bringers to weak-willed—albeit noble—natives and catatonic kidnapped Africans. Aping this tone, Martínez openly borrows historical documents and events and places them within a frame that itself stages history as fictions paired with facts: the story of conquest and empire consolidation—from the underside.

Similar to the *Popul Vuh* (1613) and Miguel Leon-Portilla's *Broken Spears* (1959),[12] this chronicle represents an adaptation written from the point of view of the vanquished—probably not good reading if you are a Spaniard—as jarring as it is unthinkable.

> As is well known but quickly forgotten, the victors ordinarily write history. The losers are usually silenced or, if that is impossible, they are dismissed as liars, censored for being traitors, or left to circulate harmlessly in the confined spaces of the defeated. Bringing marginalized perspectives to light is therefore a revolutionary act of some importance: it can subvert dominant understandings, it might inspire other victims to raise their voice and pen their protests, and it always forces old histories to be rewritten to include or at least respond to the vision of the vanquished.... Traditionalist authors wanted us to understand that Spaniards had triumphed against great odds and had succeeded in bringing about not only the military and political conquests but also spiritual, linguistic, and cultural ones. A defeated, silent people, we were asked to believe, had been reduced to subservience and quickly disappeared as Indians to become mestizos, or had simply retreated into rural landscapes. (J. Jorge Klor de Alva xi)

Notwithstanding, as a genre learned or taught under the aegis of the official church, in the earlier instance, the chronicle necessarily carried within it a priori aesthetic requirements and assumptions into which the aborigines had to fit their story, in order to make their tale understandable to the Spanish, including the emphasis on lineage (*limpieza de la sangre*, the nobility of the blood line), valor in battle, and fairness in triumph. Thus, the writers of the adapted chronicles had to constantly "translate" their own cultural system of meaning—and its own epic forms—into the "idiom" of the conqueror. Something, however, remains outside—glaringly outside—the dominant system of meaning. In the *Popul Vuh*, for example, the spatial arrangements of the drawings that accompany the text defy the perception of acquiescence on the part of the vanquished and, in fact, tell not just the simplistically opposite version of the tale, but, in the insistence on their native system of meaning, are slyly belligerent.

Likewise, the kidnapped Africans and transplanted *ladinos* likely adjusted the Spanish chronicle form to the familiar functions of the griot as historian who similarly plays fast and loose with fiction and fact:

> If one places the notions of history and literature into one category broadly defined as interpretations of the past, the griot as historian emerges as a "time-binder," a person who links past to present and serves as a witness to events in the present, which he or she may convey to persons living in the future. In this sense, the griot's role as historian is somewhat more dynamic and interactive than what we have in the Western tradition—the scholar who spends years in libraries going through archival sources. (Hale 23)

Thus orality again invades the writerly exercise, insinuating both synchronicity and interactivity—"traditional techniques of creativity"—in the production of "a multigeneric narrative that includes genealogies, praises, songs, etymologies, incantations, oaths, and proverbs" (Hale 23).

In this manner, Martínez cleverly "paints his own picture" by learning to curse in the bifurcated and bound languages of the chronicle: mastering in parodic fashion the accursed conventions of the one and playfully improvising on the other. Having thus set the stage, his characters can perform with bravura and a largeness/largesse usually reserved for the Prosperian entity. Two main threads, the first alluded to earlier, which follows the segregationist-insular "Esclavos y cimarrones" and a second, which traces the integrationist-assimilative strand between Black and Indigenous, celebrate belligerence as a national treasure, as in the case of central figure Bartola Aviles Chacaltana, mother of twenty-five sons (by the same husband) and social activist:

> Ya tenía ella todos los diablos de sus ancestros entreverados en la sangre. Tenía de negro y de indio, una rabia doble que la atiaba por dentro cuanto presentía el atropello. Antiguos rumores hervía bajo su piel y sentía que algo iba a ocurrir. Apretó los dentes con fuerza hasta que rechinaron con un temple más duro que el hierro. Si el capitán Eudocio Tarquino la tocaba y ella no movía un dedo, juró en nombre de todos sus antepasados que la tierra iba a tener que abrir y sorbérsela entera. Tragó saliva y apretó con más fuerza su resolución. (78)

> [She already had coursing through her blood all of the demons of her ancestors. From the Black and the Indian, she had a double dose of fury that beat inside her. Ancient rumors boiled under her skin and she sensed that something was about to happen. She clamped her teeth forcefully until they became harder than steel. If captain Eudocio Tarquino touched her, she did not move a finger, she swore in the name of all of her ancestors that the earth would have to open up and swallow her whole. She swallowed hard and pressed even more firmly her resolve.]

Absent the angst typical of the nineteenth-century creations, Oscar-winning performances abound. The bigger-than-life pioneer woman, who births her sons and continues on her way, participates in the struggle to follow the law's ruling regarding the eight-hour work day, not just for factory workers but for farm laborers as well.

Just as she embodies the Black Earth Mother, a figure popular in the length and breath of the Americas and in Africa as well, other personae in the novel deliberately recall other figures, in their improvised American reincarnation: the epic leadership of *cimarrón* Antuco Luccumi, "el pretendido alcalde del palenque de Huachipa" (67) [the acting mayor of the Huachipa fugitive settlement], reenergizes the griot figure in his roles as advisor, spokesperson, diplomat, mediator, interpreter and translator, teacher, exhorter, warrior, witness, ceremony participant. There is also the extraordinarily gifted Catalino Advíncula "alias el Nasqueño" who, "[p]ara cualquier indagción, pregunta o comentario, disponía siempre de una respuesta versada que como mandada hacer la tenía pendiente en la punta de la lengua" (66) [(f)or what-ever question or commentary, he had ready on the tip of his tongue a rhymed answer as was his rightful duty]. This description echoes that of a case of real-life verbal virtuosity recorded in *Erasmo* (Matos Mar and Carbajal):

"Aquí ha habido muy buenos negros decimistas. Eran mozos que habían nacido para esto. Figúrense que en Caqui Juan Zambrano un negro, que no sabía ni la O por redonda, analfabeto, hacía décimas que nadie las ha podido igualar. Este negro lo veía a uno y en ese mismo momento le sacaba una décima que hablaba de su cara, de su cabeza, de su ropa, o sino iba a cualquier casa y si veía algo que le gustaba: un buen caballo, un gallo, ahí mismo le sacaba su décima. (63)

[There have been very good Black dueling-poets here. For example in Caqui, Juan Zambrano, a Black guy who was completely illiterate, made up verses that no one could equal. This guy would look at some-body and in that very instant spit out a poem that spoke about his face, his head, his clothes or if not he would go to whichever house and if he saw something that he liked, a fine horse, a rooster, then and there he would make up a verse.]

In a very profound sense, these figures cannot narratively contradict the epic expectations of the chronicle genre.

Similar to Martínez, Zapata Olivella in *Changó, el gran putas* paints ex-ceptional characters, yet he will go further. His creations cannot discursively betray the universe set up for them. Rather than posing an interruption at a particular historical moment as did Ortiz or an insertion into an already-set story and by extension into its discourse, as did Martínez, the Colom-bian author establishes a cosmic, mythical justification based within African cosmological imaginings for the Africana presence and ensuing experience in the New World. This backdrop is especially important since more often than not, even when acting as the featured player, the African-descended character was always, already fundamentally misplaced in the master nar-rative of the dominant group, as in *O mulato* (1881) by Aluízio Azevedo, *Ecué-Yamba-O* (1933) by Alejo Carpentier, and *Pobre negro* (1937) by Rómulo Gallegos, to name a few. That is to say, Blackness was incorporated into the "Western architecture of signs" (Wynter "Eye," 10) as an "upside-down" fig-ure: enslaved while others were free; poor while others profited; artless while others schemed; sincere while others were unctuous. This upside-downness provided the proscenium from which to comment and denounce behaviors and practices deemed discursively unbecoming of the dominant group/discourse. Thus, Caliban's unthankfulness pointedly indicates a problem with Prospero's lax leadership style—not so unrelated to his ouster from Milan—while the knave's final gratitude signals that the hegemonic order has been reestablished. Similarly, Lastre Asunción and his aimless wandering embody a critique of the callousness of incipient multinationals and colluding petty officials, and, likewise in *Crónica*, the high level of order, justice, and well-being in the *palenque* with its cimarron-denizens, despite the most basic of conditions, stands in marked contrast with the pusillanimous opulence and self-interested greed of the *latifundistas* [land barons] and local authorities with whom they therefore rightfully and righteously feud.

Zapata Olivella cleverly creates a complete environment: a cosmology, panoply, a philosophical vision of existence, a transcendental explication of human conditions. Intriguingly, that brave new world, while formed in the image of more familiar spheres, represents neither a simple inversion of the European nor a faithful copy of the African (*see* Captain-Hidalgo 135). For example, at the end of the text, in the "Cuaderno de Bitácora: Mitología e historia," he offers a list of terms, names, and concepts used throughout the novel and their definitions. In another example, the writer creates a language and with it a mode of being/thinking by fusing multiple notions into a single word, for example, *sombraluz, sonidovista* [shadowlight, soundview]—concepts that in Western parlance stand as exclusive or antithetical. Thus this polyglot language—"made up of words, in many cases taken from European language, on a structure, a linguistic structure that is not European" (Goveia 8)—suggests a polyglot *narrative*, made up of *conventions*, *tropes*, and *formulae*, staged on narrative structures, heretical and orthodox. Latin American Blackness is just that: polyglot. And its improvisation is also a very effective way to curse.

Afterword

Parting Salvo

For Professors Sylvia Wynter and Kimberly Nance

The reasons for studying Blackness in Latin America are many: perhaps chief among them, the resolve to face a problem that proverbially poses Black-as-nothingness and to entertain the supposition of Blackness-as-being. In turn, that discussion centers on two motivations. On the one hand, if knowledge is power, undoubtedly something can be learned by knowing the dynamics of race and their impact in the cultural arena and on the cultural agenda. On the other, the specific dynamics of Blackness are arguably a measuring stick along which to gauge the depth and veracity of those stories/histories that purport to narrate the participation and contribution of given groups, their cultural production, and, ultimately, their social worth.

Yet, coming to terms with Blackness in Latin America, as elsewhere, often defies reasoned explanation. However, Wynter manages to refashion nothingness into being by affirming uprootedness—the displacement of kidnapped Africans—as "the original model of the total twentieth century disruption of man" that "anticipated by a century the dispossession that would begin in Europe with the Industrial Revolution [and] anticipated, by centuries, that exile, which in our century is now common to all" ("We Must Learn" 307). Similarly, uprisings against the institution of chattel slavery and the sojourn of peoples of African descent into and throughout the so-called New World provided stark contrast to grandiose claims of liberty, equality, and harmony and fueled the polemic regarding the very meaning of being human. The expression of Blackness—played out in the scripted or unscripted life—is then a state of out-of-awareness anticipation and an ongoing challenge to global and local knowledges.

The *need* to study Blackness in Latin American is even more compelling. The varied narratives that have been examined here eloquently argue that, in order to achieve a meaningful conception of humanness, it is necessary to recognize and decipher those embedded paradigms that systemically and systematically demonize an unprivileged other or that teasingly misshape the nonideal being into "harmless" caricature. On a first level, the need involves acknowledging the peculiarities of experience and expression by presenting a challenge to the overrepresentation (and repetition) of European/Western discourses and also of the distorted/distorting terms of North American Blackness, each taken globally as a universal interpretation of being, in one case, and Blackness, in another. Such a rethinking first disarms slave-based explanatory models content with tales of empty-handed arrival and empty-headed existence. Secondly, such a repositioning takes the wind out of the sails of a tardily rejected, segregationist paradigm against which is venially measured the harshness or blandness of racial prejudice and discrimination.

On a second level, the reiterated fragmentation of the *negro* from *lo negro*—of Black experience from Black expression—needs to be seen as a part of a discursive necessity to subvert Blackness *and* being. The effort to eclipse the relationship between peoples of African descent and their innovative cultural production signals an *absented* locus, the center that has been taken *out* "and yet is still there, dominating and dominated by the soloist's performance" (Benítiz-Rojo 20). Within the Western system of signs, Blackness remains largely "dominated by the soloist's performance," whether "soloist" refers to the liberal human individual or the exceptional Negro-citizen, a darkened figure constructed on that model. As a result, allusions to wistful metaphoric invisibility (a misreading of Ellison's original intent) and expeditions to "recuperate" mythical or esoteric beginnings share in a (deliberate) fiction, masking the ways in which history, social science, and political entities engage to a greater or lesser extent in narrative flourishes—and necessities.

However, as the texts here make clear, visibility is not the problem—Blackness is the elephant in the room—and unearthing something in plain sight artfully dodges more pressing concerns. What is needed is to make *apparent* the obvious: that, in Latin America, peoples of African descent are "still there," dominating and dominated, not by a privileged or gifted individual, but rather, as Chinweizu asserts, by a community's *collective* cultural performance of being, improvised on a sometimes ragtag array of its own peculiar references and necessities.

Accordingly, the discussion of Blackness and being cannot stop short of the kind of challenge so stridently urged by Harold Cruse in *The Crisis of the Negro Intellectual*: a critical project that could "connect up" narratives across disciplines, from "low" to "high," across time and space. Such a challenge would enlist strategies and would enunciate a critical vernacular that anticipates "opportunities for sly commentary on the master race, for riffing and improvising off the man's tune and making it fun" (Hunter Lattany, qtd. in Spencer 138). In that spirit, this project has juxtaposed, compared, and contrasted the narratives of the West, North, and South—and those of the often-elided or too romantically imagined Africa—because they are inextricably bound up together despite the interested overrepresentation of one or another version.

The artistic production of peoples of African descent is "still there" because it uniquely captures and conspires to represent the human condition—and the human comedy. Between whimsy and sobriety, propelled by anticipation and challenge, the improvisation on uprootedness reveals, in a way that staid niceties and canons cannot, a culture's deepest and most closely held beliefs about the ideal and nonideal conceptions of being. And the strategies of improvisation—off-timing, riffing, answerback, contest, versioning—make available a methodology that challenges the reiterated assertions of Black-as-nothingness and anticipates assaults on Blackness-as-being, wherever and whenever they arise. And they will continue to present themselves. Thus, both Blackness and being—each a state of being "*possessed* of soul" (Bone 156)—enable "contemporary man to be at home with his sometimes tolerable but never quite certain condition of not being at home in the world and . . . also dispose him to regard his obstacles and frustrations as well as his achievements in terms of adventure and romance" (Murray 277). Uprootedness refashions territories; improvisation plays with conventions, strategically constructing a respite, a corner of reality—and fantasy—that offers well-being and celebration. Clearly, Blackness and being are not about survival; they are about transformations. Anything else is nothingness.

Notes

In the fine tradition of e. e. cummings and bell hooks, i do not capitalize the personal subject pronoun. Unless otherwise noted, all translations are mine.

Introduction

1. One popular tale that surfaces to adjust the glaring material discrepancy is that of Cinderella and the fairy godmother, continually rescripting a common rags-to-riches plotline. For example, one version celebrates the ascension of Afro-Peruvian Susana Baca who after many years of local fame is "discovered" by David Byrne of the Talking Heads, who produces an album that hits the World Music charts, and the rest, as they say, is history (or legend, as the case may be). Likewise, the biography of Bahian singer Virginia Rodrigues has all the drama of the classic Hollywood plot where the hero overcomes a lack to arrive at a happy ending, reconfirming societal order: "Growing up in extreme poverty (her mother was a street vendor), Rodrigues sang as a youth in church choirs and ceremonies of the 'candomblé' religious cult, while working as a beautician and a domestic. Progressing to work on a production with the Olodum Street Theatre company she was spotted by Caetano Veloso who, impressed by her rich pure and passionate vocal style, acted as artistic director for her debut recording *Sol Negro*, that also featured guest appearances by Gilberto Gil, Milton Nascimento and Djavan" (search Virginia Rodrigues at http://www.keepmedia.com/pubs/Muze/2005/02/01/634508?from=search&criteria=Virginia+Rodrigues&refinePubTypeID=0). Accordingly, the "class not race" premise follows a narrative necessity to reach an a priori conclusion: economic mobility as panacea, racial harmony through the back door.

2. Since the central premise of this project is to renarrativize the usual meanings and connotations of a dehumanized Blackness, i capitalize the proper noun *Black* when the term refers to a community of humans. That "semantic" gesture underscores a difference in pre- and postconsciousness in the 1960s, which transformed peoples of African descent from passive object to active subject. In other words, black shoes may be a fashion choice, but "Black" people reflect a discursive and political position. The use of uppercase Black therefore signals and affirms the humanity and culture—and no less the struggle to achieve both—of this community.

3. See Hans Blumenburg, *The Legitimacy of the Modern Age*.

Chapter 1. Coming to Terms: Uprootedness

1. Epigraph translation note: "zauro" zorro; "zamuros" zamarros as hick or peasant.

2. Manoel [*sic*] Fraginals, quoted in Luz (21), argues a more mercantile vision of this same concept: "[D]esculturação é o processo consciente mediante o qual, com fins de

exploração econômica, se procede a desagregar a cultura de um grupo para facilitar a expropriação de riquezas naturais do território em que está estabelecido e/ou para utilizá-lo como força de trabalho barata não-qualificada. O processo de desculturação é inerente à toda forma de exploração colonial ou neocolonial" (16) [Deculturation is the conscious process by which, with the goal of economic exploration, culture becomes disassociated from a group in order to facilitate the expropriation of natural resources of a territory in which a community is established and/or in order to use its members as a source of cheap, untrained labor. The process of deculturation is inherent in all forms of colonial or neocolonial exploration].

3. See for example the fictional text *Dreaming in Cuban: A Novel* (1992) by Cristina García or the nonfiction essays *Next Year in Cuba: A Cubano's Coming-of-Age in America* (1995) by Gustavo Pérez Firmat.

4. Both Ilie's and Benítez-Rojo's texts, in their English versions, translate "desalojamiento" as uprootedness.

5. See James Gleick, *Chaos: Making a New Science* (New York: Penguin, 1988); and Paul Davies and John Gribbin, *The Matter Myth* (New York: Simon & Schuster, 1992).

6. See C.L.R. James who, writing in the appendix to the republished edition of *Black Jacobins* (1938), includes the essay "From Toussaint L'Ouverture to Fidel Castro" (1963), describing the peculiarities of Caribbean history as: "a series of uncoordinated periods of drift, punctuated by spurts, leaps and catastrophes" (391).

7. A more successful approach to the relations between humans and machines is that of Sidney Mintz in *Sweetness and Power* (New York: Penguin, 1985), which traces how the human in the differing cultural contexts of the Caribbean and Europe reacts to the technology of sugar production and the changes wrought in social order, eating habits, and systems of mercantile and cultural value. See also Mintz's *Tasting Food, Tasting Freedom: Excursions into Eating, Culture and the Past* (Boston: Beacon Press, 1996).

8. See Benítez-Rojo, especially "From Literature to Carnival" (22–32) and "Nicolás Guillén: Sugar Mill and Poetry" (112–49).

9. A first version was published in Mexico's magazine *Plural* 99 (Dec. 1979). These quotations come from the expanded version published in 1979.

10. "Professionals" here refers to the educated elite, e.g., intellectual bureaucrats and technocrats, such as those discussed by Uruguayan Angel Rama in *La ciudad letrada* (1984) and Hungarians Konrád and Szenlényi in *Intellectuals on the Road to Class Power* (1995).

11. As Hobsbawm writes in the introduction, invented tradition "includes both 'traditions' actually invented, constructed and formally instituted and those emerging in a less easily traceable manner within a brief and dateable period—in a matter of a few years perhaps—and establishing themselves with great rapidity" and "is taken to mean a set of practices, normally governed by overtly or tacitly accepted rules and of a ritual or symbolic nature, which seek to inculcate certain values and norms of behavior by repetition, which automatically implies continuity with the past" (1).

12. I paraphrase Even-Zohar who asserts that "there is no symmetry in literary inter-ference. A target literature is, more often than not interfered with by a source literature which completely ignores it" (qtd. in Moretti 56).

13. Moretti reconsiders the study of world literature, which i replace with cultural text.

14. See Robert Bone's anticipation of Gates's signifying monkey.

15. Zenón Cruz is, in this grouping, the sole representative of inner exile, marooned by his caustic observations.

16. An equally errant C.L.R. James acknowledges the Western influence in "Discovering Literature in Trinidad."

17. DeCosta concludes the passage with the sentence: "Then rebirth, re-creation, conversion and fiery baptism" (6). This redemptive tone of a phoenix rising from the ashes of the holocaust, of a people newly remade in a fit of Christian ecstasy, underscores how the African descended are often conflictingly "totally at [the] disposal" of alienating paradigms.

18. Jackson attributes "vulturistic isms" to Malcolm X. The phrase is from his February 14, 1965, address, "The Last Message," delivered at the First Annual Dignity Protection and Scholarship Award Ceremony, Detroit, Michigan.

19. A recent inundation of writing on Blacks in Argentina includes national and international efforts: George Reid; Marvin Lewis; two books by Picotti, one that actually focuses on Africa or africanisms, *La presencia africana en nuestra identidad* (1998), and the second, an anthology of seminar presentations, *El negro en la Argentina: presencia y negación* (2001); and by Liboreira, *(No) Hay negros argentinos* (1999). The reasons for the reappearance of Blackness and the language and tone of that apparition deserve further study and critical comment.

20. See discussions of intellectual indenture, the inability to enunciate a critical vernacular that analyzes the dynamics of victimization, in Wynter's "Beyond Miranda's Meanings" and "We Must Learn" and in Cruse's *The Crisis of the Negro Intellectual*. See also Francoise Lyotard's *Postmodern Condition* (1979, 1984) where the French intellectual discusses the resulting competition between victims. In Latin America, the rivalry between the heritage of slavery and the heritage of colonization expresses itself on the one hand in Cuban (so-called) antislavery novels that paint the slaver as victim, narrating the terrorization of the weaker sex and other sensitive souls or, on the other hand, through the "opresor oprimido" [oppressed oppressor] paradigm, discussed by González in the Puerto Rican context.

Chapter 2. Territoriality: Becoming Places

1. See Hall, *The Hidden Dimension*, 7–10.

2. Palmares perhaps represents the best-known example, "subject of at least two major feature-fiction films, *Ganga Zumbi* (1963) and *Quilombo* (1984); of many documentaries, notably Linduarte Norohna's *Aruanda* (1960), Vladmimir Carvalho's *Quilombo* (1975), and Samin Cherques and Moisés Weltman's *Zumbi dos Palmares* (Zumbi of Palmares, 1963); and most recently of a TV miniseries: *Zumbi, O Rei dos Palmares*

(Zumbi: King of Palmares)" (Stam 41). However, recent research in the Brazilian state of Maranhão alleges the existence of more that 500 such communities that rewrote the definitions of wealth and land use from that time into the present. Dona Mundinha Araujo, former director of the State Archives in São Luiz, Maranhão (Brazil), is at this writing preparing a text on the subject of resistance in the many, but less-known, *quilombos* of that region.

3. Stam notes that "during the dictatorship, the leftist theatrical group Arena . . . took up the theme of Zumbi-as-anticolonialist with contemporary allegorical overtones in . . . *Arena Conta Zumbi* [Arena tells the Story of Zumbi, 1965]" (231).

4. The Cuban edition of this Colombian novel carries the curiously abbreviated title *Corral de negros* (La Habana: Casa de las Américas, 1963).

5. See the book-length study *The Culture of Fiction in the Works of Manuel Zapata Olivella* by Yvonne Captain-Hidalgo.

6. Horacio Jorge Becco, editor of the 2001 edition of Rossi's *Cosas de negros*, cites the eclipsed sources.

7. The Fulleda León play *Plácido* was made into the 1984 film directed by Sergio Giral, *Plácido, the Blood of the Poet*. Of the rebellion Carpentier writes, "When the colonial authorities undertook the barbarous repression of the Escalera Conspiracy in 1844, all the whites involved were absolved, with one or two exceptions. Blacks, however, paid for all the supposed faults. The poet Plácido and the musician Pimienta were executed. The poet Juan Francisco Manzano, despite his good relationships with intellectual circles, was thrown in jail. After dedicating his best compositions to high-ranking Spaniards and writing sonnets to aristocratic ladies, Claudio Brindis de Salas, the father, was arrested and tortured by O'Donnell. After being amnestied, when he wanted to reorganize his old orchestra he found out that almost all of the musicians had been executed" (165).

8. See also Robin Moore, *Nationalizing Blackness,* and Wimberly, "The Expansion of Afro-Bahian Religious Practices in Nineteenth Century Cachoeira."

9. This umbrella group in 1998 was composed of several small Afro-Ecuadorian associations including Nelson Mandela (50 members), Martin Luther King (20), Martina Carrillo (28), Concepciones de Residentes en Quito (20), Afro-29 (39), Mujeres Africa Mía (15); and groups including Kathelete Africa Club (40), Alonso de Illescas (10), African, Son y Tambor (18), Franqueza negra (20), Canela (30), Malcolm X (25), Las Hijas de Daniel Comboni (12), Raíces Africanas (16), Negra Bonita (24), Dispierta Negro (12), Conciencia (19), Café (35). Activities varied and included dance, theatre, small business, sports, solidarity campaigns, genealogical investigation, youth workshops, and diverse seminars. Asociación Negra de Defensa y Promoción de los Derechos Humanos (ASONEDH) directed their efforts toward legal aid and human rights. Some of the groups published educational material and newsletters: *Voces negras* (Peru) and *Palenque* (Quito).

10. In just one example, Thales de Azevedo notes in *As élites de cor numa cidade brasileira*, "[O]s clubes socias e recreativos são o setor de mais difícil acesso às pessoas de cor mais escura. . . . são muito fortes os obstáculos à entrada em tais organizações

por influência de preconceitos de cor e, simultaneamente, porque as mesmas são domi-
nadas por famílias tradicionais que resistem à admissão de sócios que não sejam do seu
grupo social e económico." (141)[(S)ocial and recreational clubs are the sector of most
difficult access for people with the darkest pigment . . . the obstacles for admission in
such organizations are very strong because of color prejudice and concomitantly because those groups are dominated by traditional families that oppose the membership
of those not of the same social and economic class.]

11. See for example *Historias de vida*, a series of interviews compiled by Teresa Porze-
canski and Beatriz Santos (Uruguay); *El negro en Esmeraldas* by Julio Estupiñán Tello
(Ecuador); Cuadra's *El montuvio ecuatoriano* (Ecuador); *Erasmo* by José Matos Mar
and Jorge A. Carbajal H. (Peru); *Pasado y presente de los negros en Buenos Aires* by Juan
Carlos Coria (Argentina); and the "testimonio" of Esteban Montejo as told to Miguel
Barnet (*Biografía de un cimarrón*) (Cuba).

Chapter 3. Coming to Terms: Improvisation

1. Interview with Dorothy Parker in *New Yorker*, November 30, 1929.

2. In later texts from his Black nationalist period (*Black Music* [1968], see *Reader*,
179–209) or from his Marxist period (*The Music* [1987], in *Reader* 400–49), Baraka
will become more strident in his remarks on and framings of the "exploitation of en-
ergy for profit" (*Blues People* 187).

3. See Lemuel Johnson, *The Devil, the Gargoyle and the Buffoon* (1977) and João
Carlos Rodrigues, *O negro brasileiro e o cinema* (1988), especially the opening chapter
that discusses a dozen archetypes and caricatures.

4. See Jean Paul Sartre, "Réflexions sur la question jüive" (Paris, 1946).

5. Hippolyte Brice Sogbossi condenses the argument presented by Suzanne Lallemand (1974: 20–21).

6. This observation refers to the long-lived and ongoing discussion regarding the
Africanness of literary endeavor.

7. Hall explains, "Tradition is equated with *experience*, and experience is thought
of as being very close to if not synonymous with know-how. Know-how is one of our
prized possessions so that when we look backward, it is rarely to take pleasure in the
past itself but usually to calculate the know-how, to assess the prognosis for success in
the future" (*Silent Language* 8–9).

8. A similar phenomenon takes place in the U.S. context as evidenced in treatments
factual and fanciful of the Jazz Age. See for example the play (1975) and movie (2002)
Chicago, F. Scott Fitzgerald's *The Great Gatsby* (1925), and Ann Douglas's study *A Ter-
rible Honesty: Mongrel Manhattan in the 1920s* (New York: Farrar, Straus and Giroux,
1995).

9. The absented locus here, the reference that is not cited, seems to be Ellison and
his notion of "retreat." Note that Benítez-Rojo's (and similarly Gilroy's) emphasis on
the soloist also echoes Charles Edward Smith who describes "the art of improvisation"
where "As in folk music, two creative forces were involved, that of the group and that
of the gifted individual" (qtd. in Baraka, "Swing" 35).

10. Tine suggests that "oralite feinte" (10) represents the central characteristic of African literature in "Pour une théorie de la littérature africaine écrite" (1985).

11. See Derrida, *Of Grammatology*, qtd. in Julien 17.

12. Examples abound of that predilection for orality on display, largely unrecognized in wider cultural expressive practices: e.g., *Pregón de Marimorena* (1946) in which Uruguayan poet Virginia Brindis de Sala echoes the market call of an impoverished newspaper hawker in order to discuss the heedless comfort of her potential clients. The description of ritual, or what might be termed spirituality on display, can be found in Quince Duncan's short story "La rebelión Pocomía" and in Nsue Angüe's novel *Ekomo*.

Chapter 4. Temporality: Telling Times

1. Spencer's "our" references U.S. North American Blackness, but the possessive can fruitfully embrace the "our" of diasporic Blackness.

2. See Peter Brooks' discussion of the transformation from passivity to mastery, "Freud's Masterplot," in Shoshana Felman's *Psychoanalysis and Literature: The Question of Reading, Otherwise* (Baltimore: Johns Hopkins University Press, 1982).

3. In this passage, Hall references the geneticist Theodosius Dobzhansky.

4. See also his *Silent Language*, 7.

5. This idea of machine-made temporalities represents a popular filmic theme. Consider Charlie Chaplin's *Modern Times* (1934); the impact of the introduction of the sugar mill in *La última cena* (Gutierrez Alea, 1976); and the topic of production quotas in rare U.S.S.R. musicals featured in the documentary *East Side Story* (Ranga, 1997)and in Wajda's *Man of Marble* (1977).

6. See especially *El negro uruguayo (hasta la abolición)* (1965) and *El Carnaval de Montevideo* (1967).

7. This material is in part fruit of a panel discussion by African graduate students during African Culture Week, April 3, 2000, Indiana University, Bloomington.

8. In "Constructing the Jazz Tradition," Scott Deveaux warns of too essentialist a view of musical histories: "The envisioning of jazz as an organic entity that periodically revitalizes itself through the upheaval of stylistic change while retaining its essential identity resolved one of the fundamental problems in the writing of its history: the stigma of inferiority or incompleteness that the notion of progress inevitably attached to earlier styles. . . . Of course, this requires a conscious decision to overlook the obvious discontinuity in musical language—to say nothing of the social and cultural contexts for the music—in favor of a transcendent principle of continuity. That so few objected to this project shows how powerfully attractive a unitary narrative was" (in O'Meally, 495).

9. *African Collage*, a music workbook i believe to be the joint effort of South Africans Dorette Vermeulen and Riekie van Aswegen (University of Pretoria) (http://www.name2.org.uk/cgi-bin/robbd2/robboard.cgi?action=display&num=70), explains, "The unique sound of 'township' music is partially due to the creative way in which townspeople invent original instruments from so-called waste materials, for

example old oil cans, bottles and soda cans," (5) coupled with the use of more traditional guitar and kwela flute and, attesting to the influence of North American Jazz,
the saxophone. Likewise, African instruments that made the Middle Passage to Latin
America face the challenge of new resources and influences. As a result, some African
inspired instruments disappear because of material conditions and those that remained
faced social censure against what were considered raucous demonstrations of Africanness. See Fryer, "Three Vanished Instruments," (*Rhythms of Resistance*, 78–85), Moore,
Nationalizing Blackness (24), and Carpentier, *La música en Cuba* (chapters seven and
sixteen, "Los negros" and "Afrocubanismo" respectively).

10. Continental African urban musical forms include High-Life in Nigeria, similar
to North American jazz; juju, based in traditional Yoruba forms; and in Kenya, the
Twist and Benga. Along with the adopted electric guitar, the Benga dramatically de-
parts from call-and-response form. More teleological than circular, it builds from slow
to ever-faster rhythms without refrains. This admixture recalls a similar transformation
in Black North American music where the acoustic guitar and piano cede to the possibilities of electric guitar and organ in the development from blues to jazz, spirituals
to gospel.

11. This transition implies issues of ownership, distribution, and exploitation, ex-
acerbating these same unresolved questions in the context of traditional and popular
music. Questions revolve around respect, dubbing, and copyright. The infrastructure
for culture production and legislation—and compliance with such legislation—has yet
to be more fully, more meaningfully addressed.

12. The marketed management of taste is also the theme of Sidney Mintz's *Sweetness
and Power* (New York: Penguin, 1985).

Chapter 5. Talking Drums or Trying Times

1. In that proverbial vein, in "El factor religioso" (one of seven essays in his foundational work, *Siete ensayos de interpretación de la realidad peruana*), Peruvian Carlos
Mariátegui claims that "el negro prestó al culto católico su sensualismo fetichista, su
oscura superstición" (114) [the Black lent his fetishism and his dark superstition to the
Catholic religion]. Underscoring his point, he quotes Javier Prado (*Estado Social del
Perú durante la dominación española* [Social State of Peru during the Spanish Domina-
tion]), who offers this harsh assessment: "Embriagados completamente por el abuso
del licor, excitados por estímulos de sensualidad y libertinaje, proprios de su raza, iban
primero los negros bozlaes y después los criollos danzando con movimientos obscenos
y gritos salvajes, en las populares fiestas de diablos y gigantes, moros y cristianos, con
las que, frecuentemente, con aplauso general, acompañaban a las procesiones" (115)
[completely inebriated by the over-use of liquor, excited by the stimulus of sensuality and scandal innate to their race, the African-born first went, then the native-born
Blacks, dancing with obscene movements and savage shouts, in the popular festivals of
demons and giants, Moors and Christians, with which, frequently to general applause,
they accompanied the processions].

2. In *The Wife of His Youth*, by North American writer Charles Waddell Chesnutt

(1858–1932), a mulatto character observes: "I have no race prejudice, he would say, but we people of mixed blood are grouped between the upper and the nether millstone. Our fate lies between absorption by the white race and extinction of the black. The one doesn't want us yet, but may take us in time. The other would welcome us, but it would be for us a backward step. 'With malice towards none, with charity for all,' we must do the best we can for ourselves and those who are to follow us. Self-preservation is the first law of nature" (49).

3. These observations are in larger part based on the generous guidance of Ángel Acosta Martínez, Uruguayan percussionist, drum maker, and teacher who resides in Argentina, and the instruction of Mestres Francisco Pinheiro and Arlindo Carvalho in the workshop "Ritmos e Percussão" during the Tenth Congresso Brasileiro de Folclore, June 2002, São Luíz, Maranhão, Brasil.

4. After such an introduction, students will fail to query source texts. For example, a student from Oberlin who had obviously read Carlos Rossi's openly racist *Cosas de negros* concluded that tango and candombe were essentially one and the same. This is akin to stating that torch songs and folk music or opera and rock aren't that far apart, forgetting differences of high and low, the purloined roots, the prohibitions in the one case and the support in the other.

Chapter 6. Orality: A Word-Worldview

1. On October 12, 1492, Columbus writes in his log: "At dawn we saw naked people, and I went ashore in the ship's both, armed," later adding, "I made all the necessary declarations and had these testimonies carefully written down by the secretary." Of the natives he records, "No sooner had we concluded the formalities of taking possession of the island than people began to come to the beach, all as naked as their mothers bore them, and the women also, although I did not see more than one very young girl"; further, "They are friendly and well-dispositioned people who bare no arms except for small spears, and they have no iron," with this ominous note, "They ought to make good and skilled servants, for they repeat very quickly whatever we say to them" (1613–14).

2. Leslie Wilson in fact comments that "The feigned Puerto Rican song that Sor Juana Inés de la Cruz composed for the vespers held in honor of Saint Peter Nolasco in 1671 compares quite favorably, from the standpoint of rhythm, to Nicolás Guillén's 'Black Chant' ('Canto negro')" (93). Medieval Spanish literature transcribes African/ Black orality highlighted in dialects laced with unintelligible tribal syllables or Portuguese (as if to prove that Spain had nothing to do with slavery or the sacking and looting of Africa and its peoples). See also Horacio Jorge Becco, *El tema del negro en cantos, bailes y villancicos de los siglos XVI y XVII* (Buenos Aires: Editorial Ollantay, 1951); Howard M. Jason, "The Negro in Spanish Literature to the End of the Siglo de Oro" (in DeCosta, 29–35); and Leslie Wilson, "La Poesía Negra: Its Background, Themes and Significance" (in DeCosta, 90–104).

3. On the subject of how to approach a historiography of Afro-Hispanic literature, see Yvonne Captain, "Writing for the Future: Afro-Hispanism in a Global Criti-

cal Context," *Afro-Hispanic Review* 13.1 (Spring 1994): 3–9; Richard L. Jackson, "The Emergence of Afro-Hispanic Literature," *Afro-Hispanic Review* 10.3 (September 1991): 4–10; Edward Mullen, "Afro-Hispanic and Afro-American Literary Historiography: Comments on Generational Shifts," *College Language Association Journal* 38.4 (June 1995): 371–89; and Laurence Prescott, "Afro-Hispanic and Caribbean Literature in Recent Theory and Criticism: Affirmations and Implications," *Latin America Research Review* 31.1 (1996): 148–61.

4. This spatial fluidity recalls Faust's roots in *volk* tales and the nefarious doctor's mobility from Christopher Marlowe's England to Goethe's Germany to Klaus Mann's Austria to Hungarian director István Szabó's filmic adaptation *Mephisto*, set in Nazi Germany but with clear parallels in totalitarian regimes before and since.

5. It is quite possible that the roots of these tales go even further back or that their travels are more extensive than "North Africa." Such queries, however, go beyond the modest scope of the present examination.

Chapter 7. Refashioning Spoken Souls

1. See also Carámbula's *Negro y tambor*, 1952.

2. Caroll Mills-Young notes that the birth date varies as 1908 or 1920. In an introductory note to Young's contribution, Miriam DeCosta-Willis notes that Iris Virginia Salas took some poetic license with her name, concomitantly appropriating "a relationship with a noted Black family" (2). As in the case of North American Black poetess Phillis Wheatley, questions have arisen regarding the authorship of her work (3).

3. The title is sometimes translated as "The Call of Mary Brown."

4. The 1961 Nuevo Mundo publication of *Cuentos negros de Cuba* compiles selected stories originally published in two earlier collections, *Cuentos negros de Cuba* (1940) and *¿Por qué?...* (1948), the latter confusingly subtitled "cuentos negros de Cuba." The three works are separate albeit slightly equal.

5. Juan Liscano records 1946 as the original publication date for Arráiz's *Tío Tigre y Tío Conejo*. This project uses the sixth edition (1995) of the Monte Avila Editores 1975 reprint. I think it an interesting coincidence that the original publication date is current with the appearance of Cabrera's works, while the latest edition is current with that of Julia Cristina Ortiz Lugo's *De Arañas, Conejos y Tortugas* (1995).

6. Wynter discusses the relationship between book and text, writer and critic: "For what they show us, these essays, is that the books, as the products of the writers, have a function, at least in academic circles. There they are transformed into texts. West Indian books have a function in West Indian society. West Indian writers have none" ("We Must Learn" 308).

7. Wynter's original asserts, "Since the texts are there, to be explained, interpreted, accepted, dismissed, the interpreter replaces the writer; the critic displaces the creator" ("We Must Learn" 308).

8. The contest between documentary verité and staged document can be seen in stereotypical native Americans variously portrayed in films such as *Stagecoach* (John Ford, 1939) as the Western-genre Indian, either the civilizationally challenged warrior

(Geronimo) or the scout (cigar-store grunting stoic) or as Disney's bronze Barbie-doll Pocahontas who sings of her simpatico relationship with nature. The critical reaction to *Yo soy Rigoberta Menchú y así me nació la consciencia* exemplifies this diverging stance. In the realm of *testimonio*, the eyewitness account offers to some the "authentic" voice of the silent indigenous subaltern; for others, the autobiography is fraught with editorial interference and/or the half truths or outright lies of an unreliable narrator. The Diaries of Carolina de Jesús (Brazil) would meet with the same scrutiny as would the poetry of Phillis Wheatley (U.S.).

9. See also Gayatri Chakravorty Spivak, "Can the Subaltern Speak?" in *Marxism and the Interpretation of Culture*, ed. Cary Nelson and Lawrence Grossberg (Urbana: University of Illinois, 1988).

10. See discussions of the carefully preserved colonial documents that register complaints and growing sanctions regarding Black ritual and artistic production (e.g., music) in Bahia (Kraay), Cuba (Moore), Argentina, and Puerto Rico.

11. See Alejo Carpentier and Robin Moore on the tenuous balancing act required of these musicians to play a music not too Black.

12. In the same short story collection, Cartagena Portalatín employs this same methodology in "Tête-à-tête con Teresa de Ávila" and in "Tire el juego," a tale that confronts "Mr. Hemingway" with his betrayal of Gertrude Stein.

13. Satiric indirection is evident in the short stories of Charles Chesnutt (U.S.), the tales of Simple by Langston Hughes (U.S.), and the disarming tone often employed by Zora Neale Hurston (U.S.). The same strategies of indirection, staged as a response to totalitarian and paternalistic governments, are a part of Eastern European artistic discourse: see for example Elmér Hankiss's critical exposition and the films of Hungarian István Szabó and Polish Andrzej Wajda (e.g., *Man of Marble*).

14. The juxtaposition of practical and fantastic solutions represents a telling difference, indicative of a trend in Black women's writing in novels such as Toni Morrison's *Beloved* and Nsue Angüe's *Ekomo* that, despite the desperate realities with which their novels deal, resolve the central conflict of the narrative with a fantastic denouement. A similar example whose meaning nevertheless diverges can be found in *Como agua para chocolate* by Laura Esquivel (México, D.F.: Editorial Planeta Mexicana, 1989), and the later film version directed by Alfonso Arau (1992).

Chapter 8. Blackness Unbound: A Tale of One's Own

1. An early version of this material was presented at the Latin American Studies Association, Washington, D.C., September 2001, as part of a panel organized by Denise Corte of the University of Maryland; it benefitted at that time from the encouragement of fellow panelist Patricia Gonzalez, Smith College.

2. These plays take inspiration from Bertolt Brecht, featuring characters who possessed a growing self-awareness of the need for a proper course. See for example: *Three Penny Opera*, *Mother Courage*, and *Galileo* (which examines Soviet show trials in the thinly veiled context of the Italian inventor's condemnation for heresy for his assertion of the earth's roundness).

3. This character, reminiscent of the griot-guide, can be found in prose (Zapata Olivella) and is favored in theatre as well, e.g., Wensley in *Cabaré da RRRRRaça* and Caliban in Césaire's *A Tempest*.

4. I believe this last line is borrowed from Aimé Césaire.

5. Off topic but still intriguing: John Ford's 1939 classic western *Stagecoach* starring John Wayne reenacts a similar case of mistaken female identity where the protagonist, the Ringo Kid, seemingly never realizes that his new-found love is a saloon "hostess" of dubious reputation, who has recently been railroaded out of town by the ladies' auxiliary.

6. A version of this material was presented at the Midwest Modern Language Association, November 2000, in Kansas City, Missouri. Prepared during a residency at Center for Cultural Studies, Oakes College at University of California, Santa Cruz, the text benefited from comments by panel organizer James Pancrazio and editorial suggestions from fellow panelists.

7. When real-life personalities are painted with the brush of the folk negro or the material negro, the protagonist seems to behave according to form because narrative and discourse tend to restrict other interpretations. Thus the exceptionalism as described by Du Bois does not prove the openness or the permeability of systems plagued by systemic racism, but rather acts as a carefully regulated release valve alleging that some can make it and insinuating that those who do not are not applying themselves.

8. Caracas: Dirección de Cultura, Universidad Central de Venezuela, 1996.

9. San Juan: Instituto de Cultura Puertorriqueña, 1979.

10. Cambridge: Cambridge University Press, 2002.

11. This quotation i believe can be found in Miguel Leon-Portilla's 1959 *Broken Spears*.

12. The original title of Leon-Portilla's *Broken Spears* is *Visión de los vencidos; relaciones indígenas de la Conquista* (Mexico: Universidad Nacional Autónoma, 1959).

Bibliography

Achebe, Chinua. *Morning Yet on Creation Day: Essays*. Garden City, N.Y.: Anchor Books, 1976.

———. *Things Fall Apart*. 1958. New York: Fawcett, 1989.

Aguilera-Malta, Demetrio. *Infierno negro*. *Teatro completo*. Mexico: Finisterre, 1970. 291–343.

———. *Canal Zone*. México: Mortiz, 1977.

———. *El tigre*. 1955. Dauster and Lyday, 91–110.

Allende, Isabel. *Eva Luna*. 2d ed. Buenos Aires: Editorial Sudamericana, 1987.

Andersen, Benedict. *Imagined Communities: Reflections on the Origin and Spread of Nationalism*. London: Verso, 1983.

Andrews, George Reid. *The Afro-Argentines of Buenos Aires: 1800–1900*. Madison: University of Wisconsin Press, 1980.

Annaud, Jean-Jacques, dir. *Noirs et blancs en couleur* [*Black and white in color*]. France, 1976.

Armendáriz, Montxo, dir. *Cartas de Alou* [*Letters from Alou*]. Spain, 1990.

Arraíz, Antonio. *Tío Tigre y Tío Conejo*. 1946. Caracas: Monte Avila Editores, 1975; 6th ed., 1995.

Arriví, Francisco. *Vejigantes*. 1958. *Máscara puertorriqueña*. Río Piedras: Editorial Cultural, 1971. 245–366.

Ayestarán, Lauro. "La Música Negra." *La Música en el Uruguay*. Montevideo: SODRE, 1953.

Azevedo, Aluízio. *O mulato*. 1881. São Paulo: Livraria Martins Editora, 1964.

Azevedo, Thales de. *As élites de cor numa cidade brasileira: um estudo de ascensão social & classes sociais e grupos de prestígio*. Rio de Janeiro: Editora Nacional, 1955. First published Paris 1953 by UNESCO as *Les élites de couleur dans une ville brésillienne*.

Baker, Houston A., Jr. *Blues, Ideology, and Afro-American Literature: A Vernacular Theory*. Chicago: University of Chicago Press, 1984.

———. *Modernism and the Harlem Renaissance*. Chicago: University of Chicago Press, 1987.

Baldwin, James. *Notes of a Native Son*. Boston: Beacon Press, 1955.

Baraka, Amiri (née LeRoi Jones). *Dutchman* and *The Slave, Two Plays*. New York: Morrow, 1964.

———. *The LeRoi Jones/Amiri Baraka Reader*. Ed. William J. Harris. 2nd ed. New York: Thunder's Mouth Press, 1995.

———. *The Music: Reflections on Jazz and Blues*. New York: William Morrow and Company, 1987. In Donnell and Lawson Welsh, 400–49.

———. *Black Music*. New York: William Morrow and Company, 1968.

———. "Swing—From Verb to Noun." *Blues People*. New York: William Morrow and Company, 1963. In Donnell and Lawson Welsh, 33–50.

———. "African Slaves/American Slaves: Their Music." Originally from *Blues People*, 1963. In *Reader*, 21–32.

Barnet, Miguel. *Biografía de un cimarrón*. La Habana: Academia de Ciencias de Cuba, Instituto de Etnología y Folklore, 1966.

Barnstone, Willis, and Tony Barnstone. *Literatures of Asia, Africa, and Latin America*. Upper Saddle River, N.J.: Prentice Hall, 1999.

Bastide, Roger. *African Civilisations in the New World*. New York: Harper & Row, 1971.

Benítez, Daniel. *Tarmas: historia y tradición*. Caracas: Dirección de Cultura, Universidad Central de Venezuela, 1993.

Benítez-Rojo, Antonio. *The Repeating Island: The Caribbean and the Postmodern Perspective*. Trans. James E. Maraniss. Durham: Duke University Press, 1992.

Blumenburg, Hans. *The Legitimacy of the Modern Age*. Cambridge: MIT Press, 1983.

Bogéa, Lopes, and Antônio Viera. *Os Pregões de São Luís*. Brazil: Cultural Foundation of Maranhão, 1980 (book)/1988(LP). Audio CD released 1999 as *Pregoeiros*.

Bollaín, Icíar, dir. *Flores de otro mundo* [*Flowers from another world*]. Spain/Dominican Republic, 1999.

Bone, Robert. *Down Home: A History of Afro-American Short Fiction from Its Beginning to the End of the Harlem Renaissance*. New York: Putnam, 1975.

Bottaro, Marcelino. "Rituales y Candombes." In Nancy Cunard, ed., *Negro Anthology*. London: Wishart and Company, 1934. 519–22.

Brindis de Salas, Virginia. *Cien cárceles de amor*. Montevideo: n.p., 1949.

———. *Pregón de Marimorena*. Montevideo: Sociedad Cultural Editora Indoamericana, 1946.

Burton, Julianne, ed. *Cinema and Social Change in Latin America: Conversations with Filmmakers*. Austin: University of Texas Press, 1986.

Cabrera, Lydia. *Ayapá, cuentos de Jicotea*. Miami: Ediciones Universal, 1971.

———. "Contes cubains." *Revue de Paris* 42.1 (1935): 905–26.

———. *Cuentos negros de Cuba*. (Compilation) La Habana: Ediciones Nuevo Mundo, 1961.

———. *Cuentos negros de Cuba*. La Habana: La Verónica, 1940.

Calvino, Italo. *The Uses of Literature: Essays*. Trans. Patrick Creagh. San Diego: Harvest/Harcourt Brace, 1982.

Captain-Hidalgo, Yvonne. *The Culture of Fiction in the Works of Manuel Zapata Olivella*. Columbia: University of Missouri Press, 1993.

Carámbula, Rubén. *Negro y tambor: Poemas, pregones, danzas y leyendas sobre motivos del folklore afro-rioplatense*. Buenos Aires: Editorial Folklórica Americana, 1952.

———. *Pregones del Montevideo Colonial: Candombe, Comparsa de Negros Lubolos, Poesía, Música, Prosa*. Montevideo: Editores Mosca Hermanos, Sociedad Anónima, 1987.

Carbonell, Walterio. "Birth of a National Culture." Trans. Jean Stubbs. Sarduy and Stubbs, 195–203.

———. *Crítica: Cómo surgió la cultura nacional*. La Habana: Ediciones Yaka, 1961.

Cardoso, Jorge E. *El desalojo de la calle de los negros*. N.p., 1992.

Carpentier, Alejo. *Music in Cuba*. Ed. Timothy Brennan. Trans. Alan West-Durán. Minneapolis: University of Minnesota Press, 2001.

———. *Écue-yamba-ó!* Barcelona: Bruguera, 1979.

———. *La música en Cuba*. 1946, 1979. México: Fondo de Cultura, 1988.

Carroll, Patrick J. *Blacks in Colonial Veracruz: Race, Ethnicity, and Regional Development*. Austin: University of Texas, 1991.

Cartegena Portalatín, Aída. *Culturas africanas: Rebeldes con causa*. Santo Domingo: Taller, 1986.

———. "La llamaban Aurora (Pasión por Donna Summer)." *Tablero: Doce cuento de lo popular a lo culto*. Santo Domingo: Editora Taller, 1978. 13–17.

Carvalho Neto, Paulo. *El Carnaval de Montevideo*. Sevilla: Publicaciones del Seminario Antropológico Americano, 1967.

———. *El negro uruguayo (hasta la abolición)*. Quito: Editora Universitaria, 1965.

Césaire, Aimé. *A Tempest: Based on Shakespeare's The Tempest: Adaptation for a Black Theatre*. 1985. Trans. Richard Miller. New York: Ubu Repertory Theater, 1992.

Chinweizu. "Deriding the Derridians." *Decolonising the African Mind*. Lagos, Nigeria/London: Pero Press, 1987. 231–41.

———. "Literature and Nation Building in Africa." In *Decolonising*, 211<n>30.

———. "Pan-Africanism and the Nobel Prize." In *Decolonising*. 175–83.

———. "What the Nobel Is Not." In *Decolonising*. 184–200.

Chirimini, Tomás Olivera, and Juan Antonio Varese. *Memorias de Tamboril/Memories of the Drum*. Montevideo: Editorial Latina, 1996.

Clave, Luís Miguel. "A ti si te cumben. Una historia de lo afroandino en el Perú." *El Comercio* (Lima), 26 agosto 1995.

Cleaver, Eldridge. *Soul on Ice*. New York: McGraw-Hill, 1968.

Cobb, Martha. *Harlem, Haiti, and Havana: A Comparative Critical Study of Langston Hughes, Jacques Roumain, Nicolás Guillén*. Washington, D.C.: Three Continents Press, 1979.

Cole, Catherine M. *Ghana's Concert Party Theatre*. Bloomington: University of Indiana Press, 2001.

Columbus, Christopher. "Excerpts from *The Log of Christopher Columbus*." Trans. Robert H. Fuson. Camden, Maine: International Marine/McGraw Hill, 1992. In Barnstone and Barnstone, 1606–28.

Condé, Maryse. *Tree of Life* [*La vie scélérate*, 1987]. Trans. Victoria Reiter. New York: Ballantine Books, 1992.

Coria, Juan Carlos. *Pasado y presente de los Negros en Buenos Aires*. Buenos Aires: Editorial J. A. Roca, 1997.

Crouch, Stanley. "Blues to Be Constitutional: A Long Look at the Wild Wherefores of Our Democratic Lives as Symbolized in the Making of Rhythm and Tune." O'Meally, 152–65.

Cruse, Harold. *The Crisis of the Negro Intellectual: A Historical Analysis of the Failure of Black Leadership.* 1967. New York: Quill, 1984.

Cuadra, José de la. *El montuvio ecuatoriano: ensayo de presentación.* 1937. Quito: Libressa and Universidade Andina Simón Bolivar, 1996.

Dauster, Frank, and Leon F. Lyday, eds. *En un acto: diez piezas hispanoamericanas.* 2nd ed. Boston: Heinle and Heinle, 1983.

Dávila (Malavé), Ángela María. *Animal fiero y tierno.* Río Piedras, Puerto Rico: QeAse, 1977.

DeCosta, Miriam, ed. *Blacks in Hispanic Literature.* Port Washington, N.Y.: National University Press, 1977.

DeCosta-Willis, Miriam, ed. *Daughters of the Diaspora: Afra-Hispanic Writers.* Kingston: Ian Randle Publishers, 2003.

Derrida, Jacques. *Of Grammatology.* 1967. Trans. Gayatri Spivak. Baltimore: Johns Hopkins University Press, 1976.

Deveaux, Scott. "Constructing the Jazz Tradition." O'Meally, 483–512.

Díaz Sánchez, Ramón. *Cumboto, cuentos de siete leguas.* Caracas: Ministerio de Educación, 1960.

Diegues, Carlos, dir. *Quilombo.* Brazil, 1984.

Dobzhansky, Theodosius. "The Genetic Basis of Evolution." *Scientific American.* January 1950.

Donnell, Alison, and Sarah Lawson Welsh, eds. *The Routledge Reader in Caribbean Literature.* London: Routledge, 1996.

Duncan, Quince. "La rebelión Pocomía." *La rebelión Pocomía y otros relatos.* San José, Costa Rica: Editorial Costa Rica, 1976.

Early, Gerald, ed. *Lure and Loathing: Essays on Race, Identity, and the Ambivalence of Assimilation.* New York: Penguin, 1993.

Echeverría, Esteban. "El matadero." 1840. *La cautiva—El matadero.* Buenos Aires: Editorial Losada, 1984.

Elgood, Rick, and Don Letts, dirs. *Dancehall Queen.* Jamaica, 1997.

Ellison, Ralph. "The Golden Age, Time Past." O'Meally, 448–56.

———. "The Golden Age, Time Past." *Shadow and Act.* 1964. New York: Vintage Books, 1972. 199–212.

Estupiñán Bass, Nelson. *Curfew.* Trans. Henry J. Richards. Washington, D.C.: Afro-Hispanic Institute, 1992.

———. *Toque de queda.* Colección Letras del Ecuador no. 69. Guayquil: Casa de la Cultura Ecuatoriana, Núcleo del Guayas, 1978.

Estupiñán Tello, Julio. *El negro en Esmeraldas: Apuntes para su estudio.* 1967. Quito: Editorial Formularios y Sistemas, 1996.

Felistoque, Edú, and Nereu Cerdeira, dirs. *Drought* [*Soluços e Soluções*]. Brazil, 2000.

Finnegan, Ruth. *Oral Literature in Africa.* Oxford: Oxford University Press, 1970.

Fraginals, Manuel M. "Aportes culturales y desculturación." *Africa en América Latina.* México: UNESCO/Siglo Veintiuno, 1977.

Franco, Aninha. *A Conspiração dos Alfaiates* [*The Tailors' Conspiracy*]. (Play) 1992.

Franco, Jean. "Criticism and Literature within the Context of a Dependent Culture." Occasional Papers, no. 16. New York University: Ibero-America Language and Area Center, 1975.

———. *Historia de la literatura hispanoamericana a partir de la independencia.* Trans. Carlos Pujol. Barcelona: Ariel, 1975.

Frigerio, Alejandro. "Estudios sobre los Afrouruguayos: Una revisión crítica." Buenos Aires: Cuadernos del Instituto Nacional de Antropología y Pensamiento Latinoamericano, no. 16, 1995. 411–22.

Fryer, Peter. *Rhythms of Resistance: African Musical Heritage in Brazil.* London: Pluto Press, 2000.

Fulleda León, Gerardo. *Chago de Guisa.* La Habana: Casa de las Américas, 1989.

———. *Plácido.* 1967–1975. *Algunos dramas de la colonia.* La Habana: Letras Cubanas, 1984.

———. *La querida de Enramada.* 1981. La Habana: TREME (Unión de Escritores y Artistas Cubanas), 1989.

———. "El rito como fuente de teatro contemporáneo." *Société suisse del Américanistes/ Schweizerische Amerikaisten-Gesellschaft Bulletin* 59–60 (1995–96): 133–37.

———. *Ruandi.* 1977. La Habana: Editorial Gente Nueva, 1988.

Gallegos, Rómulo. *Pobre negro.* Caracas: Editorial Elite, 1937.

Gálvez Ronceros, Antonio. *Monólogo desde las tinieblas.* Lima: INTI-Sol Editores, 1975.

García, Cristina. *Dreaming in Cuban: a Novel.* New York: Knopf/Random House, 1992.

García, Jesús "Chucho." *Barloventeñidad: aporte literario.* Caracas: Ediciones Los Heraldos Negros (Fundación Afroamericana), 1997.

García, Juan. "El tigre y el conejo." *Cuentos y décimas afro-esmeraldeñas.* 2nd ed. Quito: Ediciones Abya-Yala, 1988. 107–16.

———. "Introducción." In *Cuentos.* 7–8.

García Márquez, Gabriel. *El amor en los tiempos de cólera* [*Love in the time of cholera*]. 1980. Buenos Aires: Editorial Sudamérica, 1985.

Garganigo, John, et al. *Huellas de las literaturas hispanoamericanas.* Upper Saddle River, N.J.: Prentice Hall, 1992.

Gilroy, Paul. *The Black Atlantic: Modernity and Double Consciousness.* Cambridge: Harvard University Press, 1993.

Giral, Sergio, dir. *Plácido, the Blood of the Poet.* Cuba, 1984.

Godzich, Wlad. "Language, Images, and the Postmodern Predicament." In Gumbrecht, *Materialities.* 355–70.

Goldberg, David Theo. *Racist Culture: Philosophy and the Politics of Meaning.* Oxford: Blackwell, 1993.

González, José Luis. "El país de cuatro pisos (Notas para una definición de la cultura puertorriqueña).” *El país de cuatro pisos y otros ensayos*. 1980. Río Piedras, Puerto Rico: Ediciones Huracán, 1989. 11–42.

Gordon, Edmund T. *Disparate Diasporas: Identity and Politics in an African-Nicaraguan Community*. Austin: University of Texas Press, Institute of Latin America Studies, 1998.

Goveia, Elsa. “The Social Framework.” *Savacou: A Journal of the Caribbean Artists Movement* 2 (Sept. 1970): 7–15.

Graden, Dale T. “‘So Much Superstition Among These People!’ Candomblé and the Dilemmas of Afro-Bahian Intellectuals, 1864–1871.” In Kraay, 57–73.

Greenblatt, Stephen. *Learning to Curse: Essays in Early Modern Culture*. New York: Routledge, 1990.

Guamán Poma de Ayala, Felipe. *Primer nueva corónica y buen gobierno*. 1613. 1st ed., 3 vols. Edición crítica de John V. Murra y Rolena Adorno. Mexico: Siglo Veintiuno, 1980.

Guillén, Nicolás. *Motivos de son*. 1930. La Habana: Editorial Letras Cubanas, 1980.

Gumbrecht, Hans Ulrich, and K. Ludwig Pfeiffer, eds. *Materialities of Communication*. Trans. William Whobrey. Stanford: Stanford University Press, 1994.

Gutiérrez Alea, Tomás, dir. *La última cena* [*The Last Supper*]. Cuba, 1976.

Guy, Rosa. *My Love, My Love or The Peasant Girl*. New York: Holt, Rinehart, 1985.

Hale, Thomas A. *Griots and Griottes*. Bloomington: Indiana University Press, 1998.

Haley, Alex. *The Autobiography of Malcolm X; with the assistance of Alex Haley*. London: Hutchinson, 1966.

Hall, Edward T. *Beyond Culture*. 1976. Garden City, N.Y.: Anchor, 1977.

———. *The Hidden Dimension*. 1951. Garden City, N.Y.: Anchor, 1969.

———. *The Silent Language*. 1959. Garden City, N.Y.: Anchor, 1973.

Hankiss, Elemér. *East European Alternatives*. Oxford: Clarendon Press, 1990.

Hebdige, Dick. *Cut 'n' Mix: Culture, Identity and Caribbean Music*. London: Methuen, 1987.

Hiriart, Rosario. “Prólogo.” In Cabrera, *Cuentos negros de Cuba*. Barcelona: Icaria, 1997.

———. “El tiempo y los símbolos en *Cuentos negros de Cuba*.” In Sanchéz et al., 31–34.

Hobsbawm, Eric, and Terence Ranger. *The Invention of Tradition*. 1983. Cambridge: Cambridge University Press, 1997.

Hünefeldt, Christine. *Las Manuelos, vida cotidiana de una familia negra en la Lima del siglo XIX: una reflexión histórica sobre la esclavitud urbana*. Lima: IEP Ediciones, 1992.

Hunter Lattany, Kirstin. “Off-Timing: Stepping to the Different Drummer.” In Early, 163–74.

Hurston, Zora Neale. *Their Eyes Were Watching God*. 1937. New York: HarperCollins, 1990.

Ilie, Paul. *Literature and Inner Exile: Authoritarian Spain, 1939–1975*. Baltimore: Johns Hopkins University Press, 1980.

Immerfall, Stefan. “Territory and Territoriality in the Globalizing Society: An Introduction." *Territoriality in the Globalizing Society: One Place or None?* Eds. Stefan Immerfall and Jürgen von Hagen. New York: Springer, 1998. 1–16.

Isaacs, Jorge. *Maria.* 1867. La Habana: Casa de las Américas, 1970.

Jackson, Richard L. *Black Writers in Latin America.* Albuquerque: University of New Mexico Press, 1979.

James, C.L.R. "Discovering Literature in Trinidad." In Donnell and Lawson Welsh, 163–65.

———. "From Toussaint L'Ouverture to Fidel Castro." *The Black Jacobins.* 1938. New York: Vintage, 1963.

———. *Notes on Dialectics: Hegel, Marx, Lenin.* 1948. Westport, Conn.: Lawrence Hill, 1980.

———. "Triumph." In Donnell and Lawson Welsh, 84–90.

Johnson, Lemuel. *The Devil, the Gargoyle and the Buffoon: The Negro as Metaphor in Western Literature.* Port Washington, N.Y.: Kennikat Press, 1977.

Julien, Eileen. *African Novels and the Question of Orality.* Bloomington: Indiana University Press, 1992.

Kennedy, James H., ed. *Relatos latinoamericanos: la herencia africana.* 2nd ed. New York: Glencoe/McGraw-Hill, 1992.

Klor de Alva, J. Jorge. "Foreword." In Leon-Portilla, xi–xxiv.

Konrád, György. *The Melancholoy of Rebirth: Essays from Post Communist Central Europe 1989–1994.* New York: Harcourt, 1995.

Konrád, György, and Ivan Szenlényi. *Intellectuals on the Road to Class Power: A Sociological Study of the Role of the Intelligentsia in Socialism.* Trans. Andrew Arato and Richard E. Allen. New York: Harcourt Brace, 1979.

Kraay, Hendrik, ed. *Afro-Brazilian Culture and Politics: Bahia, 1790s to 1990s.* New York: M. E. Sharpe, 1998.

Laguerre, Michel. "The Voodooization of Politics in Haiti." Whitten and Torres, Tome 2: 495–540.

Lallemand, Suzanne. "'Tete en loques': Insulte et pedagogie chez les Mosi." Cahiers d'Etudes Africaines (Paris, France) (15), 1975, 649–67.

Lee, Spike, dir. *Malcolm X.* U.S., 1992.

Leon-Portilla, Miguel. *The Broken Spears: The Aztec Account of the Conquest of Mexico.* 1959. Boston: Beacon Press, 1992.

Levine, Lawrence W. *Black Culture and Black Consciousness: Afro-American Folk Thought from Slavery to Freedom.* Oxford: Oxford University Press, 1977.

Lewis, Marvin A. *Afro-Argentine Discourse: Another Dimension of the Black Diaspora.* Columbia: University of Missouri Press, 1996.

———. *Afro-Hispanic Poetry, 1940–1980: From Slavery to Negritude in South American Verse.* Columbia: University of Missouri Press, 1983.

———. *Ethnicity and Identity in Contemporary Afro-Venezuelan Literature: A Culturalist Approach.* Columbia: University of Missouri Press, 1992.

———. *Treading the Ebony Path: Ideology and Violence in Contemporary Afro-Colombian Prose Fiction.* Columbia: University of Missouri Press, 1987.

Liboreira, M. Cristina. *(No) Hay negros argentinos*. Buenos Aires: Editorial Duncan, 1999.

Liscano, Juan. "Prólogo." In Arraíz, 7–13.

Lopéz Albújar, Enrique. *Cuentos andinos*. 1920. Lima: Peisa, 1955.

———. *De la tierra brava: Poemas Afroyungas*. Lima: Impreso por Editora Peruana, 1938.

———. *De mi casona*. Lima: Imprenta "Lux" de E. L. Castro, 1924.

———. *Matalaché: novela retaguardista*. 1928. La Habana: Casa de las Américas, 1978.

Loreau, Dominique, dir. *Les noms n'habitent nulle part* [*Names live nowhere*]. Belgium, 1994.

Lorriaga, Nené. *Carimba*. Buenos Aires: Editorial Amerindia, 1988.

Luz, Marco Aurélio. *Cultura Negra e Ideologia do Recalque*. 1983. Salvador: Edições SECNEB (Sociedade de Estudos da Cultura Negra no Brasil), 1994.

Lyotard, Jean-François. *The Postmodern Condition: A Report on Knowledge*. 1979. Trans. Geoff Bennington and Brian Massumi. Theory and History of Literature, vol. 10. Minneapolis: University of Minnesota Press, 1984.

Mackey, Nathaniel. "Other: From Noun to Verb." In O'Meally, 513–32.

Malone, Jaqui. "Jazz Music in Motion: Dancers and Big Bands." In O'Meally, 278–97.

———. "Jazz Music in Motion: Dancers and Big Bands." *Steppin' on the Blues: The Visible Rhythms of African American Dance*. Urbana: University of Illinois Press, 1996. 91–110.

Manuel, don Juan. *El Conde Lucanor*. 9th ed. Ed. Enrique Moreno Baez. Madrid: Editorial Castalia, 1977.

Mariátegui, José Carlos. "El factor religioso." *Siete ensayos de interpretación de la realidad peruana*. 1928. Caracas: Biblioteca Ayacucho, 1979. 105–25.

———. "El proceso de la literatura: las corrientes de hoy." *Siete*, 216–28.

Mariñez, Pablo A. *Nicomedes Santa Cruz: decimistan poeta y folklorista afroperuano*. San Luís Potosí, Mexico: Instituto de Cultura, 2000.

Martínez, Gregorio. *Crónica de músicos y diablos*. Hanover, N.H.: Ediciones del Norte, 1991.

Matamoro, Blas. *Historia del tango*. Buenos Aires: Centro Editor de América Latina, 1971.

Matos Mar, José, and Jorge A. Carbajal H. *Erasmo: Yanacón del valle de Chancay*. Lima: Instituto de Estudios Peruanos, 1974.

Mbiti, John S. *Introduction to African Religion*. 1975. 2nd rev. ed. Melbourne: Heinemann Educational Publishers, 1991.

Meirelles, Márcio/Bando de Teatro Olodum. *Cabaré da RRRRRaça*. Dir. Marcio Meirelles. August 8, 1997. Program and play text. Salvador da Bahia: n.p., 1997.

———. *Essa é nossa praia*. In *Trilogia*, 53–94.

———. *Trilogia do Pelô*. Salvador: Fundação Casa de Jorge Amado, Grupo Cultural Olodum, 1995.

Mijares, María Marta. *Racismo y endoracismo en Barlovento*. Caracas: Ediciones Los Heraldos Negros, 1997.

Mills-Young, Carol. "The Unmasking of Brindis de Salas: Minority Discourse of Afro-Uruguay." DeCosta-Willis, 11–24.

Molino, Tirso de. *El burlador de Sevilla y convidado de piedra*. Salamanca: Almar, 1978.

Moore, Robin D. *Nationalizing Blackness: Afrocubanismo and Artistic Revolution in Havana, 1920–1940*. Pittsburgh: University of Pittsburgh Press, 1997.

Moretti, Franco. "Conjectures on World Literature." *New Left Review* 2 (January/February 2000): 54–68.

Muñoz, Angel, dir. *Nueba Yol [New York]*. Dominican Republic, 1995.

Murray, Albert. "Improvisation and the Creative Process." In O'Meally, 111–13, 277.

Nassy Brown, Jacqueline. *Rooted in the Global, Routed through the Local: Cosmopolitanism in Liverpool's Age of Sail*. Princeton, N.J.: Princeton University Press, 2005.

Neely, Barbara. *Blanche Passes Go*. New York: Penguin, 2000.

Ngangura, Mweze, dir. *Pièces d'Identité [I.D.]*. Belgium/Congo, 1998.

Nsue Angüe, María. *Ekomo*. Madrid: Universidad Nacional de Educación a Distancia, 1985.

Obeso, Candelario. *Cantos populares de mi tierra: antología poética de los olvidados*. Bogotá: Alcaldía Mayor de Bogotá, Instituto Distrital de Cultura y Turismo, Observatorio de Cultura Urbana: Fundación Cultural y Ambiental Candelario Obeso, 2004.

Olliz Boyd, Antonio. "The concept of Black awareness as a thematic approach to Latin American literature." In DeCosta. 65–73.

O'Meally, Robert G., ed, *The Jazz Cadence of American Culture*. New York: Columbia University Press, 1998.

Ortiz, Adalberto. *Juyungo*. 1943. La Habana: Colección Literatura Latinoamericana, Casa de las Américas, 1982.

Ortiz, Fernando. *Los cabildos y la fiesta afrocubanos del Día de Reyes*. 1920, 1921. La Habana: Editorial de Ciencias Sociales, Colección Fernando Ortiz, 1992.

Ortiz Lugo, Julia Cristina. *De Arañas, Conejos y Tortugas: Presencia de Africa en la Cuentística de Tradición Oral en Puerto Rico*. San Juan: Centro de Estudios Avanzados de Puerto Rico y el Caribe, 1995.

Pacheco, José Emilio. *Islas a la deriva (Poemas 1973–1975)*. 1976. Mexico: Ediciones Era, 1985.

Padilla Pérez, Maybell. "Los cabildos afrocubanos: Génesis." *Anales del Caribe* 14/15 (1995): 137–41.

Peixoto, Afrânio. *Clima e saude*. São Paulo: Nacional, 1938.

Pereira dos Santos, Nelson. "Toward a Popular Cinema." Interview with Randal Johnson. In Burton, 133–41.

Pérez Colman, Mario. "La cultura negra en Uruguay: Resuena el último tambor." 56–63.

Pérez Firmat, Gustavo. *Next Year in Cuba: a Cubano's Coming-of-Age in America*. New York: Anchor, 1995.

Picotti, Dina V. *El negro en la Argentina: presencia y negación*. Buenos Aires: Editores de América Latina, 2001.

———. *La presencia africana en nuestra identidad*. Buenos Aires: Ediciones del Sol, 1998.

Pizarroso Cuenca, Arturo. *La cultura negra en Bolivia*. La Paz: Ediciones Isla, 1997.

Plácido. *Poesías—Gabriel de la Concepción Valdés (Plácido)*. Ciudad de La Habana, Cuba: Editorial Letras Cubanas; New York: Ediciones Vitral, 1980.

Porzecanski, Teresa, and Beatriz Santos, eds. *Historias de Vida: Negros en el Uruguay*. Montevideo: EPPAL, 1994.

Rama, Angel. *La ciudad letrada*. Hanover, N.H.: Ediciones del Norte, 1984.

Ramos, Arthur. *O negro brasileiro*. Rio de Janeiro: Civilização Brasileira, 1934.

Ranga, Dana, dir. *East Side Story*. Russia, 1997.

Retamar, Roberto Fernández. *Calibán; apuntes sobre la cultura en nuestra América*. 1st ed. México, Editorial Diógenes, 1971.

———. *Calibán y otros ensayos*. La Habana: Editorial Arte y Literatura, 1970.

Rickford, John Russell, and Russell John Rickford. "In Praise of Spoken Soul." *Stanford Alumni Magazine* (September/October 2000). http://www.stanfordalumni.org/news/magazine/2000/sepoct/articles/rickford.html (8aug2005)

Robinson, Cedric J. *Black Movements in America*. New York: Routledge, 1997.

Rodó, José Enrique. *Ariel*. 1900. Austin: University of Texas Press, 1998.

Rodrigues, João Carlos. *O negro brasileiro e o cinema*. Rio de Janeiro: Editora Globo, 1988.

Rodrigues, Nina. *Os africanos no Brasil*. São Paulo: Nacional, 1935.

Rojas Rodríguez, Marta. *El columpio de Rey Spencer*. 1993. La Habana: Editorical Letras Cubanas, 1996.

Rossi, Vincente. *Cosas de negros: Los orijenes del Tango y otros aportes al folklore rioplatense. Rectificaciones historicas*. 1926. Rev. ed. 1958. Buenos Aires: Taurus, 2001.

Ruíz, Rosa. "El aporte de la cultura negra en el departamento de Cerro Largo." *Hoy es História*. Enero–febrero 1993, año X, no. 55, 72–75.

Salles, Walter, dir. *Central Station* [*Central do Brazil*]. Brazil, 1998.

Sanchéz, Reinaldo, José Antonio Madrigal, Ricardo Viera, and José Sanchéz-Boudy, eds. *Homenaje a Lydia Cabrera*. Miami: Ediciones Universal, Colección Ébano y Canela, 1977.

Santa Cruz (Gamarra), Nicomedes. *La décima en el Perú*. Lima: Instituto de Estudios Peruanos, 1982.

———. *Décimas*. Lima: Librería-Editorial Juan Mejia Baca, 1960.

Santos, Milton (1926–2001). *O País Distorcido*. 1999. Org. Wagner Costa Ribeiro. São Paulo: PubliFolha, 2002.

Santos Febres, Mayra. "Marina y su olor." *Pez de vidrio*, 41–50.

———. *Pez de vidrio y otros cuentos (Un pasado posible)*. Río Piedras, Puerto Rico: Ediciones Huracán, 1996.

Sarduy, Pedro Pérez, and Jean Stubbs, eds. *AfroCuba: An Anthology of Cuban Writing on Race, Politics and Culture*. Melbourne: Ocean Press, 1993.

Sarmiento, Domingo Faustino. *Civilización y barbarie: Vida de Juan Facundo Quiroga*. In Garganigo, 221–31.

———. *Facundo: civilización y barbarie.* Edición de Roberto Yahni. Madrid: Cátedra, 1990.

Schlaich, Frieder, dir. *Otomo.* Germany, 1999.

Segal, Ronald. *The Black Diaspora: Five Centuries of the Black Experience Outside Africa.* New York: Farrar, Straus and Giroux, 1995.

Shusterman, Richard. *Performing Live: Aesthetic Alternatives for the Ends of Art.* Ithaca: Cornell University Press, 2000.

Sogbossi, Hippolyte Brice. *La tradición Ewé-Fon en Cuba.* Habana: Fundacion Fernando Ortiz, 1998.

Spencer, Jon Michael. *The Rhythms of Black Folks: Race, Religion and Pan-Africanism.* Trenton: Africa World Press, 1995.

Spielberg, Steven, dir. *Amistad.* United States, 1997.

Spratlin, Valaurez B. "The Negro in Spanish Literature." In De Costa, 47–52.

Stam, Robert. *Tropical Multiculturalism: A Comparative History of Race in Brazilian Cinema and Culture.* Durham: Duke University Press, 2003.

Stanley, Avelino. *Tiempo Muerto.* 1998. Santo Domingo: Cocolo Editorial, 1999.

Stein, Stanley J. *Vassouras: A Brazilian Coffee Country, 1850–1900.* Harvard Historical Studies, vol. 69. Boston: Harvard University Press, 1957.

Szabó, István, dir. *Mephisto.* West Germany/Hungary/Austria, 1981.

Tabori, Paul. *The Anatomy of Exile.* London: Harrap, 1972.

Tedlock, Dennis, trans. *Popol Vuh, the Mayan book of the dawn of life.* New York: Touchstone, 1996.

Thompson, Robert Farris. *Flash of the Spirit: African and Afro-America Art and Philosophy.* New York: Vintage Books, 1983.

Tine, Alioune. "Pour une théorie de la littérature africaine écrite." *Présence Africaine* 133–34 (1985): 99–121.

Todorov, Tzvetan. *The Conquest of America: The Question of the Other.* Trans. Richard Howard. New York: HarperCollins, 1984.

Uribe, Imanol, dir. *Bwana.* Spain, 1996.

Vianna, Hermano. *The Mystery of Samba: Popular Music and National Identity in Brazil.* Ed. and trans. John Charles Chasteen. Chapel Hill: University of North Carolina Press, 1999.

———. *O misterio do samba.* Rio de Janeiro: Jorge Zahar Editor/Universidade Federal do Rio de Janeiro, 1995.

Vidal, Luís Fernando. "A modo de prólogo." In López Albújar, *Cuentos,* 7–10.

Wajda, Andrzej, dir. *Man of Marble.* Poland, 1976.

Walcott, Derek. *Joker of Seville* and *O Babylon!* New York: Farrar, Straus and Giroux, 1978.

Whitten, Norman E. *Los negros de San Lorenzo: Clases parentesco y poder en un pueblo ecuatoriano.* Quito: Centro Cultural Afroecuatoriano–Ediciones Afroamérica, 1997.

Whitten, Norman E., and Arlene Torres, eds. *Blackness in Latin America and the Caribbean: Social Dynamics and Cultural Transformations.* Bloomington: Indiana University Press, 1998.

Williams, Colin N. "Identity, autonomy and the ambiguity of technological development." *Globalization and Territorial Identities.* Ed. Zdravko Mlinar. Aldershot, Hants, England; Brookfield, Vt.: Avebury, 1993. 115–28.

Wilson, August. *Ma Rainey's Black Bottom.* New York: French, 1985.

Wilson, Leslie. "La poesia negra: Its Background, Themes, and Significance." In De-Costa, 90–104.

Wilson, Olly. "Black Music as an Art Form." In O'Meally, 82–101.

Wimberly, Fayette. "The Expansion of Afro-Bahian Religious Practices in Nineteenth-Century Cachoeira." In Kraay, 74–89.

Wynter, Sylvia. "Beyond Miranda's Meanings: Un/silencing the 'Demonic Ground' of Caliban's 'Woman.'" In Donnell and Lawson Welsh, 476–82.

———. "The Eye of the Other: Images of the Black in Spanish Literature." In DeCosta, 8–19.

———. "We Must Learn to Sit Down Together and Discuss a Little Culture—Reflections on West Indian Writing and Criticism." In Donnell and Lawson Welsh, 307–15.

Zapata Olivella, Manuel. *Chambacú, corral de negros.* Medellín: Editorial Bedout, 1963.

———. *Changó, el gran putas.* 1983. Bogotá: Letras Americanas, 1992.

Zenón Cruz, Isabelo. *Narciso descubre su trasero: el negro en la cultura puertorriqueña.* 2 vols. Humacaco, Puerto Rico: Editorial Furidi, 1974–75.

Zéphir, Flore. *Haitian Immigrants in Black America: A Sociological and Sociolinguistic Portrait.* Westport, Conn.: Bergin and Garvey, 1996.

Zumthor, Paul. *Introduction à la poésie orale.* Paris: Seuil, 1983.

Index

Patricia D. Fox is an independent scholar. She has taught at the University of Missouri-Columbia; Indiana University, Bloomington; and the University of Ghana, Legon campus. Dr. Fox has traveled extensively in Latin America and the Caribbean researching Afro-Hispanic and Afro-Brazilian cultural production.